CASUALTIES

CASUALTIES

Death in Viet Nam; Anguish and Survival in America

Heather Brandon

ST. MARTIN'S PRESS / NEW YORK

The poem "Violence" by James D. Lange is from *Peace Is Our Profession,* edited by Jan Barry, East River Anthology, 1981. Reprinted with permission of the author and editor.

The Vietnam Veterans' Memorial photos used in chapter openings are courtesy of Joel Sarchet.

Design by M. Paul

Library of Congress Cataloging in Publication Data

Brandon, Heather.
    Casualties: death in Vietnam, anguish in America.

    1. Vietnamese Conflict, 1961–1975—Psychological aspects. 2. Vietnamese Conflict, 1961–1975—Casualties (Statistics, etc.) 3. Vietnamese Conflict, 1961–1975— Personal narratives, American. 4. Bereavement— Psychological aspects. I. Title.
DS559.8.P7B7 1984   959.704'3   84–15059
ISBN 0–312–12358–2

First Edition

10 9 8 7 6 5 4 3 2 1

For survivors, everywhere. And for their loved ones.

Doughboys were paid a whole dollar a day
and received free burial under the clay.
And movie heroes are paid even more
shooting one another in a Hollywood war.

—Kreymborg, *What Price Glory*

There was laughter and loving in the lanes at evening;
Handsome were the boys then, and girls were gay.
But lost in Flanders by medalled commanders
The lads of the village are vanished away.

—Cecil Day Lewis, *A Time to Dance*

VIOLENCE

violence
dog tags
red dirt
shit
olive drab
baggy pants
with baggy pockets
gook
napalm
SP/4
Ban Me Thout
Boun Ho, Ban Don
garbage
gonorrhea
grenades
siren
death
    quick death
    slow death
    crippling death
    permanent death
    $10,000
Air America, CIA
easy money
black market
number one
beaucoup fear
beaucoup anger

bullet
pain
chopper
miniguns
mistakes

1900 hours
operation
search and destroy
contact
CIB
Lifer
career soldier
Man In Service To His
    Country
Yours is but to do or die
    die
55,000 American lives
Fifty-Five Thousand
    Men
died in this country
for a rotten jungle
full of
      booby traps
      snipers
      mines
      rockets
and other absurdities

—James D. Lange

CONTENTS

FOREWORD

America has finally begun, in a variety of ways, to attempt to come to terms with the implications of the Vietnam experience. This phenomenon is particularly visible in the recent spate of articles, books, and television shows on a variety of facets of the war, including many by and about those who served in Vietnam.

Casualties by Heather Brandon adds an important new element to this healing process by letting us hear the voices of the survivors of some of those who gave the final full measure in Vietnam. Much like the Vietnam Veterans' Memorial in Washington etched with the names of the fallen for all to witness and contemplate or the noted *Life* magazine article of June 27, 1969, with individual pictures of all those killed in Vietnam during a particular week, *Casualties* personalizes the impact of the conflict in a haunting way that can cause even the most hardened to want to turn away in grief.

Casualties is a difficult book, filled with much pain. Nevertheless, its powerful, stunning message about the enormous personal torment of the war in Vietnam should be read by anyone seeking to understand the human implications of United States involvement in Southeast Asia during the Vietnam era.

—ALAN CRANSTON
U.S. Senator
Ranking Minority Member of
the Senate Committee
on Veteran's Affairs

INTRODUCTION

In December 1965, when my cousin Don was killed at Tuy Hoa, Republic of South Vietnam, I didn't cry. I thought it really didn't affect me that much. Now I know the daily letters I sent after learning he was missing in action were desperate notes. They were my attempt to know quickly if he was alive. I told myself that if one of my letters was *not* returned, I'd know he had been found, that he was okay, that he had received the letter. All the letters came back. I sent one each day; soon I began receiving one back each day. Then his body was found. I stopped writing. In 1974, I cried.

By 1980, I knew of other families feeling as torn apart and isolated as my own. Would they talk to me? Would my own family talk? They would. In many instances, no one had ever asked.

In December 1982, I began this book. Don had been dead for seventeen years.

In January 1983, Vietnam veteran Patrick Finnegan, whose brother Dennis was killed in Vietnam in 1972, shared with me something he had written on his way home from Washington, D.C., one day during the fall of 1982:

> Dewey Ruis, Larry Pypinowski, Bob Moinester, Jerry Sorrentino, Dennis Finnegan; all young men, all in the prime of their lives, all dead. Three enlisted men, two officers. Three of them never saw their twentieth birthday, one made it into his twenties, one almost made it out of his twenties. Two were friends from my boyhood days, one a brother of shared blood-

lines. Two were brothers of many humps, smokes, jokes, cups of cocoa, and terrified moments together. Four Army, one Navy. Four had enlisted; one was drafted. Three paratroopers, one regular infantry, one Navy riverboats. Four dead from fatal gunshot wounds, one dead in the flaming wreckage of a helicopter. Four of them had never married. One of them left a wife and two daughters. Three from New York, one from Georgia, one from New Jersey. Two killed in 1968, two killed in 1969, one killed in 1972. Four were on their first tour; one was on his fourth tour.

For the rest of my life I will remember these friends and brothers of mine. . . .

Their names are now etched in our nation's capital for as long as granite exists. Their names are there among all the other "Deweys" from Georgia, all the other "Skis" from Jersey, all the other "Bobs" and "Jerrys" and "Dennises" from New York, and the "Jims" from Texas, and "Reds" from California, and "Chiefs" from Montana, and "Docs" from Puerto Rico. They are all there, all these sons and daughters of small- and big-town America, for America to see.

What America doesn't see are the mothers and fathers who fainted when they opened their doors to see a uniformed military officer and their local religious leader standing there with practiced looks of sorrow and compassion. What America doesn't see is the young wife, four months pregnant, who miscarries with the news that her nineteen-year-old husband is dead. What America doesn't see are the grandparents with weak hearts who yield themselves to death because the joy of their old age has been blown to pieces 11,000 miles away. What America doesn't see are the infants and young children who were just starting to realize who the person with the deeper voice and stronger hands is. Infants and young children who now have only fast-diminishing memories.

What America doesn't see are the surviving families that now dread the unspoken words and melancholy that surround their holidays. What America doesn't see are the 57,939 shrines of pictures and medals, in houses and apartments from Maine to Hawaii, Alaska to Puerto Rico, Chicago to New Orleans.

. . . What America doesn't see are the hundreds of thousands wounded in Vietnam, men now without arms, eyes, spleens, kidneys. What America doesn't see are the 115,878 mothers and fathers, the 231,756 grandparents, the uncounted brothers, sisters, daughters, sons, friends and lovers. . . .

The material in this book comes from tape-recorded interviews with family members and Vietnam veterans who generously opened private portions of their lives to a stranger and, now, to the public. They did not do this without enduring the additional pain that remembering brings. Many of them agreed to the interviews in the belief that stories such as theirs needed telling. I thank each of them.

Of the thirty-seven voices here (other than members of my own family), I had met four before beginning the interviews, which were conducted between January and September 1983. Only two people interviewed, Opal and Grover Gunnels, my aunt and uncle, do not appear in this book. To Grover and Opal, many thanks. Their interviews were excluded primarily because of my wish not to devote an excessive portion of this book to Don.

The following people assisted me by contacting the families and the veterans and arranging for the interviews: David Kowalewski and Mafalda DiTommaso of Buffalo, New York; Rick Wideman of Washington, D.C.; George Swiers of Saratoga Springs, New York; Jim Hebron of New York City; Louis Gover of St. Thomas, U.S. Virgin Islands; Edwino Riviera of San Juan, Puerto Rico; and Roland Huth and Bill Snyder of Marion, Ohio. Edwino Riviera also helped immeasurably by transporting me around Puerto Rico and conducting two interviews in Spanish. These interviews have been translated into English for this book. Barry Lobdell of Saratoga Springs, New York, helped by making negatives and prints of the Baker family's photographs. Harold Bryant of Washington, D.C., and St. Louis, Missouri, responded to a crisis call by hand-delivering an eight-foot wooden ladder on my last picture-taking jaunt to Washington. Rick Wideman located the ladder, cutting short an anxiety attack I was fast developing!

A very special thanks to Kathy and Gary DeTample, their three daughters, and their all-too-human German shepherd, Honey Bear, for their generous hospitality during the weekend I first struggled to turn tape into manuscript. My parents gave me the same support during a very long weekend in Texas, and emotional support and encouragement all along the way. Dr. Greta Salenius provided unwavering belief in the importance of this project. Her support came directly out of her own experiences as a surgical nurse in a field hospital in Korea. Dr. Jim Mikawa provided, as he has so often in the past, whatever I needed, whenever I asked. Again and again, many thanks, Jim.

Joseph Anderson of the New York State Division of Veterans Affairs and Andrew Hughes showed me the way to the beginning. Andy Hughes has continued to provide legal advice and practical direction and support. Many thanks. My editor at St. Martin's Press, Susannah Driver, has been a jewel. She rescued my manuscript from a heap delivered one day and has nurtured it from that day forward. I could not ask more.

Finally, Vietnam combat veterans contributed to this book in ways less direct, but no less significant. In hours of conversation, often in bars, drinking and talking through the wee hours of the morning, Vietnam began to soak into me, both as the emotional experience of those who served, and as a still ill-defined national experience for those of us who did whatever we did or did not do through the long years of their struggle. I must say I knew nothing about war until these conversations began. I would have probably *said* I knew war was about death and destruction. I did not know. Not really. War was a concept; death and injury in war abstract. Combat veterans brought emotion to my ideas. Because of them, I know war in a different way. Yet, Vietnam will remain always, in most ways, a vicarious experience for me. I was not there. I do not regret that. Closer, I would not necessarily trust my sanity.

While what I have been taught has come from many voices and experiences, and while I can't pretend to sort out precisely who has taught me what, some people and events do stand out. Gary May. He taught me about grace under pressure. Jack McCloskey, to whom I can still say, "No, Jack, I never saw 'Nam!" Jim Hebron. He taught me the core of what I understand about the emotions associated with being a grunt in Vietnam and with being a survivor when others were not. Jim Lange. He helped in so many ways, but mainly by teaching me that I, too, had something to teach. Someone from Seattle, whom I met once, and whose name is lost to me. He taught me how to pronounce "Tuy Hoa," where Don was killed. Others taught me about betrayal. And my cousin Don. He taught me, in a horrible way, how much I loved him.

HEATHER BRANDON
New York City
December 1983

TIMOTHY DALY · RAYMOND C D
EAR▮W JENNINGS · AU▮UST D J
CASIMIR NIESPODZIANY · WILLI
WENDELL SPENCER · JERRY L SPI
MORTON E TOWNES Jr · ROBER
SALVATORE CAMMARATA · ALLA
CHARLES S HYMERS · KENT L JO
WILLIAM L LOWMAN · THOMAS
FRANK M PIPKIN · RUSSELL A PO
FRANKLIN B WILLIAMS · JOHN S
WOODROW H WILBURN + ROB
JAMES E BOSTOCK · JOSEPH M
ROBERT B ECKER · ROBERT L ELG

SALVATORE PETER "SAMMY" CAMMARATA

Born: February 2, 1947
Montedoro, Sicily
Killed: February 4, 1967
DaNang, Republic of South Vietnam

WILLIAM E GRAY · DONALD J
JAMES A LASCHE · JAMES O MIL

Sammy Cammarata

Left to right: Carmen Cammarata, Sr., Kathy and Gary DeTample

Mr. and Mrs. Cammarata

Salvatrice Cammarata

Sammy's monument in Sicily

KATHERINE MARY "KATHY" CAMMARATA DETAMPLE

Born: September 4, 1946
Lackawanna, New York
Widow of Salvatore Cammarata and wife of Gary DeTample

GARY ARTHUR DETAMPLE

Born: February 24, 1941
Lackawanna, New York
Friend of Salvatore Cammarata and husband of Katherine Cammarata DeTample

---

Together

KATHY: Gary is a Vietnam vet. He was in the 196th Light Infantry Brigade with my first husband. They were together in Vietnam. Gary was at Sammy's side when he was dying, so I know exactly what happened, but I didn't know until three years after I was married to Gary, and Gary didn't tell me. I'm glad I know.

DaNang. It said on the death certificate, "DaNang." He was not killed at DaNang. He was killed in the field. He was supposed to be in charge of the ammo dump and never leave base, but it was one of those days, I guess, that they needed men. He went out and was killed, and he never came back.

When I received the letter, it stated he was blown up in an ammunition dump. The night before, I had dreamt. I was carrying his daughter at the time, and I had dreamt that he was killed. When I woke up and told my mother, she said, "Oh, it's your imagination. It's because you're pregnant. You're going to have a baby, and you're dreaming all sorts of things." I said, "Nine o'clock, Mom. The doorbell's going to ring, and it's going to be two officers." Well, at nine o'clock the doorbell rang, and it was two officers. They told me they weren't definitely sure, that I would have to wait for the telegram to verify it, but they were almost positive it was my Sam. A couple of hours later, it did come, and it was him. Three days later I had his daughter. She was late. She was supposed to be born on his birthday, but she was late.

They sent his body home, and they wanted to take him and bury him before I got out of the hospital. I said, "No, there's no way. I better attend; otherwise, I will never believe it." I was fortunate in that I did have an open coffin, and that I did something I shouldn't have done. I broke the glass and put him in another coffin. I was able to see where he was blown through his stomach and that his legs were blown off. Maybe I shouldn't have done it, but I did it. First of all, they lost Sam's body in transit. They sent him up to Springville and another fellow to Buffalo, so they had to open the coffins to see who was who. It stated Sam could have an open coffin, but he was sealed under glass. I don't know the reason why. They said they can bring something bad from overseas, or something. I just made up my mind: "I'm going to see him. I'm going to touch him. I'm going to know it's him. I'm going to verify that it's him." We broke it open, and we had him placed in another coffin. What could they do? After we did it, it was done.

I proceeded to find out where he was shot, because his face was completely untouched. It looked like he was perfect, and I said, "How could this have happened?" Then I saw his whole stomach was blown right out, and his legs were off, and there was all paper inside. I don't think I really should have done it, but at the time I wanted to verify why he was dead, and I felt better knowing I did it, that I actually saw him. I saw him, and I was able to touch him, to know that it was him, and to verify that it was him. Otherwise, I probably to this day would never have believed it. That was awful hard for someone who had never seen the contents of a casket.

According to stories told to me by Phillip, an army buddy of Gary's, you would not know if it was your family's remains or not, because they had to go through the field and pick up arms and legs and put them into bags not knowing. There was no way to identify them sometimes, so maybe you had half of someone else. This was the only way they could do it in the field, so I was really one of the fortunate ones. I have to honestly say I was fortunate. I can be at peace, knowing it was him.

Some women got letters from the president. They got letters from Robert Kennedy. I kept everything for his daughter, Sally. I even have the original copy of an article printed in the *Buffalo Evening News* when he was eight years old. It said the only thing he wanted to do was to get his American citizenship papers, because he wasn't born in this country. That's the only thing he wanted when he was eight.

GARY: I went over with him. A bunch of us from this area were drafted, and we all went together. That's pretty unusual for Vietnam, but we were all drafted together. We went to Fort Dix and Fort Devens, and we trained as the 196th Light Infantry Brigade. It was the first time they had formed it since World War II. We trained together, we shipped together, and a lot of us didn't come home together. It was a little harder when someone got killed, because you knew him. It was a lot harder.

He wasn't at base camp when he got killed. He was supposed to be at base camp. He wanted to go out and see what it was like, because everybody else was going out, but he wasn't ordered to go, not as far as I know. That's what happened. Mortars. I was there. I was a medic. She has one letter that tells her he was killed outside of the area by mortars. It was sent by somebody from our base camp. It was not sent from Washington or the Department of Defense or anyplace like that.

KATHY: I received a lot of letters. I was the only one carrying a baby when they went overseas. Be it a girl or be it a boy, it was to be their mascot. I got letters from all of them, asking for pictures of her. Gary tried to get a ship-to-shore phone call through to me to notify me [of Sammy's death] before the army did. Gary didn't tell me that. Phillip told me the entire story while Gary was at work. This was about three years after Gary and I were married. When he told me about the phone call attempt, I thought, "Well, if I fill him up with a little booze, I can get anything I want out of him," so I did. We sat up all night, and he told me the entire story.

When Sam was dying, Sam asked Gary to come and take care of me and the baby. Gary came home at the end of July. The first thing he did, the first day he was home, was to come over to my mother's house. We had corresponded back and forth after Sam was killed, but I'd never met him. I didn't know him, and I thought, "Well, I don't want people to pity me, because I'm an independent person. I want to be able to stand on my own two feet and take care of the baby," but for the last sixteen years, I couldn't have asked for a better person. He has become a saint in his own way. I think he kind of favors Sally over his own two. He doesn't do it intentionally, but he does.

When Phillip started talking, telling me things, I thought, "Before Sam died, he was looking out for me, making sure that somebody would take care of me. I didn't have to worry." He was choosy who he picked. He didn't send some run-of-the-mill person, but somebody he knew would take care of me and his child, and Gary has. As I always say, Gary's a saint in his own way, but I never tell him. He never told me about any of this. He didn't even know I knew, until just now.

GARY: When I see Phillip, I'm going to smack him. Fortunately, he's stopped drinking. He won't tell any more stories.

KATHY: I still have my way of getting stories out of him. I've talked to Sally about it, but I've never talked to Gary about it before this. Sally and I have talked about how lucky we are, because, compared to what a lot of people have gone through, we don't know what hell is. He's always provided and made sure we were looked after. If I'd told him I knew, he wouldn't have admitted it. He probably would have said, "You don't know what you're talking about. You're talking off the top of your head," but I know it's true. This is the first time he's admitted it in public. Sam's mother and father treat him like a son. They make sure he's looked after and has things.

GARY: Sam's dad just started talking about it the last couple of years. His mother took it pretty hard. He did, too, to the point of going over to the cemetery and trying to dig up the grave.

KATHY: Sam was gone for about four or five years then. His other son started growing up, and that son got mixed up with the wrong kind of people, and Dad felt, "I've lost one, now I'm losing another." Sam was his sidekick. Dad went hunting; Sam went hunting. Dad went fishing; Sam went fishing. He'll say, "Sam should not have gone to war. Sam wasn't old enough to go to war. Why did they take my Sammy?" He just doesn't understand why his son got drafted: "He wasn't born in this country, why did they take him?" He'd just turned eighteen when he was drafted. He quit high school and started working at the plant. He got his draft notice that fall and reported in October.

GARY: Most of our brigade was made up of people who were drafted. I was drafted two or three times. I was underweight all the time. It finally got to the point where if a guy could bend over, he went. I could bend over, so I went. Most of our brigade were draftees. It was not our decision to go. Three of us were known as the "pops" of the brigade, because we were old. We were twenty-three, twenty-four. The average age in Vietnam was something like eighteen, so we were old for Vietnam. One of the three of us died, another killed himself. He killed himself in this country, after he got back.

KATHY: When Sam died, his dad just wanted to go and bring his son back. When he was at the cemetery that day, he just started digging. His hands were all raw, sore, and he said he would rather be there than his son. He said, "I'm going to take him out of here." Now that family has a beautiful memorial. It's in Italy, in Montedoro, where Sammy was born. It's in the center of town. It's all brick and marble. It is the memorial that was built before anything was built for a Vietnam veteran in this country, and Sam's parents did it. It's the most gorgeous thing, and they built it.

GARY: We had our disagreements with them for a while, but we straightened it out, and we're close to them now. He treats all the kids the same. He might even treat Sally a little worse. I honestly think at first he resented her. It was just too hard for him to see her.

KATHY: You could feel the tension when he came to visit. He used to say, "She should sit in a chair." It was all right for the other ones to run around and do what they wanted to, but Sally should sit still. I think it was either, "She should be put in a shell so nothing happens to her," or "Put her up there, so I can see her and remember something she reminds me of." Sam's mother wears black to this day. She's constantly lighting candles, constantly sending masses to anything and everything. I don't think she will ever be able to come out of black, but she's learned to accept the fact that he's gone, and he's not going to come back.

For years they thought I killed him. For years we did not talk, because they thought I killed him. I don't know how, how I would have gone to Vietnam and killed him, but, to them, I killed him. When you come from the old country, you have funny beliefs. I'm Irish, and the old Italians don't believe in marrying outside your nationality. Sammy and I met, we started dating, and it was taboo. We were both only eighteen when we married. We ran away the first time he was home on leave. That was in 1965. When we came home, he had to go back to base. They finally got stationed at Camp Drum for guerrilla training, and I had relatives living near there. They weren't supposed to be going to Vietnam. They were told they were going to Santo Domingo.

GARY: We were trained for guerrilla warfare, but we were supposed to go to Santo Domingo. They trained us for guerrilla warfare up at Fort Drum, in the dead of winter. We'd never even seen an M-16 until we were in the ships on our way to 'Nam. Our experience was different, going over together, and in ships. The only time it started getting somewhere near the usual experience for Vietnam was when we started getting replacements as we lost people. Then, near the end of our tours, they asked us to extend in Vietnam to get an early out of the service: "Stay over here, and when you leave here, you can forget it. You're done. But you've got to stay here until we can get enough people to replace this whole unit." I didn't re-up. No way.

When I was on my way back from 'Nam, going to Fort Dix, I went AWOL. I was trying to get discharged, and a few of us got lost for a few days. We were riding around with some New Jersey cops. They were having all the riots at that time, and they were trying to get us to join the police force. Nothing doing. The day we finally made it back to Fort Dix, they were trying again to get us to sign up again. They wanted us to sign up again so they could send us right back to where we came from. They were short of people. No, thanks. I saw too much to ever want to go through it again.

KATHY: He wrote home to Jacob Javits complaining there was not enough medicine and blood and everything in the field. I still have the letter from Javits. The officers were kind of mad at him. He didn't get along with the officers, because he sent letters home saying, "Hey, I can't take care of these men if I don't have the proper medicines and equipment and whatnot." I guess you're not supposed to do that. It's going against top brass.

Well, as I said, Sammy and I got married, and I stayed up at Fort Drum. Two weeks before he was shipped out to 'Nam, I went to the doctor and found out I was pregnant. Right away, I was accepted into his family: "Oh, they got my namesake coming." Right. When Sammy was killed, I called them. I said to the officers, "Could you please go to the house and tell them?" I asked them to wait until I got a priest there, because I knew they'd never believe this, so I had the priest there, and I called them, and they said, "You're lying. Why are you joking about something like this?" I said, "I'm not joking," but the two officers couldn't even go over there. When the telegram came, someone took it over to them, and they said, "She killed my son." I didn't understand Italian then, but during the entire wake, his mother told his father, "She killed my son. She killed my son." I kept saying to myself, "Don't cry, Kathy, don't cry. You've got to be strong for these people. You cannot cry."

From February until July, when Gary came home, it was three days here, three days there, three days at their place, four days at my mother's. I didn't have a permanent address. I was back and forth, living with them both. Finally I was going to take an apartment on my own. I was going to live downstairs from Sam's parents. When Gary came home, he said, "You're not living in this neighborhood with this baby. No way." They live on the west side. It's the lower section of Buffalo. It was rough then, but it's even rougher now. It was a downstairs apartment, and Gary was afraid for the baby and me, so I told them, "No. I'm not going to live there." In August, Gary and I got engaged. They said, "Oh, my God. Our son isn't even in his grave a year yet. You must have had this planned. We know you killed our son."

They never saw Gary as part of the plot. It was simply me, because I stole their son. He quit school for me, right? I didn't tell him to quit school. He wanted to go to work and make money. At that time, the plant was hiring off the street. I worked as a beautician, and after he was killed I used to get calls from his mother. She would tell me I was going to be thrown into the Niagara River. I laughed. She would come to the place where I worked and stand in front of the doorway and call me a "black whore" in Italian. My boss would say, "Who's that?" I'd say, "I don't know. I've never seen the lady in my life." I would talk to them some during that time, but, at the same time, I figured, "Hey this is your hardship, your problem." The final blow was when Sally made her communion. They said, "Our son isn't here to see this. You killed our son."

This went on until about two years ago. That's when I saw Sam's dad at a funeral. I don't hold grudges, so I went up to him and said, "Hello, Dad, how are you? This is your granddaughter."

He said, "My granddaughter?" and the tears started coming down. I asked him if he needed a ride to the cemetery. He said, "No," but he made me promise to come over to the house and see him sometime. He and I were still arguing back and forth until about a month ago. I guess Sally got fed up with it. He'd had a little bit too much of his wine, and he started in on me again. He said, "Well, if it wasn't for you, Sammy wouldn't be dead." Sally said, "Now wait a minute, Pop. How do you figure my mother killed your son? My mother didn't kill my father. In the first place, she couldn't get over there, but how do you figure this? You're wrong." He thought about it for a minute, then he said, "You know, I think you're right." It's been within the last month that it's been totally different. You can see that it doesn't come to his mind anymore that I killed his son. It's totally different. Now he introduces me as his daughter.

Before that day with Sally, I was nothing. I was the whore who killed his son. To this day, I can remember the day I went and started taking my furniture out of that downstairs apartment: "I hope you wind up on the street begging for a dime, because I wouldn't give it to you." I said, "Well, okay. Don't give it to me, because I wouldn't ask you."

GARY: I know when it started changing. It was at the St. Anthony Festival. He called me up and said, "Do you want to go to the Italian festival?" I'd never been to it. He was laughing and joking, buying this and that for the kids, saying, "Anything you want, you can have," then he got to the statue of St. Anthony, and I saw him turn away from me. Tears were rolling down his face. He didn't want anyone to see him crying, and I wasn't going to go up and ask him why he was crying. I didn't know it was his son's saint.

KATHY: St. Anthony's is near here. Sammy was an altar boy. He followed through until he was seventeen years old at St. Anthony's, and St. Anthony was Sammy's patron saint. When Dad saw St. Anthony, he saw his son, but he's been better the past two years, and in the last month he's been totally different. He just couldn't face the fact that his son was gone. Even while he was accusing me of killing him, he thought his son was going to come back and that I shouldn't try to wipe out his memory. I shouldn't have married again. Even now, when I go someplace with him and I happen to have to sign my name, he'll say, "You know your name is Katherine Cammarata DeTample." I say, "Okay, Dad." I'll sign it like that to make him happy. I'll do anything to please him. To keep peace in the family, I'll do anything.

GARY: I've made up my mind as to that. I want peace and quiet in my life. No aggravation. No fights. I've seen enough. What I've got left of my life, I'm going to live in peace and quiet. It's as simple as that. You can't go through an experience like Vietnam and be the same. You're not going to be the same person, from any war. You're just not going to be the same. A lot of people don't understand that. They can't accept it. There's a lot of things that would have bothered me before that I just ignore now, and nothing's going to tell the whole story, not about actually being in combat. No books, no museums, nothing. They can't even tell about the environment.

They can't really tell how it feels to be walking through a rice paddy and stopping to take leeches off. They can't tell about feet being wet all the time. They can't tell about sweating all the time. They can't tell about taking barrels of shit and burning it and calling that "sanitation." Nobody can really describe a rice paddy when you're walking through it, and what happens when you get out of it. Nobody really believes that the red ants over there are ferocious. You go through the leaves and knock them off and they climb all over you. You think the things are going to eat you alive, and there's nothing you can do to protect yourself from them. When we first went through a rice paddy, nobody told us about the leeches, and we didn't know. How do you get rid of these things? Most of us smoked cigars or cigarettes, and we found if we put a little heat by them they would fall off. You'd have to go over there to know it.

There's a friend of mine who flew over that country. He'd been through World War II, and he couldn't believe it, and he's only seen it from an airplane. The only veterans from World War II who understand that kind of environment are the ones who were in the Philippines, in the jungles. They understand. They're the only ones who really do understand. Just the environment itself. It stinks. The rats. The damn environment was hostile, very hostile. Then they had the rain. The rain.

KATHY: He wants peace and quiet to the point that he won't fight with me. He won't argue. He's beyond arguing. Many times I'll be talking to him, and my voice will rise, unintentionally. He'll say, "If you're going to yell about it, we aren't even going to talk," and I say to myself, "I'm not yelling. I'm just explaining something." Sometimes I think it would be good if he would fight, but he doesn't want to be around any conflicts at all, or hassles. He just stays away from them.

GARY: A lot of things might be important to someone else, but they're not important to me.

KATHY: There were many times when I got punched in the mouth. Not intentionally. He would be dreaming, and I got punched, and I would wake up and say, "Who the hell are you to hit me? Don't hit me, or I'll hit you back." He would be asleep, tossing and turning. I don't know how many clock radios he's put his fist through. I no longer put clock radios in our bedroom. He still dreams at night.

GARY: They're not as bad as they were.

KATHY: They're bad. You just don't realize it. Many nights I get up, and I'll sit an hour. I'll crochet, or I'll do some kind of needlepoint. If he hasn't settled down in an hour, I'll sleep on the couch, because I know he's asleep and he doesn't know what's going on. He has no idea what he's doing.

GARY: The next morning, I'll just be tired. I won't remember it. She took me out to the fair one time. . . .

KATHY: Oh, Lord. He came home in July, and the fair was in August. This was the first August after he came back, in 1967. At the end of the Hamburg Fair, at eleven o'clock at night, they light up the fireworks. Well, it was all unknown to me at that time. I didn't realize what they had gone through in Vietnam. I was knocked down in the parking lot, thrown between two cars, and another woman got totally knocked to the ground. Gary tried to barricade her. I thought, "Oh, my God, I'm going out with a crazy man," not realizing at the time that Vietnam was flashing back at him. He thought we were getting hit with mortars, and he was trying to protect us.

GARY: It's an automatic reaction. I stay away from fireworks now. If I'm prepared for it, I can handle it, but I can't if I don't know they're going to go off.

KATHY: A complete stranger was walking by, and he was trying to protect her. This person got up off the ground, and she said, "Oh, my God, this guy is going nuts." In my own mind, I was thinking, "I agree with you." It was about five minutes later that he realized where he was, then he said, "I've got to get out of here. I've got to get out of here."

What was the name of that movie? The one with Henry Winkler and Sally Fields? (*Heroes.* That's it.) Well, anyway, we went to the drive-in to see that. We all went to see it because we wanted to relate it to Vietnam. We were hoping to learn more about it. The whole family went, all of us. Well, the poor guy. What he went through that night. About twenty minutes into the show, the car all of a sudden took off, and the speaker went with it. The car just went, and I thought, "Oh, my God, we're going to get killed." He just took off. He couldn't take it. It was like everything was coming back to him at the same time.

Sally understood, but the little ones didn't. They asked, "Why did Daddy do that? Did he break the speaker down on purpose?" I sat all three kids down and said to them, "Daddy went through a lot. We'll never know about all of it, but let's just give him the benefit of the doubt." Right now, Gary will go downstairs and sit at the typewriter. He'll take out his frustration by writing letters to President Reagan, to [Senator] Moynihan, to anybody under the sun. If he's down in the cellar, and he's down there for more than an hour, we know it's one of those days, and we don't bother him. I don't know if it's a day that's constantly bringing him flashbacks, either. I don't question it. I just know it's a day to let him be on his own. Eventually he'll come upstairs. Call him for dinner, but don't bother him. He wants to be alone. I don't think he's aware that we know these days are here.

GARY: I just put myself in the cellar, and I stay away from everybody. I know they're leaving me alone, but I don't think any more about it. Well, I survived Vietnam. I'm all in one piece. My head's on, and I consider I'm pretty normal. I might have bad days once in a while, but I'm not carrying an M-16, trying to wipe out the world or anything like that. Vietnam's changed both of us a lot. I think any war will change anybody's life. I don't care if it's World War I or World War II or Korea. It'll change anybody's life. It's not going to be the same. You're not going to be the same person.

It's hard, but I don't think this country should forget Vietnam. If it was a mistake, learn from it, so we don't do the same thing over again. Let's not let any American go through it again unless it is an absolute and correct necessity, based on a true threat to our own freedoms. I don't think we should forget it. I don't think we should bury it. The school books aren't even telling the kids the true facts. If someone wants Vietnam vets to come to a school and talk about Vietnam, we should be willing to go. One of our friend's kids took an American history course in college last year. In the whole book, there were two little pages about Vietnam, and they never got to those pages in the book. That's the college course. Kids old enough to be drafted not even learning about what really happened. Be honest. Let them know what it's about.

I can tell about people I remember, lying there, knowing they were going to die. They would say, "I don't want anybody to know I died this way. Don't let anybody know this is the way I died." Three minutes later, or in less time, they'd be gone. The last statement they would make would be something like that. It would be somebody who'd lost both his legs and both his arms, and there was just nothing left of him. You didn't know how they could even talk anymore. They didn't want anybody to know they died that way. The medics couldn't walk away from it. Somebody else, they could call for a medic. They could get away. A medic couldn't get away from that. You had to deal with it. There was just no way you could get away from that.

You were hoping nobody would die, but they did. They died on you. At first we weren't wrapping them up. When I first went over there, we didn't have body bags. If somebody was missing a poncho, you would try to get somebody else's. Put a tag on the body who died, wrap him in the poncho, try to get a helicopter in to get him out. Sometimes you had to wait twelve hours to get him out. The first one I saw, a mortar went right through him. There was nothing left of him, just the pieces. I can still see him. Those are the nights when I have a tough time. I'll be sleeping, and I'll wake up because it's night, and I can see it.

It wasn't just from our group. It was everybody who was there. There was some feeling of satisfaction if you could get to somebody, and you could give him some help, get him back. Most of them ended up going home. You knew then you'd done something to help, so they could get back to a hospital and be taken care of, sent home.

KATHY: On nights when he wants to talk, I'll listen. I told him, "I can feel for you, and I can relate." I can't really say I know what it was like, but I'm willing to try and understand. You can listen, you can try to understand, but when it comes right down to the nitty-gritty, I cannot picture myself being in any of the spots he's been in.

SALVATRICE "SALLY" CAMMARATA

Born: February 7, 1967
Buffalo, New York
Daughter of Salvatore Cammarata and Kathy Cammarata
DeTample, and Gary DeTample

Good Parents

When I told my granddad to stop saying my mother had killed my father, I was just sick of it. How could he say that? How was she going to get to Vietnam and kill him? It made no sense, and I told him, "I can't take you telling her that all the time." He'd been doing that for years, and I just got tired of it. It made no sense.

I've known for years about my father's wish that Gary come home and take care of my mother and me, but I haven't thought a lot about it. I was surprised my mother said anything about it today. I guess I figured eventually she would say something to Gary. I don't know. It just came out today. I'm glad I have him for a father. I could have wound up with some jerk, so I'm lucky. If I didn't have good parents, I know I'd be a lot brattier. I'm lucky to have good examples.

Sometimes, when we're arguing, one of my sisters will try to pick on me. We get in little digs at each other once in a while, but we know we don't mean it. One day I think Lisa meant it. She said, "Well, he's my father, and not yours." All of a sudden, he got into the conversation and he said, "Well, I had no choice with you. You were born to me, but I had a choice with Sally. I picked her."

Once in a while he can be aggravating, but if you just leave him alone and stay away, then everything's okay. He does have a lot of things to be aggravated about. Everything just seems normal to me. I don't know any other way.

CARMEN CAMMARATA, SR.

Born: March 7, 1922
Serrodefaleo, Callanessetta
Province, Sicily
Father of Salvatore Cammarata

The Slaughterhouse Way

Bullets, they don't respect nobody. I know, because I was there, in World War II. It was quite a thing. Starvation. Everything going on.

I came to this country in 1949. We got married in 1946, then we came here in '49, by ship. When we came, we left our Sam with our family in Italy. Ten months later, when he was two-and-a-half years old, he came in with my wife's brother. Her brother was born in this country, and he brought Sam over. After he got here, he started growing up, and he went to school. He went to church, was a choir boy. That was his life. Many times I told him, "Take the bed with you. Go sleep at the church." He was good. He was doing good in school and all of that, singing, playing the guitar, playing the accordion. I still got the accordion in back of the couch. Brand-new accordion, imported from Italy. Electric guitar. He had an electric guitar, a silver-toned guitar. That's underneath the bed. I keep it under the bed. He loved sports, fishing, hunting. He used to go with me. I have everything now. The boat. I have the boat, too, the fishing boat. I can't take anything away from here.

What did I get from the war? A gold medal, right on the nose. That's what I got. They took the diamond out of my house, the racketeers in Washington. They packed their own pockets off the war. Why do they start these stupid wars? They start shipping stuff away from the U.S.A. to make money, to get guerrillas organized to start shooting. They shoot over there, in other places. They will not shoot in this country. They won't kill nobody here. That won't make any money for them. When they get elected, that's when they grab the money. They take everything away from us. That's what they're doing.

They talk about organized crime. What do they mean "organized crime"? What do they think they are, legitimate? They put all these kids up at the slaughterhouse. That is what it is, a slaughterhouse. "Go. Go and get killed." What did I get? After he got killed, I never even got a letter from the army, from nobody. No. Nothing. The letter I received was from Rockefeller. Sure. Big deal. He was governor then. I didn't even get a telegram from the army. Nothing. That's bad.

When I came to this country, it was to establish myself, because of conditions in Italy after World War II. We didn't have no jobs in Italy after the war. Everything was destroyed. Starvation. It was going left and right. If I had a job over there, I wouldn't have come here. No way. Things were bad, no matter where you went. If the war hit it, it was bad, no matter where. It takes a long time, a long time, to resettle. They tell me a good ten years went by before it began to pick up again. I couldn't stay ten years and just wait it out. On and off every day. Nothing. Day in and day out. Do nothing. No, not me. I'm not a bum.

I started working on the farm when I was ten years old, and I worked and I worked. Over there, you work eighteen, twenty, maybe twenty-two hours a day. I worked here, too. I worked in the bakery for two and a half years. For eighteen months I even put up without cleaning myself and changing my clothes. Ninety-three hours a week for thirty dollars a week pay. That's when I first came to this country. Thirty dollars a week. Right here, on Niagara Street, in the bakery. Ninety-three hours a week for thirty dollars. Calgo Bakery on Niagara Street, right across from Columbus Hospital. I was satisfied. At that time, for thirty dollars, you could live. Oh, yes. Me and her, we could go to the grocery store. We used to spend five, six dollars, and we had a full bag of groceries at that time. Not now. Five dollars, and you won't even get a steak. One breakfast, and that's gone. That's quite a bit. That's quite a bit of a history. The kid was good in the schoolroom, in church. "Pray for me," they say. "Pray for me." Yeah. They prayed for me in church, and now, my son, where is he? BANG!

I didn't know he was going to Vietnam before he went. If I would have known, I would have kicked his clothes right off him. I would have stopped him. He wasn't born in this country. I would have held him back. "Hold it, baby. I take you, baby. I take you away." I know where to take him. To the mountains. Dig a tunnel in the mountains somewhere. Let him stay there. Give him a gun. He would have survived. Sure. On wild game, fish. He would have been in Canada, in Allegheny County, in Pennsylvania, anyplace. There are a lot of mountains in Pennsylvania. They would have never got him. No way. When he was home on leave in December after boot camp, I told him, "I'll get the lawyer. You go back to school. You don't have to go in the Army." He said, "Oh, no. I'll get it over with," but he didn't know he was going to Vietnam. He was told he was going to Santo Domingo. I said, "Son, watch out. Don't go looking for medals. Those bullets, boy, them are hard bastards." I know.

War is not a funny thing. All kinds of baloney, and for what? What you got at the end of the line? Nothing. You got nothing. Look at these boys. What are they doing in the hospital? Then they're trying to eliminate all these hospitals, all these supports, government support, federal support. What the hell is this? What are they trying to do? I can't figure out what they're trying to do. All they do is grab, grab, grab. Don't they know, by cheating and grabbing, one of these days it is going to be the end of them? Don't they know this country is in a danger situation? I may be wrong, but I think this country is in a danger situation. They keep on pushing so many countries. They're shooting all over, and one of these days one of these countries is going to be strong enough to turn it around and dump it on this country. This country is going to go down. BANG! Something is going to happen to this country.

This country is talking too much, because they never saw a bomb. They never saw an atomic bomb. They've never been attacked. They've never been running around from one town to another, from one month to another. That's why they talk too much. We never had a war here, not in internal U.S.A. Just wait. There's going to bc an inside shoot-out. Like in El Salvador. They don't want to see no Yankees out there. I listen. I listen to the TV. The pope was there yesterday. "Down boys. Get out." And this country wants to go over there and grab everything.

Reagan, he says, "Help your next-door neighbors." Ha, ha. What a laugh. He won't say, "Hey, here is a million dollars. Go and put up some macaroni. Feed them." No. He wants me to feed them. The poor has got to feed the poor. That's the way it goes. The Church. Oh, yeah. Salvation Army. Pick up a can here and there to feed the people. Oh, what a country. It's not the country, it's the politicians. We never put the right people up. Whoever pays more, we elect him, so it's like that. Some people want war. It helps them. That domino theory, they're playing it out in Central America right now, like in Vietnam. That's quite a bag. That Reagan, I tell you, he's got funny ideas. Congress has got to dump him.

When we lost our boy, it was quite a bit. We lost our minds. We lost all track of everything, went out of balance and everything, out of control, physically and mentally, all of it. His mother is still in it. This is a house that will never see light again. Since he's been dead, there's no parties, there's no weddings, there is no nothing. We are tied up in the house. We are jailed in this house, jailed in without doing anything. That's it. We can't go out. Know what I see on TV? News. Western pictures, something like that. If there's dancing or singing, I shut it off. There is no radio for singing. That is only for if I need to get up early, or to take a pill, or whatever. There is no music in this house. Everything is dead. We ain't going noplace. This is a house, after my thirty-four years in this country, working like a bull, day and night, this is a house with no light. This is a life? Better be dead. I don't know why I am alive. I feel rotten, pretty rotten inside. I don't know. I feel no

more pain. I don't know. I used to feel pain. No more. It stopped
a few years ago, about ten, but it is all right. Every day I say,
"Thank you." I say, "Good night, and thank you." That's all. I
don't even go to church anymore. What good is it going to be to
me? I used to go to church. Sure, respect. I am still respectful. I
maintain my regulation, my books. I won't get off the line. I'm not
changing my religion. That's my religion. I was born that way, and
I am staying that way.

We got a granddaughter, a nice granddaughter, to look at. A
mother. Another mother. A Gary. Another couple more kids to
look at. What I'm gonna do? I'm not going out. I got a new car,
bought it in 1978, got 20,000 miles on it. I ain't going no place.
Where I'm gonna go? Go shopping, go to the house to see the kids,
go to see a funeral. Like today, I have to go to another funeral.

Everything went. After World War II, everything went. I tell
you, between pollution, bad water, everything we had on the
farms, everything dried away. Crops were bad. We had to leave.
Everybody's disappeared. Belgium, France, Germany, Switzer-
land. Everybody moving away, away from all over, from most of
the towns, every town in Sicily. Not too many remaining, and they
are the very old ones, saying, "Hey, what am I gonna do?" They're
still there, but the young generation, they all took off right after
the war, because there was no prosperity. Nothing doing there.
Things were going bad. That's it.

In Italy, we built a monument, for my son. We built a monument up there. The land was donated from the priest, the monsignor. I knew him when he was a kid. He was about three years
younger than me. He was a good friend of my brother. They went
to school together. He became a monsignor, and my brother, he
wound up in France.

When my wife went back for a visit to Italy, she said she
wanted to do something, to build something for my kid in the
town where my boy was born, so the monsignor said, "I have a
space." He had a space about twenty-five feet square. Now, one-
half of it, the state owned, but the piece that the church owned
had had a little chapel on it years back. It fell apart, and nobody

bothered to put it back. So, anyway, she said, "I got a spot." They got in the car and went to the head of the town, and they talked to the bishop. They explained they wanted to buy the piece of land. The bishop said, "For what?" The monsignor said, "One of the boys, a friend of mine, he died in Vietnam, and the mother wants to put up a monument." He released that deed for nothing, not even a dollar. The land that belonged to the Church, and the other piece that belonged to the state, they got both of them together, and that is where they built. They go celebrate Mass there every month. It is in a small town, population four thousand. Montedoro. Montedoro is the name of the town.

The monument is made of all brick and marble. The floor and all the steps are marble, too. It was finished in 1971. We had to get a bricklayer from out of town and an engineer from out of town to put the arches up. She's been back to see it three times, but not me. *The Last Supper* is inside, and it has all gold writing, the inscription. All the landscaping is not finished yet, but the fence is up. It's wrought iron, copper plated. It is very fine fence work. And the cross, it is very delicate, very fine work. This money I spent myself. They just give me the land. We just got the land for nothing. The rest we had to pay for. Each soldier, he should have his own stone, his own grave and sculpture. He should have his own flag. Every year he should have that honor.

It's not easy. It's a tough thing to go through all that. It is a scar. How can you forget? Every time I turn around, even if I go into another room, I see something. The picture. The gun. We used to hunt together. Fishing, he was with me like a little puppy, like a puppy dog. He wouldn't get away from me at all. Anything I needed, I had from him: "Hey, Sam." "Yes, Dad." Boom. It's mine. I need that thing, and right away, it's mine. Now, what happens? So many things I remember. If he would be sick, that would be another story. Not this way. This was a slaughterhouse way.

DANNY JOE FRIES · LARRY E GLAFFELTER · LA

GE R KELLEY · LYLE A KLOEK · JOHN W KRECK

LIAM A PAHISSA · THOMAS R SCHULTZ · DO

UGHTER · LAUREN W STANDRING · DANIEL J

TLIFF · PAUL L HAINING · TERRY LEE MERRITT

NETH P TANNER · WILFRED W WARNER Jr · JO

ROBERT L BOLAN · HARRY J BORT · BILLY B BU

LENN Jr · KENNETH D. HAMMEL · BRUCE D K

WYER Jr · GREG D STEVENSON · JOHN A SUN

TIMOTHY M GREELEY · PAUL A GREGORY · H

AL Jr · DONALD R SIMON · JACK E TAYLOR ·

D · J V WATSON · MARTIN W WRIGHT · MUR

WALTER W HAMILTON · ROBERT L ASMUTH

H MERCER · STEVEN B MILLS · DENNIS R NOB

GTON · LARRY W RASEY · MARTIN L RODGER

S E TAYLOR · GREGORY C THOMPSON · CLE

RRENCE R BILLINGS · MICHAEL R BLANCHET

GREG DOUGLAS "TONY" STEVENSON

Born: August 31, 1948
Duncan, Oklahoma
Killed: July 24, 1970
Long Binh Province, Republic of
South Vietnam

RLATT · PLEASANT McCRAY Jr · RONALD F PE

NALD E AUTEN · CLYDE J BALL · DONALD A B

J · EDISON A HARKINS III · HAROLD U HAYES

Tony Stevenson

Toni Stevenson
and Carolyn Hayter

CAROLYN STEVENSON HAYTER

Born: September 21, 1949
Odessa, Texas
Widow of Greg Douglas "Tony" Stevenson

I Can't Accept It

My husband was killed in July of 1970, just a few weeks before he would have been twenty-two. He was killed in noncombat action when his tank went over an embankment. They were in elephant grass and didn't see the embankment. The tank rolled over. He was the tank commander. It threw him out. The tank crushed his head and injured the other guys, but not critically.

We'd been married for three years, but had gone together from the ninth grade on, from the time I was fourteen. I was nearly twenty-one when he was killed. I was pregnant, and his baby daughter was born two days after the funeral, which was thirteen days after he was killed. He'd been in Vietnam since December of 1969, so he was over there eight months. I was a kid, and he was a kid, so we didn't really talk about the politics of it, but he didn't really want to go. He felt it was his duty, so he went. Reluctantly, but he went. He felt it was better to do that than be branded a coward.

It's been so long that I don't really remember where he was all of the time, all of the little towns. He had me buy a map of Vietnam, and he'd write and tell me basically where they were. It was in Long Binh Province, but I don't remember all the places. He'd write and say things like, "We're so many klicks [kilometers] over from such-and-such," and "This is where we are at this time." I don't get into that often now. It's kind of hard to get into it and bring it all out again.

The way I learned of his death was sort of strange. I woke up that morning around eight o'clock. I don't remember the time exactly, but I was dreaming. I had a dream that I was with him in Vietnam. He was with the 11th Armored Cav, but I dreamed that we were in a transport plane, preparing to bail out and go into combat. I was there with him and all the other guys, and I was talking about how scared I was. I was wearing fatigues, the whole bit. He said, "Don't worry. I'm going to take care of you. Don't worry about anything, because I'll take care of you." At that instant, there was a knock on the door. I immediately knew something was wrong. A cousin of mine was staying with us at the time. She answered the door. I heard someone say, "Is Mrs. Stevenson here?" She said, "Yes, she is." My mother came from her room and said, "What's the matter?" There was an army guy standing there, in uniform. He said, "I need to talk to Mrs. Greg Stevenson." I came out of my room, putting my robe on: "Is he all right?" He said, "How are you doing?" I was huge, carrying my daughter. "I'm fine. Is he hurt?" He said, "Are you okay?" "He's dead, isn't he?" "Yes, ma'am, he is." That was it. He told me it was a noncombat death. That was it. He went over and told Tony's parents.

They were affected by his death, too. I think it's painful for them to see his daughter. They love her, and they were close to her for a while, but I've always made a point to see that she would be around them, that she would know them. Now they've drifted apart. They live in Oklahoma part of the time, since his father's retired. They write her and say, "We do love you, and we want to keep in touch," but I feel it's too hard for them to realize it's their son's daughter who's living, and he's gone. They do keep in touch, some.

Their other son was in Vietnam, also. He was injured there. I think it was about a year before Tony was killed. He was hurt pretty bad. He's partially disabled. Shrapnel hit him, and he has only partial use of the fingers on one of his hands. They were touched by Vietnam twice, but their older son is living.

The days between hearing of Tony's death and the day of the funeral are a blur to me. I remember the telegrams, and receiving some of his possessions. I was told that Gary Dan, one of his friends, wanted to come home with him. We said okay. It was hard to think of him being sent home alone, so Gary Dan brought him home. We all went to the airport the night the casket arrived. There was an instant bond between me and Gary Dan, this boy I knew absolutely nothing about. I had written to his wife a few times. Tony had mentioned him vaguely in his letters, but when he came up to me at the airport, there was an instant bond. We held each other, and we cried. I talked to him a little that night, but not a lot, I think. As I said, I really don't remember a lot about it.

I have a good friend who told me I spent one entire day with her after I received word that he was dead, before the funeral. She said she took me to her house in Goldsmith to get me away. To this day, I don't remember that. I vaguely remember the funeral. They had a flag on his casket. I didn't want it, but I did want it. I wanted people to realize he went over there. He didn't die in combat action, but still, he did go over there, and he was over there fighting. He did earn that respect. I didn't want a military funeral, really, but his parents did. I don't even know if it would be called a military funeral. He had a flag on his coffin, and I think that taps was played, and a twenty-one-gun salute, but I don't really remember. He's not buried in a military cemetery; he's at Sunset Memorial Gardens, but, as I say, the funeral is a blur. I don't remember all of it, probably because I don't want to.

I have talked about it some, but only once, in 1979. I remarried in 1976. We had one child, a boy. In 1979 we split up. My husband then asked me if I would go to marriage counseling to see if we could save the marriage. I said okay, and, after about three visits, the counselor told him, "Look, you're wasting your time. This marriage will not work." Then he looked at me and said, "But you need some help, don't you? I feel there's something bothering you." I talked to him and started seeing him on my own. He helped me to somewhat accept Tony's death.

I went through a period when I really didn't think he *was* dead, because I didn't see him. When they sent all his possessions back, I tried to postpone the funeral, because I wanted his wedding ring buried on him. We had some problems before he went to Vietnam. We were fighting one time, and he took his ring off and threw it at me. He said, "You know, this is it. You take it." When we got back together, he said, "I'll put it back on, but only if I never, ever have to take it off again." I said, "Never. This is it. Never. It's all okay." That kept going through my mind before the funeral, and I kept thinking, "When will all his things be here? I want his ring on him." They told me they were trying to rush it to me, so that it would be there on time, but they didn't make it. The funeral was on Tuesday. I went into the hospital on Wednesday, and Wednesday afternoon my mother went to the post office and picked up the ring and brought it to me. It was close, but they didn't get it to me before the funeral.

Receiving the ring did help some. I thought, "He wouldn't have taken it off unless he *was* dead." That did help, but it didn't help, because I didn't *see* him. I would think, "How do I know that he wasn't hurt badly, lost an arm, maybe, or lost a leg, or was just disfigured in some way, so that he didn't want to come back and put a burden on his family?" That was really basically the way he was. He didn't want to be a burden to anyone. So I said to myself, "What if something happened to him, and he couldn't come back in one piece, and he just decided to go somewhere else?" As I said, it wasn't until 1979 that I accepted that he really was dead. I didn't want him to be dead. To this day, I don't.

I watched the POWs [prisoners of war] come home. It was early 1973, and I sat there and watched. Part of me felt good. I could think, "I'm so happy for each of you. You're coming home." Then, another part of me would say, "Why in the name of God isn't that my husband coming off that plane? Why couldn't they have been wrong? Maybe I'm going to see him step off this plane."

That was in 1973, and I was still saying, "Maybe, maybe, maybe. Maybe they *were* wrong; maybe he is going to step off." I watched them stepping off the plane, and I cried all the way through it. It's a hard thing to live with.

I received a letter last December from a boy who served with him in 'Nam. He had gone to the dedication of the Vietnam Memorial, and he wrote me at my mother's address. He said, "I know this seems strange, after twelve years, to write, but I went to the memorial, and I saw Greg's name, and it finally hit me." He said, "I never admitted how much of a loss it is to me until I saw his name. I cried. I want to know how you are and how the baby is. I do remember you were pregnant. How is the baby? How is the family? I hope your life has been happy." It just killed me.

I intend to answer the letter, but I haven't yet. His parents received a letter, also. My daughter told me. They've answered it. I want to, but I don't want to, because, when I talk about it, it doesn't affect me for just the time I'm talking or sitting there, writing. It affects me for days or weeks. It's not something I can talk about and immediately dismiss. Nearly thirteen years have gone by. I should be able to handle it better, but I can't.

When he left for Vietnam, he didn't know I was pregnant. I found out about a month later. One time, before he was drafted, but when we thought it was inevitable that he would be drafted, I told him, "If you do get drafted, I want to be pregnant when you leave, because, God forbid, if anything happens to you, I want something of yours to have always." He said, "Okay," then he said, "No. I don't want that, because I don't want anybody else raising my child." I told him, "Well, that's the way it's going to be, but you don't have to worry, because you're coming home to raise it. It's going to have to put up with you as an old man. When you go, I want to be pregnant."

I really think we both felt that if he went, he wouldn't come back. We didn't talk about it, but the last time I saw him was in Hawaii. It was exactly three months to the day before he died. He received an early R & R, because I was pregnant and wouldn't be able to travel when his original time came up. I met him in Hawaii on the eighteenth of April. The morning we left, we went to the airport without having talked about many things. When we said good-bye, though, I think we both knew it. I thought about it later, and I think we both realized that was it, the last time we would see each other. And it was. There was nothing said, in fact, it was just the opposite. He told me, "There's nothing that's going to stop me coming home to you. I'm going to be home Christmas. You've always been like a little kid. You're so excited at Christmas. I won't miss it. I'll be there, so don't you worry. By God, nothing is going to stop me. I'll be there." I said, "Okay." My plane left about thirty minutes before his did. I looked out of the plane and saw him standing there. That was it. I know that everyone, when they see their spouses and tell them good-bye, they cling . . . but this was such a different type of clinging. Like a farewell: "This is it. I know it is." But nothing was said.

All of his things are in a footlocker in one of my closets. Every now and then I'll feel brave, and I'll open it and look through it. I'll look at the pictures from our wedding, or notes we wrote one another in high school. I have the map of Vietnam. I can look at that, and at his picture album. His dad was taking pictures and sending them to him. Most of them showed my progress from flat belly to pot belly. I can look at that, and I can look at the postcards he sent me from Hawaii on his way to Vietnam, but I can't read any of the letters he sent from the time he actually reached Vietnam. Part of me says, "Burn them. Just get rid of them." I can't do it. I think I need to do it. I need to try to finalize in my own mind that he is gone, that part of my past is dead, that it's over. His moods would fluctuate in the letters. Some of his moods were very light, something about how happy he was that he was going to be a father. His very next letter might be sour on the world, sour on us, and reflecting on the problems we'd had. He just seemed very moody, which would be understandable, with the pressure he was under over there.

In Hawaii, when we talked, he talked about his baby, and about a little Vietnamese girl, one of his scout's daughters. She and Tony were close. She'd given him a necklace, and she'd wait for them at the base when they'd come back in. He told me that one day he came back and had to tell her that her daddy would never come back again. Her father was killed. He'd also talk about some of his buddies who were killed. In one letter he wrote shortly after he arrived there, he told me how pretty the nighttime was, which sounds ironic. He said, "It's beautiful. The sky lights up in an orange blaze, and it's hard to believe it's causing such destruction where it's hitting, because it's so pretty to watch. That sounds kind of cruel. It is, in fact, but you've just got to make light of where you are."

I've had several people who were extremely close to me die. Father, grandfather, my grandmother, not to mention my husband. They were all centers of my life. In two cases, though, there were illnesses, and you know what's going to happen. You can start trying to prepare for that, and maybe in some way you can even be glad that it's coming, because they're out of their pain; but this, you can never really accept it. Number one, he was just a baby. Twenty-one years old is really a baby. His life had barely started. I cannot get a grasp yet on how this could have happened, how a tragedy like that can happen when he'd done no one any harm. He wasn't sick. There really wasn't even any reason to send him over there. It's just that one day he's alive, and the next day, he's dead. It's very hard for me to accept. I cannot justify it.

I still haven't accepted it. In fact, just last year I saw a guy and did a double take. I thought, "God, it looks just like him." For that instant, I thought, "Could it be?" Then I thought, "No, no, no." The sensible side of me says that he's gone: "He's dead. Accept it." Then there's that part of me that just doesn't want to let it die. I don't want him dead. I try not to think about the memorial in Washington. My daughter and I discussed it a little. She said, "Mama, I'd like to go see it." I said, "Someday I would too." I mean, I thought it was great. I think they deserve more than they got, sort of getting pushed under the carpet. . . . All of the vets have. It's an embarrassment to the government, but I'm proud of it, and I would like to see it someday. About a month ago, I saw pictures of it, and it's beautiful. Someday I'll go see it. I'll take my daughter and go see it.

Before he was killed, I guess a couple of years before he was killed, his parents had gotten back into church. They were going to church all the time. Every time it was open, they were there. After he was killed, they quit going. To my knowledge, neither of them has been back since he died. We saw each other a lot right after the baby was born. I would tell his mother, "I know he loved his baby." Then I moved out of town when she was about six months old. I didn't want to stay where every time I turned around I drove by an apartment where we used to live, or I'd go to his parents' house and remember things that happened when we were there. But, when I started visiting his parents again, I told his mother, "I know you want to see the baby. I'm going to let her stay over as much as I can." She needed to be around the baby. She's all they have left of their son. I spent a great deal of time with them, and then, all of a sudden, about five years ago, it started slowing down. It was about the time I got married. I talked to them several times. I'd say, "You just don't want to see her." She'd say, "No, no. I want to see her." I told her, "Well, you know I want you to see her as much as you want to. You know I'm not trying to push her off on you, but I want you to see her." I thought that she was the only living thing they had left of him. To be honest, that's the only reason I stayed alive. Because I had her.

I thought about killing myself. I had told my mother several times, "He's not going to come home. I can't handle it. I don't want to." She said, "No, no. You're carrying his baby." And I would say, "I don't have him." I think that's why they took the baby as early as they did. The doctor told me about a month before she was born that she was breach, and that he was going to have to take it by cesarean. She was a big baby. I had a broken tailbone, and all these complications. I think that's why the sergeant who came to tell me he was dead kept asking, "Are you all right?"

I had written to Tony and told him I was scared, because I was. I'm petrified of surgery. The baby was not actually due for about a week or two more weeks, but, all of a sudden, a few days after I found out he was killed, I had to go in for a checkup, and the doctor said, "I'm going on vacation, so I'm going to go ahead and take the baby. I'll take it on such-and-such a date." I feel that probably what happened is my mother went to him and said, "This is what she told me." I think that's why they took the baby when they did, because they didn't know what I would do. I was in a state of shock.

I do remember being in the hospital. My husband's funeral was on Tuesday, and they put me in the hospital the next day. The following morning they knocked me out, and when I woke up I had a daughter. When we were in Hawaii, we picked out two names. If it was a boy, it was going to be Scott Anthony, and, if it was a girl, it was going to be Kelly Lee. I named her Toni, which was his nickname. I thought, "I'll name it Toni Lee, and I'll always have him. I'll always have a part of him." I thought that was significant. I don't know whether it was or not, but it was a part of him that would live on.

I moved out of my mother's house the latter part of October. During late November, I started getting our apartment ready for Christmas. I really felt he was coming home Christmas. In the back of my mind, I thought, "He'll be here. He promised. He'll be here." When he didn't show up, I thought he *must* be dead. I thought it, but I never would accept it. To this day, in April every year, I'm in another world. I met him in Hawaii in April. Then, probably from the first part of July until after my daughter's birthday, I'm always very depressed. Everything upsets me, because that's when it all began to go into motion and everything went downhill. I usually pick up after her birthday. Then, beginning with Thanksgiving, I'm depressed until Christmas is over. I hate the holidays. Three or four months out of every year, I'm depressed.

When I used to go to the psychologist . . . one day he asked me, "Have you ever thought that possibly you're mad at him?" I said, "What do you mean?" He said, "Mad that he didn't come home." I said, "No. It wasn't his fault." But the more I thought about it, the more I thought, "That *is* the feeling." I didn't want to admit it, because I thought that seemed cold and callous. I went to his grave about six months ago. I went to his grave at night and sat there and talked to him. When I was ready to go, I was crying.

I kicked his headstone and said, "Damn you, why did you die? You promised to come home." That's how I felt, and that was twelve years after he died. I never had been in touch with that at all, not before that counselor brought it up. I had never thought about it in that context, but it is anger. Anger, resentment, a whole bunch of emotions rolled into one. Probably a little bit of selfishness, too: "Why didn't you come home? How could you do this to me? How could you let yourself get killed?"

The guy who brought him home told me if Tony had been a split second faster, he could have gotten down into the tank. He would have been hurt, but it probably wouldn't have killed him. He said he could have fallen back into the tank and not been crushed. He didn't want to die. I know he didn't want to die, but I kept saying, "Why did he do it? Why couldn't he have been quicker?"

I didn't go to work until my daughter started kindergarten. I received compensation from the VA and Social Security. I didn't have to work, and I thought, "By gosh, you owe it to her. If he'd come home, I wouldn't have had to work, so I'm going to stay home with my daughter as much as I can. You support me." I was mad at the government for being in a war that accomplished nothing except getting people killed and helping our economy by having all those boys gone. I resent the government. I don't think there's a family involved in that war that doesn't. We were butting in some place we really had no reason for being. Still, we went over there, and we let our men get killed, and we pulled out and let the enemy take over in the long run. We got all those boys killed for no reason.

Last Thanksgiving, I was in one of my moods. Very down, very depressed. I had been going to this doctor, and I had been on mood pills. Mother got upset and talked to my girl friend; she's the doctor's nurse. My girl friend said, "Don't you realize what's affecting Carolyn? Carolyn's not affected by anything that's going on in her life right now. She's affected by the things that happened in the past. Do you realize that she's never even accepted that Tony's dead?" My mother said, "Oh, but she has." My girl friend

said, "No. She never has. I don't think she ever will. She's not
ready to. She doesn't want to." Not many people realize how I did
feel about it and why I want to stay away during holidays. I'll go
to family gatherings and be there . . . well, like Christmas. I go
to my mother's house at Christmastime long enough to open
presents on Christmas Eve, then I'll leave. Or Christmas dinner.
We go long enough to eat, then leave.

When I left Odessa when my daughter was about six months
old, I went to Colorado. I stayed there for about a year, then came
back here, stayed for a while, and went to Houston. I stayed in
Houston for two years. I didn't really work there, but one of the
girls that lived next door to me in the apartment complex was a
librarian in an elementary school. I did volunteer work with her
three days a week, but I never really worked for money until my
daughter was five and started kindergarten.

It was so strange, because all the time I was gone, when I was
in Colorado, when I was in Houston, I usually had a three-hun-
dred-dollar phone bill every month. Calling home, talking to my
mother every day almost. I wanted to be away, but I didn't want
to be away. I was trying to run away from it, and was finding out
I couldn't. When I was away, there was no one that knew him to
bring back the past. I thought I could start over that way, be
someplace where I didn't have to talk about it; but I had to think
about it. I came back home, and it is difficult. I'll drive down the
streets and look at places where we used to live, and it's like I have
a vise on my heart. I can feel it gripping. But there are times when
I can talk about it. I might tell my daughter things that happened,
and have good thoughts about the past, talk about some things
about the past happily, about when he was here, and not want to
ignore it.

The day I got the letter from that friend he'd served with I
had gone to an open house. I had a nice time at the party and was
feeling good. I went to my mother's house to pick up Toni and my
son. My daughter said, "Here, Mama, you got a letter." I thought,
"Who can it be from? Who would write me a letter addressed like
that, to Carolyn *Stevenson* at my mother's house, after all these

years?" I read it, and I just went to pieces. My daughter said, "Mama, what's wrong?" I said, "Nothing." I just threw the letter down. The next day, when I went back over there, my mother was there. I said, "I came after my letter. Do you still have it?" "Yes." "It's from a guy that was with Tony." That's it. That night I let my daughter read it. She said, "Mama, what bothers you? What's wrong? What happened?" I said, "I'll show you what bothers me," because she was real upset. She hates to see her mama upset. She read the letter, and she started crying. She grabbed me. She said, "Oh, Mama, why didn't he come home? I'm sorry." I said, "It's not your fault, but I don't want to think about it." She said, "I know."

I know it affects her that her daddy is dead, but I don't know if it affects her naturally, or whether she just sees how much it bothers me, because she was not emotionally attached to him. The fact that she doesn't have a daddy bothers her, but basically, I think, she sees how it bothers me. Sometimes I can talk about him, and we'll laugh. We'll get out the picture album, and we'll look at the pictures. It's pictures of her when she was a tiny baby, and pictures of him that he sent me from over there. Sometimes I can sit and talk to her about it, and other times she'll ask me questions and I'll try to get her mind off it, and my mind off it. It's affected her, even though she was not born when it happened. She did not know him, but she's still very much affected by it.

She's lacked male companionship. She's not that close to her grandfather, and my dad's dead. I have two brothers, but they have families of their own. She has never experienced closeness with a man. She'll get down sometimes. Maybe she senses my feelings. She'll cry, and she'll say, "I wish I could have known Daddy." Her grandparents evidently talk about him some. She came home one day from their place. Her grandmother had been cleaning out closets and gave her a beaded Indian neckpiece, Indian beads that he made in Boy Scouts. Boy, did she treasure it. You know, it's really kind of amazing that she is such a loving person, that she loves him, even though she never knew him. I told her when she was sixteen I was going to give her a pearl ring her daddy gave me when I was sixteen, and she said, "Oh, Mama, Mama, please, can I have it?" This is so neat, because the child never knew, yet something that he gave to me is so important to her.

When I got married—what led to me getting married—my daughter had been hurt in February of 1976. She fell at school and fractured her skull, and it hit me that I came very close to losing her. She was hurt in the head, just like her father was, and it scared me. As I said, I had gone to work in October of 1975, right after she started kindergarten. I started working her school hours, from eight-thirty to two-thirty, and I felt, "Well, this is good, because I'm not taking any time away from her, yet I still have an outlet." In February of 1976, she fell at school and fractured her skull. They had to rush her to the emergency room. When I got there, they were X-raying her. I think she was conscious, but she crushed her mastoid on her right side, and she had drainage coming out of her ears. She was in the hospital about three days, then they let me bring her home. There was no damage to her brain or anything, and the drainage was supposed to stop in a couple of days. Well, the drainage went on for almost a week, and I was paranoid. I thought, "I could lose her." The doctor had told me if it didn't stop draining on its own, he would have to go in and do surgery on her head, open it up and close it. I thought, "No. I'll lose her. You can't do this." Well, as it turned out, it finally quit on its own, but she's deaf in her right ear.

After it happened, I kept thinking, "I need to be at home. I need to stay home so if she needs me, I can be there." Well, I had known this guy some, and we started dating. He was just all "Oohs" and "Aahs," and good to her and good to me. I got sick, and he came over when he got off work. He cooked for me, actually cooked and cleaned up. When I'd get ready for bed, he'd go home. If I ever needed anything, he was there to help, and I thought, "Well, maybe what I need is somebody to take care of me. Then I can stay home, and I can take care of her." I know

now that's why I got married. I felt I needed somebody to help take care of us, because I wasn't doing too good; if I'd been doing good, she would not have been hurt.

I know now that's a bunch of baloney, but then it even went through my mind that maybe it might have been my fault that my husband got killed. Part of me felt, "Well, it was my fault, because if I hadn't got pregnant, he would have come home." As I said, we had had trouble, and he was excited about the baby, but, at the same time, he was not. I think he felt, "Maybe this isn't mine. Maybe she's been messing around, and maybe this is somebody else's." That was wrong, and I told him so. Still, some of his letters do mention that. That's part of why I can't look at the letters. I know it's different, being over there and going through all the pressures he was under. Everything went through his mind. One letter would be degrading, and the next letter would be great, how he loved me and could hardly wait to get home, and we'd have a family. I think that's why I thought maybe he faked the death, that maybe he felt, "Well, with those troubles we had, maybe she was messing around. Maybe it's somebody else's. I'm not going home."

Still, I really know he loved me and wanted to come home. Even with the troubles that we had, we still had the love. We were kids, but we still had the love, and there was nobody else. It was just that he had those thoughts because he was miles away. I think everything went through their minds over there. They were under such pressures that they thought things like, "I'm not there to watch over you. I don't know what you're doing. You're probably doing this to me, and you're probably doing that to me." Had the circumstances been different, had he just been overseas and not in the war, I probably would have had the same thoughts about him: "Are you being faithful to me?" We talked about it in Hawaii. I said, "You know that it's not anyone else's. It's yours." He said, "I know it." Then he said, "When I'm over there, all these thoughts go through my mind. I don't know what I'm thinking half the time, because I'm scared, and I want to come home." He was apologizing for it. I never have talked to anyone else, any other widows, but I feel that probably they're going through the same things I have, the same feelings: "Was it something I did, something I said? If I had done this different, that different, could he have come home?"

The loss of my father and grandfather and Tony has always been . . . I've never fully understood them, and I've never fully accepted them. My father died first. He was thirty-one when he died. He had his own plane, and he was flying. We lived in New Mexico at the time, and he was flying down here to Odessa. My grandmother was having surgery. The weather got bad. It started snowing, and his wings froze. I think he was trying to land on a dirt road, because he was a quarter-mile from the dirt road when he caught on the power line. It killed him instantly.

After that, we moved back to Odessa. My grandparents were always there. They were more like parents than grandparents. We were all very close. It was just very special. I was the only grand-daughter, and I was spoiled rotten. My grandfather and I were very close, and he died of cancer when I was only twelve. A year to the day after he died, I started going with Tony. He was just a little kid that I started going with, yet I always thought that was significant. I thought, "Well, now he's taking over." He was like a father image to me. We went together all that time, and it was really kind of a strange relationship. We never did anything until we got married. We kissed a lot, but we never went to bed until we got married. He always referred to me as his "little kid," his "little girl friend." Then, when he died, it was as if my whole life was gone. I was seventeen when we married. Ten days out of high school. Ten days. I thought I was really old and knew everything. I was a baby. I still have a picture of him in the house in my bedroom. Sometimes I wonder if that's wrong. I wonder if every-one in my position still does that.

I was reading in a book about an airplane they found last year. It crashed in 1946, in the Philippines, I think. They were talking about the mother of one of the guys and the ex-wife of one of the guys, talking about how, especially the mother of one of them, about how she'd never given up hope. In a way, I felt I kind of related to it. I thought, "I'm sort of the same way." I think, "Well, maybe. Maybe he's not dead. I just hope he's happy. If he didn't want to come back for some reason or other, I don't understand it, but if he's happy, it doesn't matter." Sometimes I think I'll go crazy. I know I am almost obsessed with finding someone to love me and my kids and have a family with. Mother has never acted as if it bothered her that she was alone. I'm sure it did. I'm sure that it did, but she's never really acted like it bothered her. I think, "There's got to be somebody. Why isn't there somebody? Where is somebody that wants to be with me and my kids? Someone that's good enough. Good enough to love my kids, to take care of my kids."

I've looked at that letter that guy wrote last November. I've looked at it several times. It's on my dresser, and I keep thinking I may write. I need to write, for common courtesy if nothing else, because he did write to me. He lives in Minnesota. His letter was really very touching. He said he didn't realize how much Tony had meant to him, how much the loss of him meant, until he saw his name. He said it was as if twelve years had just come back to him. He said, "I cried like a baby." My heart went out to him, because I thought, "Yeah. I know what you're going through." I've thought several times about him. In fact, I think a lot about the boy who brought him home. I wonder how he is, how he's doing. He was from Pennsylvania.

That boy said Tony didn't have to go out that day. He could have waited another day, but he told Gary, "I want to get out there. I can't stand just sitting here. The sooner I get out there and get all this over with, the sooner I can go home, and I am going home." I think he was two minutes out of camp when it happened. I think it was seven-ten in the morning. The tank just rolled over. There was no enemy fire, no nothing. No. It just rolled over. They were in elephant grass, and they couldn't see the embankment because of the grass, and it went over.

The Beatles had a song out, "Here Comes the Sun." He wrote me and said, "If you'll play this in the afternoon about five o'clock, that's the time I'm getting up and starting to go. Think about me, because that's just one more day that I'm okay." I bought the album. The other day, I played it, and I thought, "One more day, and he's okay." Every now and then I hear it, and I'll think it's okay; I can listen to it. Usually, though, things like that bother me too much, and I can't listen. There's another song. Tony was a lineman for the telephone company. He was on the construction crew. Glen Campbell had a song out called "Wichita Lineman." That was ours, because he was working for the phone company. I reached the point where I couldn't listen to that one at all. It still comes on now, and I turn it off. I don't want to hear it. I don't want to think about it. I guess I'm too emotional a person. There's a lot of friends of ours that I love a great deal. I feel very strongly for them. I'd do anything for them if they asked me, but I stay away from them. It's too painful, being around them.

I'm sure I cannot imagine how his parents feel, because there's a big difference in losing a husband. There's a feeling that I have that they don't have, and there are feelings they have that I'm sure I don't have. For his mother, he was something she carried for nine months. I'm really sort of surprised at his parents, that one of them did not die, especially his mother, because of the pressure and the pain. She has changed a great deal, and I have, too. We've really grown apart, and I think it's because neither of us wants to talk about it. They did sit me down one time when I came back from out of town. They said, "Carolyn, do not think that we want you to lead your life by mourning Tony. You have a life of your own, and you need to get out. We want you to be happy. We don't expect you to sit at home and mourn from now on. That's not right." That's the closest we've ever come to talking about it.

I have thought, "You know, maybe all these fears that I have felt all these years, maybe everybody has gone through it, everybody who has lost a husband." I would like to talk to some people who are widows. Whatever. A woman. I have got to. I realize it. I should be able to accept it better and be able to carry on my life without it being so prevalent in my mind, after all this time.

TONI LEE STEVENSON

Born: August 6, 1970
Odessa, Texas
Daughter of Greg Douglas "Tony" Stevenson

I Wish

I don't know much about my father. No one talks about him much. I don't know how tall he was, or anything like that.

My mother tells me some things about him, but just a little bit. I don't really know anything about what he was like, what kind of person he was. I don't like to talk about it. I'm afraid it'll make her cry.

I just wish I had a father. Everyone I know has a father. Even the ones whose parents are divorced, they still have a father. He's still alive.

Sometimes I don't ask about him because I'm afraid someone will say something bad about him, or something like that, that he did something wrong or something. If anyone ever said that, I'd get really mad.

SE ROMERO CASTRO · McKINLEY CAUG
WARD J HABUREY · FRANK C HUFF · CLE
AROLD K KETNER Jr · LLOYD M KUEHN ·
ORMAN G LOZEAU · JOHN M MANSFIELD
ONNIE RAY PITTMAN · CHARLES L PUTNA
OBERT J SOMMERER · WOODROW J MUE
OSS J WALKER · JAMES M ALBRIGHT · DAV
EL A BROWN · CECIL L CHAPMAN · JOHN
HN H FLYNN · BERNARD A FREYNE · EDW
MES J L JOHNSON · WARREN E KECK · RO
UIS P MERINO · CHESTER A MYERS Jr · D
COB F STEPAN · HARRY RAY STEWART · C
REN·A ARMLIN · WILLIE J BAKER · EDWAR
KE ARMENDAREZ · FORREST D HOEME ·
ANK C ESPOSITO · GARY W FRIEDMANN
LVIN K GRAESER Jr · GUY P GUADAGNO
ANCIS R CONCANNON · JAMES M HOLS

JOEL ANDREW BROWN

Born: **August 27, 1946**
Lackawanna, New York
Killed: **March 10, 1967**
Somewhere near the Cambodian border,
Republic of South Vietnam

ARLES W BARRETT · BOYD G GARNER ·
BERT E JOHNSON · RONALD L JOHNSTO

Joel Brown *(left)* and friend

Kenneth Brown and his
daughter Melanie

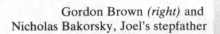

Gordon Brown *(right)* and
Nicholas Bakorsky, Joel's stepfather

GORDON P. BROWN

Born: June 22, 1935
Buffalo, New York
Brother of Joel Andrew Brown

Still, He's Not Around

When he first went over, he was a grenade launcher. Then he got that fungus or something all over him from being in the swamp. It was all over his body. When he was a baby, he had delicate skin. A wool blanket would make him break out. One year, when he was a kid, he was just all full of sores, and we had to get sulfur powder. I used to have to go to the drugstore and get it. I had to walk about two miles for that when I was a kid. Maybe that's why he and I were close. I used to go get his medicine for him. He had that awful dripping and itching for over a year when he was younger, and he got it over there, so he left the grenade launcher and went to the APC [armored personnel carrier], so he didn't have to be in the swamp. Then he got hit with a mortar, and he had a big hole in his chest, and his hands were burned and his legs were burned, but his face was perfect, just like himself. The coffin was open.

He received the Distinguished Service Cross, the second-highest medal, under the Medal of Honor. He saved about fifteen lives, and he was killed saving them. He received the medal post-humously. According to this captain's letter and other letters my mother received, they were in an APC. There were sixteen of them. There's a gunner on top of a driver and fourteen soldiers in it. He was the gunner, and they became surrounded by a group of 'Cong. They all got blown off and were running and hiding. Then they heard screaming. One of the men was wounded, lying by the APC. Joel went back up, got him, and brought him back to safety, the one that was wounded, but they were still being pinned down. I guess he thought the only way out, or one of the ways out, was to make it back to the APC, get up on the gun, and start spraying, and that's what he did. He was safe twice, and then, when he went back the third time, that's when he got hit with a mortar. He had a big hole in his side from the shrapnel, and his hands and legs were burned, but he got all the other guys out of there. I don't know how many he killed while he was getting them out. They went back in later and got his body out.

All the boys that were affected or were in his platoon wrote my mother a letter and said, "What a great thing your son did for us." One said, "I'm going to come see you," but, you know how young boys are when they come home and everything, none of them ever came by. One letter from a kid from North Carolina said that if it weren't for my brother, they'd all be dead. That made me feel good, anyway. He didn't get killed for nothing, but, still, he's not around.

This captain who wrote said he was going to put him in for the Distinguished Service Cross. He said it didn't mean he was going to get the medal, but he was going to submit his name for it. He said, "Now, don't get your hopes up. We very seldom give a medal like that." My mother got it at the ceremony at the armory here in Buffalo. I didn't attend. My other brother didn't, either. I didn't even see the medal. Still haven't. Haven't seen it to this day. It's just a piece of iron. A piece of iron doesn't do anything for me. He isn't here. I'd rather have him around, but it didn't work out that way. Anyway, my mother and my stepfather went down to the armory. They had the whole squad or whatever, the whole company of them, full dress, top brass, a representative from Washington, top brass, and they presented my mother with the Distinguished Service Cross and Purple Heart.

He was twenty-one when he was killed. March 10, 1967. That was nearly sixteen years ago. They killed a lot of good boys over there for nothing. Then they gave them the country back. The war was for nothing. Then they gave it back to them. Crazy. That war was just shitty. It was just stupid. We left them better off than when we got there. They have bulldozers and all kinds of equipment now. I also have a bad feeling about those draft protestors. They run away, and this and that, and my kid brother, twenty-one, is gone, and then they let those guys back in the country. If everybody ran away, we'd be talking Russian out there now. We wouldn't be talking English.

When my brother was drafted, I said, "Why don't you go in the navy?" I tried to tell him, but he just said, "No, I'll do my two years, and then I'll be home." My other brother was a navy man, four years. I was going to go to Korea, then my mother told me to finish high school, so I finished high school and stayed home and got married, but Joel went into the army. He finished high school, then he worked at the Bethlehem Steel plant, then he got drafted. He was in just over a year and a half. He would have had just another couple of months to go, and he would have come back to the States. In another six months, he would have been discharged.

There's another boy from Lackawanna who got blown off a half-track truck. His name was Gary, and he had just two days to go in Vietnam when he got blown off and lost his arm. There's this one little area in Lackawanna, a real close community, about four hundred houses in this one section, and the only way in there was one or two roads in, and then the railroad tracks were in the back, and there was a creek on the other side, so you were really cut off from the other part of Lackawanna. It was just these four hundred houses right in this one little area of Lackawanna, and that's where four kids came from: my brother, this Gary kid, the DiTommaso boy, who's still missing in action, and Mrs. DiTommaso's next-door neighbor, who was hit real bad. He was a captain. It was tough in the neighborhood then. You get over one, and the next thing you know, somebody else got it.

When we went into the funeral home, his coffin was open. It was about three weeks after he had been killed, and he looked just like he had been sleeping. I think they pack them with dry ice or something, to keep them. We got the body, and we never knew the coffin was going to be open until we walked into the funeral parlor. Holy Jesus. My heart stopped. My mother is Italian, and the old Italian women, they're all screaming and hollering. Holy Jesus. It just sent chills through me. I was just coming in the door when I heard them moaning. I really felt bad when I saw Mr. DiTommaso come in. His son had been missing a year already by then. The poor man couldn't even kneel down when he saw my brother. He went out on the porch, and I went with him. I let him stay by my side, and I stayed by his side. Now, this man didn't even know where his boy was, and I said to myself, "I know where my brother is." Really different, scary circumstances. I didn't know how he felt, though.

That's about it. I drank a little bit more after he got killed, then I said to myself, "If you keep drinking and drinking, *you're* going to be dead." So, I didn't quit drinking, but I slowed down. I was getting drunk all the time. I just felt sorry he wasn't around. For myself, maybe, because he and I were tight. Hey, he was a good boy, but that's the way it goes.

I have two boys now. If they get drafted, they better get their asses into the army. I feel if that's what you have to do, you have to do it, if you live here, in this country. Like I said, if everybody kept running away, we'd have Russians standing out there tomorrow morning, telling us what to do, or somebody. I have one boy eighteen and one sixteen now. If they have to go, they have to go. The eighteen-year-old went last week and got registered. His birthday was January fourth, so he's registered now.

KENNETH P. BROWN

Born: July 10, 1936
Lackawanna, New York
Brother of Joel Andrew Brown

It's a Disgrace

GI life insurance. My mother did collect the benefits from that. She never spent it. She left it for my other brother and myself when she died. I still have the check home in my jacket. I don't know what my brother did with his, but mine is home in one of my suit jacket pockets, just sitting there. I don't have money, by the way. I live week to week. I work in the steel plant, and we're going under. I live week to week. I could very easily use that money, but I don't know what it is. I hate to cash it. I don't know what it is, but I'm still thinking about him and that money, and I don't know. I've never really sat down to think about it, to be honest, but I know once I do cash it, there's going to be some thoughts, like that his life is in that check. Like I say, my family could use that money very easily, for a million and one different things. I've got four children at home, but it's just sitting there. I'm sure I'll cash it soon.

My brother was drafted, but he had wanted to join a little earlier, before the heavy stuff started in Vietnam, before Vietnam really escalated. I feel a little bit guilty, because I advised him. I said, "Look, you're going to get drafted anyway. Why don't you just wait?" He did wait, and they did draft him, and it's hard, very hard. It's difficult to talk about even at this time.

It actually killed my mother. About two years before my brother was killed, my father died, so she didn't have him for support when Joel died, but she had remarried. She married a wonderful man, a very good man. I think if it weren't for her husband, she would have deteriorated more rapidly. My stepfather is a very emotional man. He's very warm, very feeling, very religious. Unfortunately, I'm not, quite. I have my beliefs, but he's the type of man that will not miss church. He gave her much, much support. We're still close to him. If it wasn't for him, I'm sure my mother's deterioration would have been much more rapid.

Joel's death had such an impact on her. He was the baby of the family. He was the youngest of the three of us, and she started taking all different types of medications and going to different doctors, four different doctors. They were all prescribing different medications. From the time he died until her death, which was just a year ago, she was almost hypochondriacal. She had imaginary illnesses, nerves, very bad nerves, heart problems, many different kinds of illnesses. The doctors couldn't find anything wrong, but they would keep giving her different types of medication, tranquilizers of all different types. Finally, they were giving her heart medication at some point. She had a houseful of medicines. She finally died from a stroke. She just fell down one night and went into a coma and never did recover from it. We saw the deterioration, and we just kind of went along with it. We knew then; we all knew it. We just said, "Ma's not herself," and we knew why, my brother and I. Our wives knew. She just was never the same. She just never recovered from it.

I myself have agoraphobia to a certain extent. It's very difficult to travel out of my own safe area. My agoraphobia started at the time of my father's death, which was only about two years before my brother's death. It's a terrible anxiety, a panic-feeling anxiety. It's anxiety, but it's a specific fear of travel, of leaving the home or a safe area. Even to this day, I'm receiving counseling for it. I was receiving counseling several years ago, but I'm more receptive to it now, and I have a great deal of respect for the counselor I have. She's only a young lady, but I do have a great deal of respect for her, and it's helping. That's the main thing. My brother's death just compounded my agoraphobia. I just tightened up more, became more anxious, more fearful of leaving a safe area. His death has changed my thinking drastically, dramatically.

Our family has always been, you know, God, country, the flag—I'm sure like hundreds of thousands of people throughout the United States. But this war wasn't a war to save you, it wasn't a war to save me, it was a war to save the rich. Out of fifty-nine thousand dead Vietnam soldiers, brave men, brave people, I don't think there's one whose parents have any substantial amount of money. I don't think there's one who's a congressman's son, a senator's son, a president's son. I don't think there's one that's even remotely related. It was a war for the rich. This country doesn't care about people's freedoms, but if it's going to affect the rich somehow, we're going to get involved. The rich won't. They most certainly will not. Their sons won't. Their daughters won't. Their nephews won't. They will only be involved to protect their interests. That's what happened in Vietnam, and my heart goes out to all the soldiers. It really does.

My brother was a hero; he saved his platoon. He could have been saved himself, but he chose to save his platoon. He won the Distinguished Service Cross, but medals mean nothing. I could go in a steel mill and stamp out a medal, so it means nothing. The war itself meant something. If we were so concerned about freedom, why would we let the Russians march into Afghanistan and just take it over and swallow it? You know why? We have no interest in Afghanistan. The rich have no interest in Afghanistan. It's mountains. There's nothing there. We have no oil fields, no wells, no good, no grain barrels. It's horseshit. Freedom's a word. I'm sorry to say that. I wouldn't have talked this way before. No, I was patriotic. I served four years in the navy. I was in national security, matters that I couldn't talk about to this day, and that was a good many years ago. I wouldn't discuss them today, but Vietnam's changed my thinking. I'm bitter, very bitter, and I'm no fool. If there's any way at all I can keep my son out of the military, I'm going to.

He's going to be fifteen in February, and he'll never serve in the armed forces if I have anything to do with it. I don't see any immediate problem, but we've discussed it, and he envisions the military as "glamour," because that's how we portray it: "glamour." The media, movies, films. That's glamour to the young person, and my son sees it that way, as most young men do. But if I have anything to say, he will not go. Never. I would do everything in my power to keep him out and try to talk some sense into him, especially in time of danger, war. No. No one in my family's going to fight for somebody else again unless I'm threatened, my family's threatened, my homeland's threatened.

I'm still a patriot. I still fly my flag, but I just know that Vietnam was the biggest perpetuation of a hoax on the American public that's ever come to pass. I just feel for all the families, the soldiers, and the wounded, the invalids, the POWs, the MIAs [missing in action]. It's terrible. It's a disgrace. I respect the Jews. They have a statement I've taken to heart: "Never again." Vietnam's taught me that. Never again. I'll take that from the Jewish nation. Never again. A lot of power in those words, a lot of power. And whatever I can do to persuade my son, to keep him out, I will do. I don't care if it's peacetime; I'm going to keep him out. I think there's a need for every average guy in the United States to do that.

They should draft a few men out of Harvard, draft a few men out of Yale, a few hundred out of Columbia. Draft a few hundred out of each one of those schools. Let's put those kids up at war. There won't be any more wars. There won't be. When the heads of the great families are sitting around with their caviar and whatever, they'll say, "Gee, do you know, Joe's got to go off to the war?" "That's funny, Mark might have to go to war." "That's funny, so is Terry." "You know, let's not have a war." Then, there ain't going to be no war.

It's a very simplistic way of thinking, but goddamn, if you stopped and thought about it, a lot of truth to it. A country the size of North Vietnam . . . can you imagine the size of that dump? Look at the map sometime and just take the area compared to one of our states. A nation as strong as we are? Come on. You couldn't convince a third-grader that we couldn't take that country. You couldn't convince a third-grader, no way.

I really feel for our soldiers. I really do. They did what they believed was right, and they got shit on when they came home. We're just starting to recognize them now, after how many years after the war? That's a disgrace. We know the war is a disgrace, because we treated our soldiers disgracefully. We know it's a disgrace. The American people know it's a disgrace, and they're ashamed to honor men that gave their lives for a farce that Americans all know was a farce. Somebody should be hung, literally, or, in the next war, they should be on the front lines. The sons of the rich should be on the front lines. They never will be, never, ever in our lifetime. You'll never see it. I'll never see it. Nobody'll ever see it. They're immune. They're immune from war. They've got all the loopholes. They're just immune to war. That's how Vietnam affected me, so that I talk like a revolutionary, maybe. It's the way I feel, and this war's made me feel this way.

You know, right when Joel died, I had one very eerie experience. I was working days at the steel plant, that's seven to three, seven in the morning to three in the afternoon. We were communicating with Joel. We received mail, and we would send him mail. Then one night I woke up very early in the morning, maybe three or four in the morning. I woke up, and I was in a sweat, and I started shaking. My wife says, "What's the matter?" I said, "Joel just got killed." She says, "Look, will you please go back to bed." I said, "No. He just got killed. Let me tell you something. I was in a sound sleep. . . ." I *was* in a sound sleep. He called for my mother; he called for my brother; and he called for me. He said, "Mom," and then he said, "Gordy," and then he said, "Kenny." Then he said, "I'm all right now. I'm okay now."

I went into my kitchen, and we had a little closet, a little cupboard, where my wife kept her mops and brooms and stuff. I opened the cupboard. We had a calendar there, and I circled the day. I said, "He's dead today," and I closed the cabinet. My wife said, "Would you please go back to bed." Needless to say, I couldn't.

I went to work, didn't hear anything. We didn't hear anything for a few days. It was maybe four or five or six days after this incident that we got a letter saying he was missing in action on March tenth. I went to the cupboard again. March tenth was the day I circled, the day he got killed. Coincidence? Sure, probably. Natural fear, natural worry maybe. Then again, maybe there's something to it. What I'm saying is not a lie. What I'm saying happened. What I'm saying woke me out of a sound sleep and was very distinct. I know the exact moment he got killed. It was the exact moment. His voice woke me. His voice called my mother, called my brother. It called me, and it was very much in danger. But very quickly, almost instantly, after he called the three names, he said, "I'm all right now, Kenny. I'm all right now." That was it.

It was four or five days later that we received the telegram that he was missing in action. I still get a chill when I even think about this, because it's very real. I mean, it wasn't an imaginary thing. It was like he was right there. His presence was there, and it was very clear. I think his calling me actually gave me some sort of comfort. I really believe that. It did, because he told me he was all right, and I'm sure he is. That really gave me some type of comfort.

Yeah, I still fly the flag, on Memorial Day, July Fourth, and I still consider myself a patriot. I did my time. My brother gave his life, my uncle served in World War II, my father was in. We're a family of "patriots," but I'll never be hoodwinked again. If I'm in danger, if they bomb New York or bomb California, then I have to defend, and I won't hesitate, but I'm no fool. I'll never do somebody else's dirty work or nobody in my family ever will. They never will. Fifty-eight-thousand families lost people in Vietnam, and none of them was worth any substantial amount of money. It's people from steel towns, lumber towns, urban cities, not Suburbia, U.S.A. Fifty-nine thousand, and they're not there, not one person of influence, real influence. Even the officers. Their fathers were probably steelworkers, too. They certainly didn't have any pull in government or any place else, or they wouldn't have been there.

My brother served with the Big Red One [First Infantry Division, United States Army], and we were . . . maybe "proud" is the wrong word, but we certainly didn't feel bad about what he did. He saved lives. It's just all the rest of it. What he did was right, what he felt was right, but that's the type of person he was. He was a good kid, a good-natured kid, good-humored, good-natured, full of health, full of spunk, just an all-around good kid. He really was. He had a lot to live for.

I was an idealist, probably, before Vietnam. It made me a realist. Now I'm a realist. Vietnam made me a realist. It did that to me. I'm no longer an idealist, and I never will be.

BELL · JAMES E BENTLEY Jr · FREDERICK A B
ON W BROOKS · JOE H BROWN · JAMES F
F CHASTINE · KENNETH W CLAIRE · RON
OLLISTER · PETER J FILIPIAK · LARRY A DE LA
RD J FAULKNER · THOMAS J COONEY · C
YES III · ROBERT L HEARD · MANUELITO L
UGHES · DONALD JACQUES · STANLEY J
RAFT · RONALD L KUSTABORDER · MICH.
ASSITER · LESLIE R LEWIS · JOHN J MAGEE
DS · LLOYD W MOORE · GEORGE McCLE
D W McKENZIE · WILLIAM L NEWSOME ·
LIAM T PITTMAN · ARNOLD J RIVERA · CH
UFF · RICHARD M SCALA · DAVID C SCA
N A SHELLEY · ROBERT L SIMMONS · EDW
W SMITH · FORREST F S SPITLER · JOHN R
ON J THEYERL · JAMES V THORNTON · NA

DONALD JOSEPH JACQUES

Born: April 23, 1947
Rochester, New York
Killed: February 25, 1968
Khe Sanh, Republic of South Vietnam

LINK · BILLY DALE LIVINGSTON · PHILLIP
LVIN R BROWN · MONTE E VANSKIKE ·

James Hebron
(photo by Joel Sarchet)

Don Jacques

Left to right: Mr. Jacques, Jeanene, Vallette, Mrs. Jacques, and Don

VALLETTE J. MURRELL

Born: March 8, 1938
Wellsville, New York

JEANENE M. FORREST

Born: July 9, 1944
Rochester, New York

Sisters of Donald Joseph Jacques

All Together

VALLETTE: Don was in Denver going to school the year before he joined the Marine Corps. My mother and father didn't have a whole lot of money, so he didn't have much money while he was out there. That was also a time when everybody said you were going to college because you didn't want to go to war. He went to school there for a year. His roommate was a TV producer's son, who probably had all kinds of money. He came home and worked during the summer, then went and joined the marines. He didn't want to ask Mom and Dad for any more money to go to school.

It seemed that everybody in our family wanted to join the marines. My cousin was a marine, and I was a marine. I went to college, a teachers' college in Buffalo, but I didn't want to teach. The recruiters came to the college and talked about being an officer, so I joined and went to the officer's school at Quantico. I met my future husband there, and I really didn't want to go into the marines by the time I finished there. I also didn't want to teach. My father wanted me in the marines, and my husband didn't want me in the marines. My father had never served in any branch of the service. I don't remember exactly why now, but I think he was 4-F. Anyway, I solved the problem. I joined the marines, was commissioned at graduation, married in July, and was pregnant by the time I had to report for active duty. I just got pregnant right away.

JEANENE: I also think that Don joined because he didn't like the talk that was going on at the college. He didn't like the talk that everyone was against the war. That was at Denver University. I don't think he enjoyed the controversy over the war. He felt he wanted to go. That is why he enlisted.

VALLETTE: There was never any question of any other branch of the service. Even now, with both of our sons. They're both in the marines.

JEANENE: Hers is in, and mine is going in October. They never thought of anything else. They looked into it, but were not impressed by anything else. My son Billy looked into the army. He wasn't interested in the army at all. He wanted to go into the Marine Corps. We both tried to talk him out of it, or at least to see what the other services offered.

VALLETTE: When my son Matthew was home Christmas, he spent a month helping recruit in all the high schools. One night while he was home, we were having dinner at my father's house. My father is dead now. My stepmother was in the house, and my brother's uniforms were still there, everything except his dress blues. Matthew was checking them all out to see if he could use them. He came downstairs with a white shirt that my brother never had a chance to wear, still in its original wrapping paper. He said, "You know, this is kind of scary," and I said, "I hope you remember it. From now on." Because my brother was here, and then he was gone.

Don was in Vietnam five months. He went through training at Parris Island. He graduated with high honors. Then he went to Camp Lejeune, and then on to Quantico, to be an officer. He went straight to Vietnam from there. That was in October of 1967. Then he got his platoon.

JEANENE: He would write letters saying that Johnson was doing well, that he was doing the right thing, that they were there for a purpose. All his letters were "up."

VALLETTE: When they're in boot camp, they don't know anything else but "up." Before Matthew enlisted, I couldn't even get him to church, but down there, they even work on them when they are in church. I don't know, it's not like a revival, but they are working on them even in church. They think Marine Corps morning, noon, and night.

JEANENE: I don't think it hurts anybody to have pride in themselves or their country. If they can build on that in a person, that's good. Like the kids of today, they aren't like the kids were when Don went in. They don't have very much self-esteem, I don't think. Our brother did. He knew he was really something when he went in there. He just wanted to build on it. We thought the marines were the best. They were considered the best, therefore, there wasn't any possibility Billy and Matthew would do anything else.

VALLETTE: This is all propaganda and salesmanship. Three-quarters bullshit. The rest of it may be truth.

JEANENE: When Don finished his schooling, he was the youngest second lieutenant in eighteen years. He got a little cockier than normal, I guess. He really thought he was something else.

VALLETTE: My son called me one morning recently. He said he was coming home for twenty-two days, then he was going somewhere. Maybe to Okinawa, maybe to Beirut, who knows?

JEANENE: The Beirut thing is boring to the marines, though, just sitting at the airport, doing nothing.

VALLETTE: Boredom causes accidents. I think my dad wanted Don to go into the marines, but I don't really know. My father blamed his death on me. When Don was dead, in the funeral home, he blamed me. He said it was because of me he went into the marines, but it wasn't. Yet he did blame me on that particular day. He didn't on other days. I don't think he had any reason not to want him to go into the marines.

JEANENE: They were very proud of him. Definitely. While he

was over there, he wrote. His letters were up and down. When we met Jim Hebron, who was in his platoon, he came to the house, and he and I stayed up until five o'clock in the morning, and we read Don's letters. Jim's being there to explain what had happened made a difference. He had a very vivid memory of what happened each day. He could tell me if Don was writing the truth or not on any one particular day. It made quite a difference in the letters.

When we first read the letters, a lot of us thought it sounded like he was all gung-ho, and he was doing this and doing that and being very proud of it, all the time thinking he was doing the right thing, which he was. But there were underlying things, like he had lost so many men on a particular day. His letter was up, but you knew he wasn't really up, because Jim had said to me that he lost so many men that day that things were closing in on him. That was not evident in the letter when I read it by myself. So it made quite a difference to me when I went through the letters with Jim.

VALLETTE: Well, they were cooped up in this place. Jim said they had fences in front of them from the enemy, and the marines put fences in back of them. So they couldn't run, I guess.

JEANENE: They were isolated for days and days. In fact, for months. When Jim explained what was going on at the time, I realized there was a lot of depth to Don's letters. I don't think I realized it until he explained what had happened and the circumstances on a particular day. It was really amazing to me.

VALLETTE: You couldn't help watching Khe Sanh on the news. It was on every night. It was terrible. I was baby-sitting for a captain in the army, and it was in the newspaper that a second lieutenant was killed, and several members of his platoon with him. When she came to pick up the kids that night, I asked her just how long it took to hear if somebody had died. She said, "Well, probably about twenty-four hours." Well, twenty-four hours later, my mother called with the news. I knew who it was the day I read it in the paper. It sounded like him.

JEANENE: He was under a lot of stress. When we found out what was behind the letters he wrote, that made a big difference to me. We knew he was cocky, and he knew he was a big shot, or thought that he was. So, when we heard about it, we were not surprised, but it was knowing the circumstances that led to that day that made a difference. You could see from reading the letters with Jim that it was caused by all the stress and strain.

He had started out with sixty men, and he was down to twenty-five, or something like that. Morale was down, because they were closed in. Knowing the circumstances brought it to light why he took the platoon out. They had been pounded for days and days and days with artillery and everything. He saw a chance to fight back, and took it.

VALLETTE: Talking about the news coverage. About nine months after Don's death, I was pregnant and I was at the doctor for a checkup. I was in the waiting room reading a magazine and saw my brother's picture. My brother, dead in *Newsweek!* The doctor couldn't quite figure out why my blood pressure was as high as it was. I didn't say anything to him. I didn't want to break out in tears. I just went in and saw him and took the magazine and went home. Then I wrote to Jeanene: "Don't tell Mom, but . . ."

JEANENE: And I was reading the letter to my mother, out loud. I didn't know what was coming. I read right into it. When I got to "Don't tell Mom," my mom said, "What is it you're not supposed to tell me?" I had to go right on through it, then. She would not let me get out of it. I read through it, and she said, "I'll see you later." She went right to the library and got the magazine. She didn't even tell me she was going there. She just left my house, went to the library, and got the magazine.

VALLETTE: There wasn't any name on the picture, so she wrote to find out if the photographer could confirm that it was really Don. She wanted his confirmation. They wrote a letter back saying the photographer was killed right after that.

JEANENE: I was working at Rochester Products then, and one of the engineers took the picture and blew it up. We could tell for sure from that that it was Don. We really knew before then. We could tell.

VALLETTE: There was a radio man near him. A second lieutenant always had a radio man near him. It was really strange, seeing that picture. It was like watching a movie or something. The picture itself, or the taking of the picture, was not the problem. It was how fast we saw it. Not expecting it. It was the shock. I mean, even on TV. The bodies were not cold yet, and it was on TV at six o'clock, while you were eating supper.

JEANENE: At every meal, you had to have dead silence, so you could hear names. I always listened for names and different places that I recognized. It had to be quiet in there so you could eat and hear all this garbage that was coming over the TV. That's all I could think of. Your stomach was always in knots while you were trying to eat your dinner and watch that TV. You could hardly keep your mouth going. Just always watching to see if there was any word about coming home, or anything happening to him that day, because you knew that it was always right there, and they were going to be on TV. It had to make things kind of hard on everybody, because even if your son wasn't killed, or your brother, or whatever, he could be, and be on the news tomorrow night.

VALLETTE: It was that instant coverage of war. I don't think that it is necessary that we know everything up-to-date like that. Let me read this from the newspaper:

> North Vietnamese troops ambushed and overwhelmed a United States Marine platoon 800 yards outside the barbed wire of the Khe Sanh combat base today. . . . Senior Marine officers said the young lieutenant leading the platoon went beyond the distance set for him. . . . A survivor said the patrol's point man spotted two North Vietnamese soldiers and the platoon gave chase. The two enemy soldiers lured the Marines into an ambush. . . .

I think this put the fear of God into all of us. Before that, we had always been a fairly lucky family. No major illnesses or anything like that. We always seemed to escape.

JEANENE: My mother was home alone when the car came to

the house with the telegram. I was working. My father and I worked at the same plant. They called me. He said it was "Sergeant so-and-so," or somebody. Then: "I'm at your mother's home. Would you get your father and come home?" I thought it was a cop. They didn't say, "U.S. Marine Corps," or anything like that. I thought my mother was sick or something. I think I was defensively blocking Don out of my head. I went down to get my father. When I told him, he looked me straight in the eye and didn't say a word. We went out, got in my car, and left. Dead silence, all the way home. I think I was *hoping* my mother was sick, or in an accident, or something like that. Then we saw the Marine Corps car in the driveway, and that was it. We both started crying. But Mom, she got it all by herself. The whole thing. It was a terrible day. Terrible.

It must have been about seven days after that that we got his body, because the funeral was on March ninth. It was open casket, but the casket was glass-enclosed.

VALLETTE: Because it came from out of the country, it had to be sealed. So the body was down. You know how they usually sit bodies up, so you can see them. Well, in this case, the body is down, with glass on top, and nobody can see him until they're right on top. And he's lying there, down, with the glass on top. You got the whole effect all at once. There wasn't any standing in the hallway, looking in and getting prepared. All you saw was this box, until you were actually over it and looking at him. He was in dress blues. He looked good. That helped my mother, to have his body. Believe me, it helped. I really think you have got to see them, no matter how bad it is. You've got to see.

JEANENE: Don was shot once. His face wasn't disfigured, and he was brought right back after he died.

VALLETTE: My first thought was that I didn't have enough children. I needed another one. A year and a day later, I had Mary Jo. My mother and father had four children. My baby brother died in 1943, when he was nine months old, and Don died at twenty, so even four wasn't enough. My mom lost both of her boys.

JEANENE: I think the hardest part of the whole deal, other

than the fact that he was dead, was when we went to the cemetery and bought four plots. My baby brother was buried in another cemetery, so we decided that he should be put with Don.

VALLETTE: This woman who was selling the plots was a tape-recorder-type person. If you pushed a button, she might shut off a minute or so. She needed to know which son was going to be beside each parent. I mean, who would have thought they would have to make a decision like that right there on the spot? They didn't say anything, and finally I said, "Put the baby near the mother." That's where a baby should be. I can remember all of that very clearly. Neither Mom nor Dad wanted to make that decision.

JEANENE: The hardest part just recently was over my father. My mother died in 1977, and my father died in 1980. Now, to go and see all of them there, it's really hard. After a while, I got used to seeing Mark and Don there. Then it was Mom, and now, with Mom and Dad there, it is just unreal. To see all four of them there. At least they're all together.

My son has to graduate from high school first, then he goes into the Marine Corps in October. He is in a guaranteed program, supposedly, going into administration. October is when they leave for that particular program. It's a little different from before, when they just went for infantry. Now, they are telling him that he can go to school, he can do this, he can do that, so, hopefully, he won't be in a combat situation.

VALLETTE: My boy is in Camp Lejeune, finishing up his training. Then he will be going someplace overseas. They wouldn't have given him a twenty-two-day leave if he weren't going someplace overseas. He's not sure where yet. I'm not sure how I feel about all this. My whole head is mixed up between Don and these boys. I don't know. I didn't raise my brother, but I was the oldest, and I was the one who was always baby-sitting, and I get the families mixed up, really, in thinking of it.

I personally would rather he be in the marines than sitting home doing nothing or driving his car like a bat out of hell or doing pot or something like that. I don't care what they do, as long as they are doing something positive. Right now there isn't much that kids can do if they don't go on to school, and he didn't want to go to school. He can get training in the Marine Corps, and there aren't many jobs available in the economy right now. He's going to be a clerk. He's in Supply right now, and, hopefully, if he's in a combat situation, he will be the one bringing in supplies, or ordering them, or something like that. I don't know.

In the back of his mind, I think, he's planning a career. He loves it. He loved boot camp. When he came home for that month, he was recruiting like crazy, and he loved it. He loved every minute of it. The best kid in their platoon gets his dress blues, which I was hoping he would do, but he didn't get it. He was number two.

When he came home, in my mixed-up mind, he wasn't *Don,* because he didn't have dress blues. Now, Don didn't have dress blues on, except in the casket, but, I don't know. It gets confusing for me. Not that I don't recognize my own son, but time goes by so fast. It seems like only yesterday that Don was around. It's been fifteen years.

JEANENE: Billy was three and Matthew was four when Don was killed. They went to the funeral, just like we did. They don't remember it, but they were there the whole time. My husband died of a heart attack three years ago, so we've had a lot of death, one on top of the other. I don't know what we would do if we didn't have all these kids. When Don died, nobody could talk about it to Dad. He couldn't talk about it for years. If you mentioned it, he'd cry.

VALLETTE: He never talked about anything. He kept everything in. When Mom died, he never talked. My mother and father made a trip to Arizona while I was living there. She died right in the car, looking for my house. She didn't just die; she must have had problems all the way out there on that trip. He never, ever mentioned anything about her death. Don's death affected my mother. I'm sure it shortened her life. She didn't change so much, she just got old all at once.

JEANENE: There were over four hundred people that came to

the funeral parlor. She stood right there in front of that casket all of the time. She had terrible arthritis in her legs and hips, and she stood right there, and wouldn't sit down. She had to be there every minute, all the calling hours and everything. She stood right there and talked to everybody that came in.

JAMES MARTIN HEBRON

Born: July 20, 1949
The Bronx, New York
Friend of Donald Joseph Jacques

A Tragic Mistake

I was sixteen, attending high school, and decided I wanted to escape from home. I don't think I thought of it in those terms then. I just thought that the war was on, that it was exciting, and that it seemed like a patriotic thing to do, so I made up my mind to join the Marine Corps. I was raised by my mother, and I asked her if it would be okay if I joined. We argued about that for a number of months. Finally she gave in and agreed to sign the papers that would allow me to enlist. I took my physical when I was sixteen and was sworn in on my seventeenth birthday.

I went to boot camp at Parris Island, from there to Camp Geiger, which is the post–boot-camp training facility of Camp Lejeune. From there I went home on leave, then to California for more training prior to being sent overseas. Because I was only seventeen, they couldn't send me to Vietnam, so they sent me to Okinawa. I spent six months on Okinawa. When I turned eighteen, they sent me to Vietnam, to an area called Khe Sanh, with the first battalion, 26th Marines. I was in Vietnam close to seven months. Then I returned. I found it out later, but it was on the day that I returned that my platoon was ambushed, and twenty-five people were killed out of twenty-nine. I guess that's been one of the motivating factors in my life for the last fifteen years or so.

When I returned from Vietnam, I had twenty days' leave and travel time accrued, then I reported back to Camp Lejeune. That's where I found out about my platoon being ambushed. When I was home on leave, I didn't watch much television. I think I already felt the pain of separation, and it was just too much to watch Khe Sanh on TV every night. I just partied for a month. I talked to some people when I was home, but it was very superficial, because they weren't vets and I felt very estranged. I felt out of place being back in Queens after being in a war. There was one incident that occurred that kind of highlighted that sense of isolation.

My peers at the time were in their freshman year at college, and a friend of mine invited me to go to his college to pull a prank on one of the teachers there. The idea was for me to go into this classroom, wait for attendance to be taken, and, after attendance was taken, to leave the classroom, thereby confusing the teacher, who would take attendance again, finding nobody missing. It was supposed to be a big joke or something. I wound up going to the college, and we were sitting in the cafeteria for a while. I just looked around and noticed everybody having a good time, relaxed and everything. Nobody seemed to even know what was going on in Vietnam, or care. They just seemed to be going on vapidly, living their own lives. I guess I felt a sense of betrayal on their part, that we weren't in this together. I didn't feel like I belonged, so I left. I didn't go through with the stunt, or prank, or whatever you want to call it. That's sort of how I felt during that period when I was home on leave. The people who had been my closest friends really knew nothing about Vietnam. They were only inter-ested in what the war was like in terms of their preconceptions of what war was about: "How many people did you kill?" That kind of thing. Not really interested in the intense experiences that we'd undergone, and how that might affect somebody. They were eighteen-year-old college freshmen, out for a good time.

In one sense, I think I was lucky, luckier than those who were discharged directly from the battlefield. Thirty-six hours after they left Vietnam, they walked in the front door, and they were home for good. I still had almost two and a half years left to go in the Marine Corps, so when I went back to Camp Lejeune, I felt I was among peers again. People understood what I had been through. That allowed me some time to decompress in a way that is necessary, coming home from those kinds of situations. During World War II, you know, it was sometimes six months from the time the war was over until someone ended up back home. That was the average time. There was really time for decompression then. The same kind of thing happened with the Iranian hostages. They spent a week in Germany before they were allowed home. They were debriefed, and they had some time to come to terms with some of their experiences before they wound up on the streets. They also received a different kind of welcome home than Vietnam vets. The tickertape parade in New York City for the Iranian hostages, for example, in contrast to Vietnam vets, who were sneaked back in the middle of the night, ashamed to even wear uniforms because of the way they were treated at airports and bus terminals. As for me, I was lucky that I had the two and a half years to work my way back into the rest of society, but that really wasn't enough. Not for me.

I wasn't dealing with the fact that my platoon had been ambushed in my absence. I felt a great deal of survivor guilt that I didn't even recognize, that I ran away from. I should put it this way: I *un*consciously ran away from. I also associated myself with Vietnam veterans affairs from the time I got out of the service on through until now. It wasn't until about 1978 or so that I could actually start reading anything about Vietnam at any great length, even though all that time I'd helped Vietnam vets. I'd counseled them as a peer counselor or in an official position as a veterans' counselor, but what I'd been doing all that time also was reading a lot about World War II and the Holocaust, particularly the Holocaust in terms of how people coped with having survived when so many other people didn't survive. Survival. Death. What have you.

When I did start reading some books about Vietnam, and becoming more reflective about life in general, that's when I came to see the association between what I was doing and why I was doing it, hooking up working in veterans' affairs with my experience as a marine. I realized how touched I was by that war in so many ways. I hadn't been aware of that up to that point. I guess in one sense I thought it didn't affect me. I thought, "I came out with all my parts." All my physical parts were intact. But I had a sense of guilt about surviving. And I realized that I'm the only person who served in my outfit from the opening of the Tet offensive at Khe Sanh who didn't receive a Purple Heart. I was the only one who wasn't wounded. That set me thinking. I guess I felt guilty about that in some respects, too.

When I came back to Camp Lejeune from Vietnam, after my leave at home, a friend I had served with, in Okinawa first, and later in Vietnam—he was in another company—came up to me and told me that my platoon was gone, that they were ambushed. At first I thought it was some sort of joke or something. I didn't believe him. He obviously was telling the truth. He was right. Actually, the moment when I did believe it, I turned it all off. I turned the emotions off about it. I just couldn't bear to deal with it, I guess, because I felt guilty for not having been there that day. That set off a whole series of things in terms of how I suppressed it. My attitude was: "To hell with them. They were stupid. They deserved it." Or even worse. I tried to dismiss it. I tried just to not think about it, tried to force it away from my mind. Whenever it did come up in my mind, in a conversation or something like that, I found it easy to blame others—the platoon commander, Don Jacques, for instance—for getting people killed. I wasn't dealing with other aspects of it, like my own feeling that I should have been there. For many years I was bitter at the platoon commander. He didn't use the best judgment that day and led the platoon into an ambush.

Don made a mistake that day. That's clear. I think that going

up to Rochester to visit his sisters and reading his letters helped
me to deal with that a little better, helped me to come to terms
with the fact that he was under a great deal of stress then, too.
Prior to that visit, I had always viewed him as the leader, and
therefore absolutely responsible. I didn't recognize his own individual foibles and weaknesses, or his humanity. Seeing, from his
letters, the kind of stress he was under, and having to remember,
too, that he was only twenty years old, helped me. He was not the
god-figure that we might want people to be, particularly in that
type of situation. He was a human being who made a terrible
human mistake. He was rash and impetuous.

After going to Rochester, I felt I knew Don better. I think
his sisters knew their brother better, too, in the sense of knowing
what his life was like while he was at Khe Sanh. They really had
no idea what was going on. Don, in his letters, would be purposefully misleading. In a nice way. The traditional: "Don't let the
folks at home know how bad things are here." I think they got a
fuller appreciation of their brother during our visit, too. I sensed
they were grateful for that. I was grateful, too, to learn more about
who Don Jacques was. Don and I were not peers in Vietnam. He
was an officer, and I was a PFC [private first class], but I always
sensed something in common between us. I was never sure what
it really was. He was different from many marine officers who
follow the strict segregation rules between officers and enlisted
men. I think that was probably because of Don's youth. He needed
friends also.

When I say I understand it better now, it's also because I'm
aware of a number of things that happened at Khe Sanh that I
didn't realize at the time. I think Don was not qualified at that
time to make the judgment he made, and for a number of reasons,
not just because he was an impulsive person. He didn't know what
day of the week it was, he was so damned tired. It's a question of
how much judgment anybody could have had. A lot of other
factors also came into play. Like how long it had been since they
had been on patrol. There's that idea of "patrol-ready," "combat-
ready," that was missing. They hadn't been on patrol for a month

at that point. They hadn't been on patrol because they couldn't go outside the gates. So there were a number of things that came into play. Don was absolutely dead tired. He wasn't sharp. He wasn't combat-ready for patrol. He was keyed up because of all the casualties we'd been taking. All of those things came into play to affect his judgment.

I think what I'm trying to say is that I think I've gained more understanding of Don as a human being. On the other hand, I felt a great deal of loyalty to my platoon, also. I feel that it was a silly, tragic mistake. Some of that I lay at the Marine Corps' doorstep. I guess that's because of the story I got about one of the lines Don used when he was told that he shouldn't follow those two NVA [North Vietnamese Army] troopers, because the platoon was already worried about the possibility of an ambush. Don told them that he was an officer in the Marine Corps, so "Do as I say." The scout warned him, as did Doc, our medic. He didn't take guidance and counsel from others. He was an almighty Marine Corps officer: "Do as I say." A seasoned officer would have been less likely to have made the same mistake. But people learn from experience about things like that. Don didn't live to gain that experience. Had he survived that ambush, I doubt that he ever would have pulled anything like that again. What a waste. It was a very human thing. It happens in every war, but what a waste.

I've gone through a long process in learning what exactly happened that day. Originally, what I heard, when I first found out, was that he had been checking the perimeter for bangalore torpedoes, spotted two NVA troopers, and gave the order to get them. Subsequently I found out, and I don't even remember how I found out, that when he led the platoon out that day the mission was to knock out a mortar that had been inflicting a lot of casualties at Khe Sanh, on our platoon in particular. There were mortars and artillery everywhere, but this one that was particularly effective was landing right on our trench. They decided to go out there and take that mortar out. On the way out, they spotted two or three NVA troopers who stood up and were spotted. Don Jacques ordered his platoon to give chase by fire and maneuver. That's a particular infantry tactic, "fire and maneuver." What actually happened is that they went in a mad rush to grab these two guys, two or three. I'm not clear whether it was two or three. Prior to giving the order to capture these NVA soldiers, Don was warned by the Kit Carson Scout and one of the corpsmen not to do so, because of the possibility of being led into an ambush. He told them to go ahead and give chase, that he was telling them by virtue of his authority as an officer in the United States Marine Corps, and they better do what he said. They did. He charged out after the NVA, and everybody followed. They were ambushed.

It was a crescent-shaped ambush, a variation on the U-shaped ambush, and twenty-five out of twenty-nine were killed. A corpsman friend of mine told me about this, about the conversation and everything. He was there. He was hit that day, also. He was shot through the chest, and a grenade took off part of his knee, but he managed to crawl back. It took him about six hours to crawl back to the lines. He made it back and survived. He lives in Detroit now.

So. But when I read the letters up in Rochester, I understood exactly how Don felt, just how young and vulnerable he was, that he shouldn't have been a platoon commander, perhaps. He didn't have enough seasoning, and he didn't show good judgment that day. He was only two years older than I was, and I know how young I felt. I didn't really think of it like that when I was over there. Even though I was eighteen, I was only a year younger than most of the people that were over there. Many of the guys in our outfit were eighteen, too. I don't know that that's all that unusual. War's a young man's game, as they say. In this particular war, it was a very young man's game. I didn't feel odd when I was over there, because everybody else was my age. They were my peers. I think it's more in hindsight than anything else that I realize how young I was. There's not much you can do about it, about how old you are, once you make the decision and go.

There were so many phases of it, of the Tet offensive up there. The first week of Tet, up at Khe Sanh, we were receiving extremely intensive shelling. Artillery shelling, rockets. You name it, we got it. The concern at that time was that we would be overrun by the NVA. There were four NVA divisions up there, approximately forty thousand people. There were only fifty-six hundred of us inside the line at Khe Sanh. There was concern that we would be overrun. They were labeling Khe Sanh as another Dien Bien Phu, and we were aware of that. We didn't know, really, what Johnson's policies were or anything, but we were aware of the comparison to Dien Bien Phu. We'd get the papers, but by the time they reached us, the news was old. Mail wasn't the highest priority, either, if you were living up at Khe Sanh. Beans, bullets, bandages. Those were the priorities. They made an earnest effort to get mail in. That's always good to boost morale, but it just doesn't have top priority.

What happened initially, because of the concern that we might be overrun, was that barbed-wire barricades were built behind the troops on the front lines. Behind us. Behind the marines. Although there was barbed wire in front of us, because they also put barbed wire behind us, we felt cut off and isolated from the pogues [soldiers in the rear] behind us. It was psychological, too; we were not only cut off from those behind us, but from those back in the United States. This was something that I had never seen, not even in a John Wayne movie. You don't isolate your troops that way. But at Khe Sanh, the grunts, the infantry, were in front of barbed wire. There were all kinds of people behind us. Supply people, vehicle drivers, tanks, the artillery. All kinds of artillery pieces and people were behind us, but those were the rear troops. There were two sections of barbed wire between us and them.

The reason we were so upset by them putting the barbed wire behind us was that we felt that they were writing us off. It was clear: "You're the first priority to die. You go first." I guess we all knew that, anyway, as grunts, that we would always be the first to go, but it was another thing, seeing it put so clearly, in front of you like that. Why put barbed wire there, if they didn't expect it to happen? We tried to look at it as a challenge: "Was that a comment? Did they think we might try to get out of those trenches ourselves? Were they questioning our ability to stand there and fight?"

There was another thing, too. Prior to the first shell landing at Khe Sanh, we had prepared a number of protective firing lines. We had prepared positions where tanks could come in and provide direct support in case we were being overrun on any particular section of the line. With the barbed wire behind us like that, the tanks couldn't get in to give us help, so it was clear that there was only a limited amount of support that we were going to get. It wasn't a case of absolutely no support, but it was less support than might have been. The tanks were something that could have made a difference. With some of those pieces that we had, you could fire a beehive round and you could send twelve hundred darts out there. Very lethal darts. That could easily be the difference between breaking up a charge or assault, or not breaking it up. That was just something less that we could count on because of the barbed wire.

We were understaffed at that time, too, on the lines, because of people being killed or wounded. It doesn't take much to make a line empty. Take somebody who's sick, for example. He can't fight. A wound is better than a kill in the jargon of the military. You hit somebody in the field, and it takes two people to take care of him. That takes two more out of the field. If somebody's dead, you don't worry about him. So. That's the mathematics of war. It's better to wound somebody. You use more resources that way. Medicine, whatever. Food. If the person's still alive, he's got to eat. You have to devote more personnel to that, and less to the war effort, the direct war effort, so it's much more expensive to keep the person alive. That's true for the insurance industry, too. They'd much rather you'd kill somebody in a car accident than just injure them. It costs a lot more in pain and suffering payments than if you'd just kill somebody outright. I learned that in an insurance adjusting course.

So. The upshot of that, the barbed wire behind us, was that it knit us closer together, if that would be possible. We were pretty tight at that point, anyway, but I remember that a bunch of us in the squad got together and made note that we wouldn't leave the trenches alive. Because we felt isolated from everybody else, our attitude was: "Screw 'em. We're here by ourselves. They're pogues in the rear." It was us versus the NVA, but we were fighting for ourselves, not for the people behind us. That's how we felt.

As the weeks wore on, we were less concerned about being overrun. We had beefed up our positions in front. We set up more mines, booby traps, stuff like that, up in front. Rolls of barbed wire, stuffed with C-4, a plastic explosive that was used as an antipersonnel mine if we were being assaulted. We also had fifty-five-gallon drums filled with diesel oil and kerosene that they mixed together and set a primer in. If you were being overrun, you just set that thing off, and it would have the effect of napalm on people, take care of any overachieving NVA. What I'm saying is that as the weeks wore on, the concern about being overrun lessened. We felt then that if they were going to do it, they should have done it that first week. That would have been their best opportunity, if they were going to do it. As time went on, air support got more and more coordinated, and the opportunity to mass for attack against us became less and less likely. I sensed that at the time, on the inside, but I know more about that now, after reading about what happened at Khe Sanh. The extraordinary efforts that went on, for example, to pull together the air support. I found out about that later from reading about it, but I also felt it then.

So as the weeks wore on, and I was getting shorter and shorter, closer and closer to the end of my tour in Vietnam, I felt there was no chance that they could overrun us. The only way we were going to get killed was if an artillery round came in on top of us. That's pretty much it. An artillery round landing on top of someone. It was during that period, when I was getting short and getting ready to go home, that I felt a little guilty about leaving everybody there. I talked to people in my squad about it. They said, "Hey, get the hell out. Don't stay here." "Okay." That made sense, you know. I didn't think there was any chance they were going to be overrun at that point, so I rotated home, and just when I got home, that's when it happened. The day I landed in New

York City is the day they got ambushed. I left Khe Sanh on the eighteenth, but then I went down to Phu Bai, then to DaNang. I spent a night in each place, or two nights in each place, then three nights in Okinawa, so it took me a week to get home. They were ambushed on the twenty-fifth.

I landed at Kennedy. No one was there to meet me. My mother didn't know I was coming home at that point. She knew I would be home soon; my thirteen months were up, but she didn't know exactly when I would be home. I hadn't asked for anyone to meet me. I took a cab from the airport. Mother was in the house. She was painting the house at the time. I walked in and said hello, and that was it. It was good to be home, but I think my mind was still back there. It was still back there. Everything here just seemed different. I'd been gone at that point about fifteen months. Things had changed, I guess. I'd been away so long that I didn't have any sense of continuity about the neighborhood or anything that was happening back in the world. I partied for a month.

I ran across a guy in 1968 that had served with me at Khe Sanh, but not as a part of my platoon. He told me about three people that made it back: Chief, the FO or forward observer; and both corpsmen. Eddie Rayburn also made it back. Rayburn had his jaw shot off over there. I don't think this guy mentioned Rayburn. I think I first learned about Rayburn in 1972 when I went cross-country and ran across another guy, Muir, who had been with our platoon earlier, but had transferred out to another unit. He left Vietnam before I did. His parents showed me the *Newsweek* magazine. That was the first time I had seen it. It was four years after the event.

So. In 1972 I knew that the two corpsmen had made it back, and I knew that Chief had made it back. I hadn't really known Chief all that well. He wasn't a part of the squad, and the squad is the basic unit, really. The forward observer calls in the artillery, mainly; he doesn't necessarily go out with the squad. He's more in the command party, with the platoon commander. He's in that section, so he's not necessarily tied in with the squad. There's three squads in a platoon, then you have your radio man, and your platoon guide, and the FO, that kind of thing, and they make up the command party.

When I ran across Muir in Arizona, he told me that Rayburn was in bad shape, that he had his jaw shot off, all of it shot off. That literally all he had left was his two front teeth. He showed me a picture of him. They had their picture taken together. I remember he reminded me of those Bazooka bubble gum commercials, where you see the guy with the turtle neck on. That's how he was bandaged up. In a two-dimensional picture, that's what it struck me as, because he was taped up all around. When Rayburn had visited Muir, they had gone out to get something to eat. They stopped at a fast-food place, and all Rayburn could get was French fries. He had to mash them with his thumb against his two front teeth to eat. They had tried to do a skin graft for him. They sewed his face to his shoulder for about six weeks, but the graft didn't take. Because there was no hinge left to his jaw, they couldn't wire it to put a new one in. That was at that point. I don't know what's happened since then. Maybe technology has improved enough so they could do something for him. I just don't know. I'd like to track him down. I'm sure he's still getting disability from the VA, but I've been told that unless I have his social security number, there's really no way to track him down.

Anyway, 1972 is when I first saw the *Newsweek* magazine article, and I've always kept that magazine. I contacted *Newsweek* and requested that they send me a copy of it. I paid a dollar, or whatever it cost at that time, and it arrived, so I had my own copy. At that point, I still didn't know that one of the guys that I thought had been killed up at Khe Sanh was a POW.

This was a guy on my fire team. The fire team is the smallest unit in the Marine Corps. The sequence starts out with the fire team, then three fire teams make up a squad, three squads make up a platoon, three platoons plus the weapons platoon make up a company. A weapons platoon is made up of mortarmen and machine gunners. A regular platoon is called a "rifle platoon."

There are four members of a fire team: the leader, two riflemen, and an automatic rifleman. The fire team is actually the smallest military unit in the Marine Corps. Anyway. I didn't know this one guy was alive until I was watching the news on TV one night in 1973. They were releasing the prisoners, the prisoners of war. They had this story on Ronald Ridgeway, a prisoner who the government thought had been killed. They thought they had buried him at St. Louis in a mass grave.

What happened was that after the ambush occurred, people couldn't go out and get the bodies right away. There were too many NVA. You'd end up just playing into the NVA's hands, just feeding people piecemeal to them, into ambushes. So they left them out there for a while. I guess that when they finally were able to collect the bodies, they were too decomposed to identify, so they had a mass grave. Subsequently I found out that Ridgeway's mother didn't believe that her son was killed, because they couldn't find any piece of him, dog tags or anything else. She told them that she didn't want the ten thousand dollars, because they hadn't proved that her son was dead. Then, in 1973, there he was, on the evening news, the seven o'clock news. There he was, on the seven o'clock news, and there I was, watching TV, and I said, "Wow."

They had a special story on him, because it was so unusual. They thought this guy was dead. They showed his headstone, in St. Louis, then here he came, walking off a plane. I tried to contact him at that time. He'd been in the ambush, but he was captured. He spent five years as a POW, because he was released in about March of '73. The *Daily News* did a piece on him, too, at that point, with a picture of him. I think another story surfaced in a California magazine. They did a story on him, also: "Lost Platoon Survivor," or something like that. I contacted his mother when I saw him on TV. She told me she would give him my phone number. When I finally did speak to Ridgeway, in 1982, I found out that he had never gotten the message. When we spoke, he was quite surprised to find out that Eddie Rayburn was still alive. He told me how he saw Ed get hit, and that he thought that Eddie was dead. He didn't know why he had been taken prisoner himself, in light of what had happened to everybody else.

Over the years, slowly but surely, I've been able to put all these pieces back together again, finding out who had lived, who had died. In 1979 I went to a board meeting of a veterans' organization in St. Louis and decided to look at the mass grave they had there. Not the whole platoon was buried there. They were able to identify, I don't know, seventeen or eighteen of the bodies. They were able to identify that many, and so they were buried, I guess, in their hometowns. There were about seven or eight they couldn't identify, for whatever reason.

After they had gone out, and got ambushed, another unit went out there to rescue them, to try and pull them back. Some of them were killed, too. The *Newsweek* picture is of Don and Chief, on the same day of the ambush, with these people from the other unit, and they're bringing Don back in. The photographer who took the picture was right behind the line. A couple of hundred yards past where the picture was taken is where the rest of the platoon was. The photographer who took the picture was killed later, too. So. The picture shows guys from the platoon that went out to try and pull the fat out of the fire. They had to turn back. Chief was bringing Don back in, and they joined up with the rescue platoon that was going back in. That's what the picture is about.

Also, the unit that went out there to rescue my platoon had to call in artillery on themselves, because while they were out there, they could hear the screams. They could hear the screams of the people who were wounded, and the NVA going around, making them scream even louder, torturing them, so that it would put pressure on the marines inside to come out and save their buddies. That's what they wanted them to do. They didn't want to come over the wires at Khe Sanh. They wanted to engage you outside, to draw more people out. They had their own trenches, just a few hundred meters from where the picture was taken. It was their trenches, then space, then our trenches. When my platoon was hit, there were people still alive. The NVA were torturing those people, and when the guys from the other unit went out there to try to help them, they ran up against a wall of fire, but they didn't get into the same kind of ambush.

I guess with Ridgeway what happened was that when they went in to get the bodies, they could identify some, and they couldn't identify some. The ones they couldn't identify, they put in a mass grave in St. Louis. They looked at the unit diary, I guess, and saw who went out that day, and who came back, and they subtracted and they said, I guess, "Well, we better put another name on this tombstone in St. Louis, because this many people went out, we identified this many bodies, so whoever's left on the list here has got to be dead." Ridgeway wasn't there, and he didn't return, so they just assumed that he was one of the ones who was killed. Why should they think anything else? He was only a PFC, and what good is he to anybody? But I guess also, at that point, the idea of keeping prisoners started striking the NVA as a good idea. It was a good PR weapon, a good political weapon.

Talks had already been going on, the peace talks were about to start in Paris, and they understood that the United States reacts to that kind of pressure. The two sides were already saying, "We have this many guys, and you have this many guys, and let's swap." That sort of thing. So I guess they recognized it as a tool. That's the only reason I can think of that he would have survived that. He'd been hit a couple of times already, Ridgeway had. He wasn't in any state of fine physical health. He was wounded. I don't know how badly. There are wounds, and then there are wounds. He'd been hit in the hip, and in the shoulder. I imagine he'd lost some blood. But there was no real reason for him to come out of it. There really wasn't. Those guys could hear the screams back there, so who would have figured he would have made it? But he made it, and I don't know how. As soon as I saw his face, I knew him, and it was a shock. That was in 1973.

I don't even know how I knew about the mass grave in St. Louis. Maybe Muir told me, but I don't know how he would know. I'm not real sure how I knew about that, but I knew it was there. Since I was going out there for that meeting, I decided I'd like to see it. There was a lot of curiosity about it: "Will I recognize the names?" We just went by nicknames, so we didn't always know everybody's full name, except for the guys we were close to in the squad itself. I also wanted to know if Ridgeway's name was still on there, if the government had had enough time to change it. It wasn't there. It was a new headstone. They had taken his name off. I guess I just felt sad looking at it, with the names all in a list there.

Part of it, too, is that, looking at those names, a lot of them I didn't know, I could just think, "Oh, yeah. This one sounds familiar." But that's a lot different. "Sounds familiar" is different from being able to look and say, "Oh, yeah. I know this guy here. That was Skinner," or whatever. I felt a lot different looking at the Washington monument, where I clearly remembered more of the names. That was different. It had all the names. A whole section with my platoon's names on it. It's a strange feeling, too, seeing all those names up there. There's sadness in it, and also a feeling of futility about why they died. It's also hoping that we don't make the same mistakes again. That we don't. That we learned something from that.

You know, I didn't become a pacifist from my experiences in Vietnam. I think I learned more about picking my fights, about being sure we have wholehearted support before doing something like that, because we have enough serious reminders of the folly of not doing it that way. I guess I still have very mixed emotions about war, and about Vietnam in particular. I think I try to separate out government folly and American policy from what we as individuals on the ground felt. Much has been made of the My Lai's in that war, and I think that many people tend to think of My Lai as symbolizing the whole war in Vietnam. That's a disservice to those who did serve. Things like My Lai were an abberation. Because they were an abberation, they received much publicity and press. I think it's terribly unfair, really unfair, to those who served. People I served with thought we were really doing a noble, noble thing. That should never be confused with nobleness on the part of government, or policy, or anything else. That's all a part of separating out the war from the warrior. War policy is conducted by the officials in charge of the government, officials in government, and, ultimately, by the people back here who decide who they're going to vote for. That's what it comes down to. I guess that in a sense, Vietnam represents to me a collective experience of Americans, not just the Vietnam vets. Individual veterans have to take responsibility for their individual actions, including participation in things like My Lai. Most Vietnam veterans did not participate in that sort of thing. But wrongs in terms of *policy* should be shared by all Americans. Vietnam veterans were not policy setters. They were instruments of policy.

I think Vietnam vets were made scapegoats for people who do feel guilty about their role in the war effort, or whatever. I'll use for an example an event that occurred just a couple of weeks ago. I was at this affair, and this guy was telling me that he was strong in the antiwar movement and wouldn't hire a Vietnam vet after the war was over. I was sort of dumbfounded by this. It's a classic case of blaming the warrior for the war. I was offended by that. He thought we were all crazy. He made his own mind up about what we were, because he was different from that. I just think that's really cheap, a very cheap thing to do.

Emotionally, to me, Vietnam is about how I served and how my peers served, and how we felt while we were over there. That's emotionally. Intellectually, I can look at the war now and say, "Gee. Why were we so stupid? Why would we be so stupid to do that? Why would we go in there, even against the advice of some of our more eminent leaders?" Eisenhower had already warned against ever getting involved in a land war in Southeast Asia. So had General Ridgeway and MacArthur. But it just seemed like we crept right into it and didn't know how to extricate ourselves. A tragic mistake. That's the way I look at it.

I also think that it was a very arrogant kind of mistake that was made there. Nobody knew anything about Vietnam. I think in this country we only had about two hundred people who were even studying the Vietnamese language and culture during that entire period of time. None of the people who knew anything about Indochinese history were in any way involved in setting the policy about Vietnam. It was just an arrogant thing to think that we could just go in there and turn things upside down and tie them in a knot. It was stupid. Consequently, how futile the sacrifice of those who believed with their whole hearts they were doing the right thing. That's what it comes down to.

I feel that war should be the absolutely last resort. It should be something that has the support of the population as a whole before it's entered into, and, once you commit, go there with a maximum of force, an absolute maximum. Do not go in there half-stepping. Anything less only leads to encouragement to resist, and that costs more lives in the long run. War is nasty. And unless you are willing to go in there with the complete backing of the people, the complete will to win, and overwhelming force, it's a mistake. I don't think, morally, that war is always improper. Attack me, and I'm going to fight back. And there are crazy folks out there, running countries. There are. Crazy folks. Hitler is a classic example. But there are immoral wars. That's something we as people have to decide for ourselves and our country.

STER A CUMMINGS · CHARLES C DAVIS
LIAM K DOWNING · KURT C EDIE · DO
ES H FLICKINGER · ROBERT W FORBUSH
ID K HOLDWAY · EARLIE RAND · CHAR
STER G JORDAN · ROY N MANNS · JOE
PH R'LAROSE · ROBERT Y LOUIS Jr · TO
N R MEUSE · LLOYD A MILLER · RALPH
ENE MURRY · LEONARD PICANSO Jr
HAEL F HUWEL · WINSTON G RAYMO
H RUSS · JAVIER A E SANCHEZ · CLEON
N E SWEESY · JULIO A TORRES-RODRIC
N W URICK · WILLIAM T WOMBLE Jr · F
ERT B BEESON · CLARENCE BLANKS · T
N F CHAVES · WILLIAM A CRENSHAW
MANUEL GOMEZ · JACK R LENNER ·
IAM E McGINNIS II · PAUL T KOHR · A

WINSTON GLENWOOD RAYMO

Born: May 7, 1945
St. Thomas, U.S. Virgin Islands
Killed: May 3, 1967
Republic of South Vietnam

S AP L MMM R · JOS PH P RANDO
H SAMANIEGO · DONALD J SHEEHY

Wilma Raymo

Winston Raymo

Leona Raymo

LEONA V. RAYMO

Born: September 6, 1944
St. Thomas, U.S. Virgin Islands
Widow of Winston Glenwood Raymo

No Problems

My husband volunteered on his own. He finished high school in
1965, and he decided he wanted to go into the service, so he
enlisted in the U.S. Marines. It was in 1966, when he was nineteen.
I had known him for eight years then. I went out with him all
during high school.

He went into the Marine Corps, then he came home, and we
got married. I was pregnant at the time. We got married in May
of 1966, so he had gone into the service in January of 1966. We
got married in May, and then he went to Vietnam, and then the
next year he died in Vietnam. They didn't say what happened to
him. All I know is that someone told me that he walked on a mine.
That's all I know. He went out on patrol and stepped on a mine.
That's what they told us, anyway, and I think his wounds were
facial. That's why his body wasn't open to viewing. It was a closed
casket. The baby was nine months old when he was killed.

It was hard at that time to know how I felt. It was really
something. I was looking forward to him coming out, because he
would have been in Vietnam nearly a year at that time. It was
maybe just a week or two before he would be home. I was messed
up, because my mind was already set that he was coming home.
I don't know how to explain it. I can remember that at that time
it was real hard. Everything had come down. The whole of St.

Thomas attended the funeral, because we were well known. My family is well-known people. So were his family, so he was really well known. My father was the marshal at one time of the Virgin Islands, so we were well known.

I would say that for a whole year I was by myself, until my friends encouraged me . . . you know, that I am young, that I have to go out, and I have to go on, because I was in my early twenties at that time. I just gave up on anything. I never used to go any place. I just used to stay home, go to work, come back, pick my daughter up, whatever, but then after a year, my friends encouraged me, and my sister. They said, "You have to go out. We've given him enough time to come back." At that time, they were saying that they had some of the people in Vietnam captive. They said they would let some of them out sometime, so my mind was like that, that he was okay and that someday he would come home.

After I got the ring, though—he had on his wedding band and his class ring—one was full of blood, so, you know, I started to think in a different way. I didn't believe he was dead, because we couldn't open the casket, and I heard so much about how they usually shipped empty caskets . . . things like that. But the marine that brought the body home told us that I could open the casket, but he would have to step off the premises, so in case anything would happen to us, whether we got a heart attack or whatever, it would be our own fault. So I told my mother I didn't want to open it. I was going to open it before that. And then someone told my mother that it was a facial affair, you know, so I didn't take a chance and open it. We felt that there might not be anything in the casket, but the fellow told me—the marine that brought the body—told us that he just came, the week before, from delivering a body also, and the parents felt that way, and they opened the casket, and the mother had a heart attack. This is what he told me, you know, because I asked him. I really questioned him right down, you know, to find out if he was sure that his body was in there and stuff like that. And from the report that came in, I felt at that time that, really, his body could have been there, because it wasn't like he was blown to bits. It was just that he walked on this thing, and it hit him in his face. They said from his chest up, you know, which means that the other parts of him were all right. It was just that his face couldn't get to look like him, so they didn't open the casket.

For a year I didn't go anywhere. I can't say for sure the time period, but I know it was within that year that I decided he wasn't coming home, although, again, after I received his ring . . . they sent me his personal belongings and different things. Then I saw that one of the rings, the class ring and the wedding band, had blood on it. But, again, when they had told that they had some soldiers captured, that they were captured in Vietnam, I figured that he might have been in one of those camps, even though they sent me the rings.

When he went to Vietnam, I wasn't afraid. I didn't even think that he would be killed, because my brother was over there, too. He was in Vietnam around the same time my husband was killed. I think it was the same year. My brother was in Vietnam, and he came home okay. My daughter has a godfather, too, who was in Vietnam, and he came back. He had been home and was going back to Vietnam when my husband was killed. So I didn't have any thoughts that my husband would be killed. When my husband died in Vietnam, my brother was getting married. My brother got married on May the fifth, 1967, and at that time my husband had died. We only got word May eighth, though, so it was that we had sorrow, but we didn't know it was sorrow. He died May third, but we were having a good time.

When my daughter was small, they told her the monster had killed him, and my mother and myself, we have just left her to believe like that. We have never gone into detail about this to her. Well, my mother and myself, we just decided if she asked us, we would tell her something, but to go into detail, why? I have all his belongings, which I show her sometimes, inside a room, but I don't unless she asks about it, because it isn't something great, you know. I look at it like that, so I never really sat down and tell her nothing.

I had no feelings about the war at all until after he died. Then I feel that . . . someone told me that the Americans didn't have no business over there from before he died. Then at that time my brother was over there, so after my husband died, and we had the next boy from St. Thomas, a very young boy, too, that got killed, it got negative for everybody, so much that I really went against it.

His parents were messed up about this. His mother was really messed up. She's still alive, but she's blind. His father's still alive, too. She was really messed up, because she looked at him for a lot of support. She's a very sick lady, also, and she was sick before she went blind. I believe his brother and sister felt the same way, like their mother, but, you know, a mother losing a son is something.

Now and again I do think about it now. It was the way that he passed, that something happened to him, you know. You try to get over it, because you feel like you have to continue your life, but some days you just sit and you think. I do right now, because my father died in March, and every now and then I just sit and think about him. And this is the same way I do about my husband. Sometimes I just think, "If he was here, how would life be?" It might have been the same that it is, or it might have been better, or it might have been worse, but you just think, "if."

After the first year passed, like I say, my family and some other people in town were telling me: "You're a young girl. You have to continue living. It isn't something that we wanted, but it don't make sense to say you give up." I had to live for my daughter, you know, and to try to do something with myself, too. It isn't something that we wanted, but, like they say, "Don't question the act of God."

I have no problems now. I have two kids since then. I still work. I work for the government still, for twenty-one years now, in the government. I'm a fiscal officer in accounting, like a business office for an agency. I send out reports and correspondence, stuff like that.

WILMA G. RAYMO

Born: August 22, 1966
St. Thomas, U.S. Virgin Islands
Daughter of Winston Glenwood Raymo

Not into That

I have a lot of friends who are signing up. A lot of them are doing it because they want an education. They aren't really thinking about war. Some of them are, though. This one friend of mine talks about shooting and war. He doesn't do that well in school, but he talks about war and stuff like that, so I think he's into that. They say that a great number of the high school graduates this year are going into the military. I don't know what's happened in the past, but I didn't expect for so many people to be going into the service.

They think they're doing it for college. They do brainwashing. They come to the school, and they tell them all the nice things. "You're gonna get this, and you're gonna get that," and they just say, "Yeah, I'm gonna get it. I'm gonna get it." They never think to ask, "Well, what am I going to have to *do* to get it?" To me, it's just like they're brainwashing them. I listened to some girls talk. They're going into the army, and they're going to get to go to this college, and after that they're going to come home. I said, "You know, you have to pay that army back with time for the money they spend on you." They said, "Yeah? I didn't know that." You know. It's just brainwashing to me, all the good things, and they don't even tell them that the army chooses your career, because if there's no room, they put you where they want you. It's brainwashing to me.

The recruiting in the high school has been at the same level, about, I think, at least for the past four years. I think it's at the same level. They have an orientation, and every year at registration they give you a little thing about ROTC, and they try to get you to join ROTC. That's another brainwashing, too. "If you're in ROTC for four years, you won't go into the army as a private. You'll be high up." So they say, "Yeah. Yeah," and they join ROTC.

I'm not into that. Nope. I say my father served my time. I haven't thought very much about him being killed in a war, really. It just happened. But it makes me think differently about joining the service. I wouldn't want to go in, just because of that, because he was killed. I don't really think about it, though.

AN Jr • RONALD G DICKSON • SHELDON SILV
• BELARSKI • DONALD G CHMIEL • JOHN S N
JOHN P HEARSCH Jr • JOHN JASSO • GARY E
ONCE • JAMES M KOZLOWSKI • JOHN D MA
OSS Jr • TERRELL L RAWLINSON • RICHARD H
HAEL E WHITE • REX T ALLEN • WILLIAM ANDE
DRE F BEDRA • KEVIN E BONJOUR • PAUL E BR
Y O CODY • ONNIE D DUNCAN • CURTISS ES
IAH C GARNETT • JAMES M GINN • STEPHEN
JACOBSON • ALBERT L JOHNSON • FRED C K
DRK • MICHAEL L MORGAN • HIMA D McDOL
OHN L PIERSOL Jr • DAVID P REESE • JOHN W
SANDOVAL • GEORGE E TEFFT • WILLIAM D T
MARTINEZ-ZAYAS • JOEL C YORK • ERNEST M
CAIN • MARCUS J HAMILTON • WILLIE H HAV
YA • CHARLES W NURISSO • RICHARD W PALO
NZA FOSTER • RAYMOND L HODGES Jr • JOE

JOHN CHARLES HINES

Born: February 22, 1947
       Hudson, New York
Killed: August 24, 1970
       Quang Nam Province, Republic of South Vietnam

TTON • HARRY C INMAN III • FREDERICK R K
ONTES • ROGER A SCARBROUGH • CRAIG A S
B THOMAS • DOUGLAS P ZERBA • RANDY C B
NVERSON • GILBERTO GARCIA • JIMMY RAY

Don Hines in Vietnam

John Hines

UNITED STATES MARINE CORPS

Corporal John C. Hines
Born Feb. 22, 1947
Died Aug. 24, 1970

Killed in action while on patrol
in the Quang Nam Province,
Republic of Viet Nam

DONALD L. HINES

Born: September 24, 1948
Hudson, New York
Brother of John Charles Hines

My Brothers

John wasn't drafted. He joined the marines, then I joined the army after him. It was a gung-ho society then, and everything was great. He volunteered in 1966. He quit high school and joined when he was seventeen. He had a job at the Cohoes Memorial Hospital. One day he just went down and saw the recruiter. He told them he liked the dress blues, and he was in.

We corresponded back and forth, then he came home on leave after training, and we talked. He had his orders and knew he was going to 'Nam, and he was . . . well, for one to be a marine and to not have a war would have been really bad. He had the war, and he was looking forward to it. He really liked the idea of going and fighting. When we were growing up, that's all we did. We played war, had the John Wayne syndrome. He went over toward the end of 1966. It was the end of the year before I quit high school. I quit high school in 1967, just walked out of high school, went straight down to the post office, and enlisted in the army. This was at the very end of April. I didn't talk to anyone about it.

We came from a broken home. There were eight of us, and my mother and father split up, and we went into the Hudson Home. I then went into a foster home for ten years, and then to a home called Vanderhayden Hall in Troy for another three years, then with my mother for about nine months. When we went into the Hudson Home, I was about two; we were all there together for a while. I left when I was about five and went to this foster home. One day they came and just said, "These nice people want to take you for a ride." I just took one look, and I thought, "Oh, oh, something's not right here." I remember saying, "I want to see my brothers and sisters," and they said, "Well, you'll see them when you come back." I said, "I want to see them now." They wouldn't buy that. They just put me in the car, and off I went. I remember it like yesterday. I couldn't get over the fact that it was so abrupt. There were no ifs, ands, or buts about it. I couldn't even see my brothers and sisters, and then, when they more or less forced me into the car, I knew something was wrong. I think I cried about five days straight. I finally started to accept the surroundings and everything. My youngest brother was with me. They took two of us. He was about three years old at the time. We were both there for three years, then they took him out and put him in another home and left me there.

I remember coming home one summer. I was about eight, and I was coming home from school. It was in the summer, and school was almost over. I think of the old stories: "Well, I used to walk a mile to school." We had something similar to that. We lived in the country, and we had this dirt road, and the bus never went all the way up it. It stopped at one single location, and all the kids had to meet it there. It was about a mile. As I came walking home this one day, I heard this tommygun go off, and I heard, "I got you." I turned around, and there was my brother John. I hadn't seen him since I was five, since I was taken away from the Hudson Home, and there he was, just standing in the bushes with a little army helmet on. He came from the Hudson Home; it turned out they had just closed the Hudson Home, so they sent him to the foster home where I was. All my other brothers and sisters were in other foster homes by this time, so this was good. I had John in the foster home with me, and we used to play war games. There were about six boys there, but the others were from other families.

John stayed with me for about four years, then he left and went to Vanderhayden Hall in Troy. It was a home for "dependent" children, that's the word they used. I felt really bad about that. For some reason, it didn't affect me when Dennis, my younger brother, left, but when John left, it really bothered me. Wow. To me he was my big brother, even though we had two brothers older than us, but, as far as I was concerned, he was my big brother. He was my big brother, and he used to help me out in schoolyard fights. Then he left.

I stayed with the foster mother for another three years. I don't remember seeing either my father or mother for the length of time I was in the Hudson Home. When I went to the foster home, it was . . . I think it was about the second year I was there, and I was playing in the playroom. It was around Christmas time, and my foster mother came in, and she said, "I want you to come out here for a moment; I want you to meet somebody." I said, "All right." I went out and there was this lady standing there, and she says, "This is your mother." I looked at her, and I looked at my foster mother, and I said, "You're my mother." She said, "No, no. This is your *real* mother." "Oh," I thought. "Hi," I said. Then I saw the bag of presents. "Mine?" "Yeah."

It was a Roy Rogers twin-gun holster set. I put that on and went about my merry way. The following year my father stopped over. He stayed maybe half an hour, something like that, and he brought us a case of soda. About eight years later, I saw my mother again. She brought the whole family down, my brothers and sisters. Most of them were at Vanderhayden Hall; some of them were living on their own. They came down around Christmas time, and I kind of zeroed in on John. We talked, and they stayed about an hour.

One day I came home from school, and my foster mother said, "Well, you've got a choice. You can either go and live with your brothers and sisters, or go to Wasaic State School." I thought, "Hey, no way you're going to get me to Wasaic State School." It's a mental place, and for hard-to-handle kids, so I said, "Hey, I want to be with my brothers and sisters." I left, and there was no problem. I went to the home in Troy. John and Dennis were the only ones there at the time. Everybody else had left already. My brother Paul was in Troy, and he would drop by to play basketball and go out with everybody. Then John quit school. He said, "The hell with it. I don't like living here." He was sixteen. He was in high school, and he never went back. He and my brother Paul and somebody else got an apartment in Cohoes. They started working over there, and John would come over and see me and Dennis. A lot of times when he'd come, we'd just get in the car and book, just leave, raise hell, stuff like that.

I can remember one incident, just before he went into the service. I had never gotten drunk before in my whole life. We told the home that we were going to see a movie, and we went to Cohoes. John was working at the hospital at the time, so there was me and another guy and my brother Paul and some other guy, and we sat down at the kitchen table and we started playing cards: "Anybody want a beer?" "Yeah, I'll have a beer." They broke out the big quart bottles of beer. I started drinking, and I was in bad shape. By the time I really got smashed, we started to leave. I was the last one to come down the stairs, and I just fell down the whole flight. As I fell, I could hear my brother John screaming, "What the hell is going on?" He got really pissed off at my other brother because he let me get drunk. I thought it was comical at the time: "Come on, John. You get drunk. I can get drunk." He said, "Will you just shut up and get in the car?" But one day he came over and said, "The hell with it. I'm going to enlist." I said, "Why?" He said, "Because I like the marines," so he went down and enlisted.

There was basic and advanced infantry training, then he came home on leave. He had his dress blues on, and he looked sharp. I said, "Hey, you know, when I get out of here, I'm going to join the marines." He said, "I'm going to tell you something right now. You can join the air force, you can join the army, and you can join the navy, but if you ever join the marines, I will kick your ass all over the place." He loved the marines, but he didn't want me in the Marine Corps. It wasn't a competitive thing or anything like that. There was never anything competitive between me and my brother John, not a thing. He told me about the training, and how rough and bad it was. He told me one time he was doing push-ups, and he thought he was doing them right, and a drill instructor came over and kicked him solid, right in the ribs, with the toe of his boot. It knocked the wind out of him, and he still made him do the push-ups, smacked him around. I feel it was a protective thing, him not wanting me to go into the Marine Corps. It was a protective thing, so I said, "Well, we'll see." He said, "No. I'm dead serious. I do not want you to join the marines." I just said, "Well, where are you going?" "I'm going to 'Nam." "Well, write to me." "Yeah, no problem. I'll write," and he used to write letters.

I was pretty well fed up with the home by that time, and I remember calling my mother. She was living over in Albany at the time, and I said, "One of two things. Either get me out of here and come over here and get me, or I'm walking out." She got me out, and I lived with her for a while and went to school and kept in touch with John.

When I quit high school, I went down to the army recruiter and just walked in and said, "I want to join the army." He said, "Sure, fine. Just take the tests, and we'll talk to you." I took all the tests, and he called me into his office and said, "Look, you scored the highest in the automotive section of the test." I said, "I expected to score the lowest there. I never even saw the inside of a car. I guessed at everything on that." He said, "All right. The second highest score was clerical." I said, "I don't want clerical." He ran down the field, and I kept saying, "No, I don't like that," so he said, "Well, what do you want?" "I want to become an infantryman, and I want to go to Vietnam." "You want to go to Vietnam?" "Yeah." He said, "You got it. Any special unit you want to go in?" "Yeah. I want to go airborne." "Fine. No problem," so I went to basic training down at Fort Jackson, South Carolina, completed my training down there, and was on what's called a two-week holdover. Usually after basic everybody got a pass to go home for a week or so, then they went to the different specializations they were going into. I was stuck in Fort Jackson, South Carolina, for two weeks, no leave to go home or anything. I guess the training class hadn't graduated yet, and there were no orders cut for me to go home. Me and about four other guys just stayed there for two weeks. We really had it good. We had the pool, and we worked details from nine o'clock until noon Monday through Friday, and the rest of the time was ours. It was fun. Finally, I got my orders to go to Fort Gordon, Georgia, airborne training.

Fort Gordon was better than basic. It was rougher training, but it was better because you weren't treated like slime or dirt like in basic. In basic, they strip you of everything. You don't even have a name. They treat you like an animal. Nowadays I hear they have two-man rooms, and you don't have to fall out for formation and stuff like that. Not back then, boy. They didn't care. They'd come up and beat the hell out of you for nothing, or if you looked cross-eyed at them, and there was nothing you could do. We had one kid who wrote his congressman that he was being mentally abused because the DIs [drill instructors] were swearing at him and calling him a "Jewboy," and, of course, the congressman's going to write the army, and the army is going to write their commander, and the commander's going to call them in and say, "What the hell is going on?" The DIs are the last ones. They say, "Hey, we'll fix it, Lieutenant," and they go back to the kid and say, "Someone in this outfit wrote his congressman." Needless to say, the kid got the hell beat out of him, and no more letters were sent. That was the way they worked it.

When we graduated from basic, it was, "How's it going, guy?" Wow. A couple of days ago, this same guy would have been calling me "Slimey." I had this one platoon sergeant, a little short Mexican, and I had to look down at him. We'd be in formation, and he would get as close to me as possible and just stand there and look up at me and say, "Are you crazy or something?" I'd say, "No, Drill Sergeant," and he'd say, "Then why are you always fucking with me?" I'd try to keep a straight face, and I could never do it. I'd always break out laughing. It was an automatic twenty-five push-ups, but that was really great.

We had this one sergeant who had just got out of the hospital, and he had come from 'Nam. An enemy grenade had landed in his position. He had picked it up, and, just as he was throwing it back, it went off. He told us his eye was hanging out, and he had more or less just pushed his eye back. He had scars all around his eye, but he didn't lose his sight. During about the middle of basic training, he became one of our drill instructors. Whenever choppers flew over or we were on the artillery range, he would tense up. I would watch. You could hear a chopper off in the distance, and he would start tensing up. He'd start looking around and everything. They told us he was from 'Nam, and we were saying, "Wow. This is really something."

While we were in basic, they asked our squad to be an honor guard for some guy who was killed in 'Nam, and we went in our dress greens. Sergeant Hill was in charge of the honor guard. He was the one that was in 'Nam. We went to this house, and it was a black guy who was killed. There wasn't one black guy in the honor guard. We went from the house to the church where they had the body at rest. We stood up front, right across from the family, and the coffin was just a little bit more to the front. I'll never forget that. That was really an emotional experience for me. I started crying, and Sergeant Hill turned and looked at me and said, whispering, "You don't cry. You better not cry, or you're in trouble." I'm trying to be cool, and the family went up to pay their last respects, and the wife was in hysterics, and she had a little boy and a little girl.

As the family was walking by us, the little boy stopped and tugged at Sergeant Hill's sleeve and said, "Why did my daddy have to die?" I said to myself, "Oh, shit, get me out of here," and I just had the tears flowing. I looked at Sergeant Hill, and that got to him. He couldn't take that, and his tears started flowing. We got to the gravesite, took the casket there, gave him a twenty-one-gun salute, taps. Boy, I'll tell you. Taps. There's nothing like taps.

Sergeant Hill said, "Come on. Let's get the hell out of here." He was really mad that there was no one black in our squad to represent the guy. No one told us it was a black family. That, plus the little boy saying, "Why did my daddy have to die?" The kid must have been about two years old, two or three.

So we went to airborne training. As I said, it was rougher, but we had more respect paid to us. They called us by our names. I was no longer "Slime." About two weeks before we took the last proficiency test to graduate from the class, we were out in the field on a work detail. I was with three other guys. About two hundred yards away, another group of guys was working on a bunker. Some of them were inside the bunker; others were just filling sand bags. They were switching on and off, doing it that way so that they could all be out of the sun some of the time. We were watching them for a while. All of a sudden, we saw the whole bunker go BOOM! It collapsed. We tore ass up there. There were three guys inside the bunker, and three guys outside trying to get the stuff off the ones inside. There were sand bags, sheet metal, beams of wood, everything.

As we were running up there, I felt a sting on my face. By then, the adrenalin was flowing so fast, I didn't know what it was. I didn't care. We knew that the three guys we saw were in that bunker, and we knew all the stuff was on top of them, so we're tearing everything off to get the three guys out. Someone ran to a phone to call a truck to come up and get them. They were just all busted up, and I started feeling woozy. I had my back to the guys, and they asked me if I was okay. I said, "Yeah. I just feel a little lightheaded," and I turned around. "What the hell happened to you?" I said, "What do you mean?" They said, "Take your right hand and touch your face." Oh, my God. I looked, and it was covered with blood. At the time I was running up there, one of the guys picked up a piece of sheet metal and flung it, and it caught me right in the corner of the eye and went on down and split my lip open. That was the sting I felt when I was running up there. The only place I have a scar now is close to the lip. That's where it went the deepest. They just told me, "Sit down. We're going to get you to the hospital."

It wasn't until I'd been to 'Nam and come back, been back six or seven years, that something I saw at that hospital, the Army Hospital at Fort Gordon, really registered on me. When they took me to the hospital that day, I walked down a corridor with a field dressing on my face, and the corridor was filled with guys laid out on racks, some missing arms, some missing legs, some all bandaged up. I was just walking through, looking at these guys, and it never dawned on me that, "Wow. These are dudes just back from 'Nam." Had I stopped and said, "My God. These guys are from Vietnam. Shit. Do I really want to go?" I think that might have changed my way of thinking. To me, on that day, that cut I had was more important than guys lying there without limbs. It just never dawned on me.

They told me at the hospital I had to have three weeks of light duty. They put me in the supply room, and it never dawned on me that this would make any difference in terms of my training. Then my captain called me into the office and said, "You're on two weeks light duty," and I said, "Yeah, but I'm okay. I'll be all right. No problem." He said, "That's not the problem. The problem is that in a week and a half or two weeks we're taking a proficiency test. You can't take it because it's against doctor's orders." I said, "Well, okay. I'll take it the next week." He goes, "You don't understand. When that test is finished, the guys go to jump school, and you go in companies, not as single individuals." I said, "So? What does that mean?" He said, "You have two choices. One, you can hang around here and redo the whole training." I said to myself, "No. I'm not going through all of this all over again," so I said to him, "What's my other option?" He said, "You can sign a statement saying that you want out of airborne," and I said, "What happens then?" He said, "It depends. I see in the record that you want to go to Vietnam." I said, "Yeah," and he said, "Do you really want to go?" I told him yes. "Sign this waiver that you want out of airborne, and you can go to Vietnam." I said, "You got a deal." I signed the papers, and within a week I had my orders for 'Nam.

I had two weeks to spend at home, then I had to report to Fort Dix to be flown to 'Nam. My brother John was in Vietnam at this time. He'd gone over in late 1966. When I got there in October, he had something like a month and a half or two months to go. The marines did thirteen months. At the time I signed the papers, it never dawned on me that he was already over there, and that his tour wasn't over. I just went on home. I didn't even stay two weeks there. I couldn't put up with it, so I took off. I said, "Well, I'm going. I've got to report to Fort Dix," and I went to Fort Dix four or five days ahead of time. There were a few of us there who just hung around the base. They tried to put us on KP, tried to make us do all these little details, pull guard duty and everything, and we said, "We ain't going to do it." They said, "Oh, yes, you are." "We are not." "You are, too." "What are you going to do, send us to 'Nam?" They knew we were on our way to Vietnam, so they just more or less said, "The hell with you guys."

I got over to 'Nam, and they assigned us to a company. After about two or three days, we went out into the field. I was stationed at Cu Chi, right outside of Saigon. My brother was stationed up north. We were out in the field something like a week. We came back, and they said, "You're one gung-ho son-of-a-bitch." I said, "I wanted to see what it was like. I got my brother fighting up north." They said, "That's your ticket out." "What do you mean?" "Only one brother can be over here at a time." The company commander called me over, and I told him, "I just got here. No sense sending me back to wait about a month and a half, two months, and then sending me back over here again. My brother's tour is about up. Why can't you arrange for him to go home?" They did. He went home early that time; I stayed over there.

I think my brother wanted me out, but at the time I enjoyed it there. It was different. While he was over there the first time, I think it was the Navy Cross he won, and I think that's the second-highest award the marines give out. What happened was

they came to a river or a swollen stream. They had to go across
to the other side and hook up a line so that the entire company
could get across. There was only one problem. The enemy was on
the other side, shooting at them. My brother volunteered. He took
the rope and went across and gave cover fire while they sent a
squad over. They got the whole company over, and they took their
objective.

My first major firefight over there lasted from seven in the
morning until about five o'clock the following morning, just one
continuous battle. We hit a hot LZ [landing zone]. They had told
us, "This landing zone is hot," and we came in on the choppers
and jumped off. We could see Charlie running all over the place,
and that really psyched me. I was really psyched. "Hey, I can see
the enemy. Wow!" I just went apeshit. I started charging, shooting
and everything, and our gunships were coming in. There was this
one VC [Viet Cong] retreating. He turned around to fire an
AK-47, and, I know it wasn't intentional or anything like that, but
it was a good hit. At the same time he turned to fire the AK-47
toward us, the gunships over our heads fired rockets. We could see
the rocket. He caught that rocket right in the chest, and it just
blew him away.

One of the guys had shot one of the VC in the leg. He said,
"I know he's in this area somewhere," so we went to that area.
It's like a swamp. Water, grass, and we know he's down there
somewhere. Someone's got to get him. I said, "I'll do it," and I
jumped in. The water was a little over my chest, and I'm trying
to find him. I guess I had gone right by him, because, all of a
sudden, he came leaping out. I just turned around, and this was
what really blew my mind: half the guys were saying, "Waste him,
man, waste him." The other half were saying, "No. Don't shoot
him," and I just stared at him. I didn't know what to do. I was
really totally confused and saying to myself, "Hey. This isn't
supposed to happen. If you're so gung-ho, you're supposed to
make a decision like that right then and there." He had no weapon
with him. He was no threat. He had left his weapon where he was
hiding; he had just jumped out of the water to surrender.

I stood there for about a minute, with four guys saying, "Waste him," and another four saying, "No. Take him prisoner." I was just looking at him, and I think that's what did it. I made the eye contact, and I shouldn't have made the eye contact. You know, it's different when someone's coming at you, charging at you, firing at you. You just shoot and kill him, but when he's standing right next to you, and you're staring in that face . . . and this guy was scared. There was no doubt about that. I just pushed him to the guys that said, "Take him prisoner," just reached down and grabbed him and dragged him out.

We threw a quick first-aid pack on the bullet wound in his leg and brought him back. I looked around, and there were about five or six VCs there, shot up. I mean, really torn up something fierce. They caught it from the rockets, they caught it from our M-79 grenade launchers, the M-60, M-16s. They were just shot to shit, and two of them were still alive. I turned to my captain and said, "Captain, we got two of them still alive." He said, "So?" I said, "Well, what are we going to do with them?" "What the fuck do you think we're going to do with them?" "Do you mean to kill them?" "Yep." It didn't bother me. I just walked over and put a few rounds in their heads. It was like, "Well, hey, he's messed up, and he probably wouldn't live anyway, so I'm just putting him out of his misery." It didn't bother me at all.

We took the guy prisoner that was in the water. We called in a chopper for him. We had him and another guy that wasn't even hit, so the chopper landed and took the two prisoners back to base camp. In the meantime, Bravo Company was pinned down on the other side of our objective, and they were getting the shit kicked out of them. Our captain said, "Bravo Company's in trouble. Let's go."

We're tearing across this field. We could hear heavy fire, and we knew that Charlie's probably really dug in over there. When we got over to the position, we started firing. Bravo Company moved out to the side of us, and we moved in to their position. We didn't know what the screw-up was, but Bravo Company was supposed to go around one side and come in from the other side, to form more or less an L shape, but they booked. They went. They had the choppers called in, and they just took off and left us there. We were pinned down, and we fought that battle. It was the first time I saw an American dead.

They had snipers in the trees. They had this one machine gun set up that no one could locate. We were leaning up against a dyke. I was facing this guy, and we were talking. He was getting ready to pop up and let off a few rounds. Well, while he was getting ready to pop up, I was putting another magazine in my 16, and I wasn't looking at him. The next thing I know, I have this shit all over me. I said, "What the hell," and I looked. He had caught a round in the head, and that was his brains on me. I thought, "I don't believe this. This can't be happening. This is supposed to happen to the enemy, not us." I said, "Shit. This is it. We're really in for it." We moved up a little, Charlie pushed us back. Finally, our captain said, "Okay, fuck it. Move back," and he called in an air strike on their positions. Well, we moved back, Charlie moved back. The air strike came in and bombed empty positions. We moved up, and Charlie moved up. He was waiting for us all over again.

When we went to Vietnam, the first thing they told us was, "Everything you learned back in the States, forget. This is an entirely different war, so don't even try to go by the book." As I said, there was this one machine gun no one could find. In basic training, there's one session where they put you in a gravel pit. You walk in, and you sit with a sergeant. He says, "They're going to open up with live rounds. I want you guys to listen and tell me what direction the rounds are coming from." We sat there, trying to figure it out, everybody pointing in different directions. "You're not paying attention. Listen to the snap of the bullets." Sure enough. I'd say, "It's coming from that direction," and the sergeant would say, "Right," or "It's coming from that direction." "Right."

So this machine gun has the whole company pinned down, and the captain was yelling down the line, "Someone locate that goddamned gun." I'm lying there, and I'm listening, trying to listen. Finally he sprayed our area, and I was listening to the bullets. I said, "I know where it is." Off in the distance was a clump of bushes. I pointed to those bushes and said, "It's in there." The guys that were out in the field longer than me said, "No. You're full of shit." I said, "Man, I remember this from basic training." "No. That's bullshit." "Okay. Watch." I was hiding behind this tree, and I threw in a twenty-round magazine and fired a twenty-round burst into those bushes. All of a sudden, no more machine gun fire for a few seconds. I said, "I told you."

The next thing, that machine gun opened up. Evidently they must have had the same damn training as me, because bullets were kicking up all around me. I felt this sting in my side. "Oh, shit. I'm hit." I look, and . . . what had happened, the bullet hit the tree and tore off a splinter a little over six, maybe seven inches long. About three inches of that was in me, so I pulled it out. The sergeant said, "You're right. The gun is over there." He radioed it to the captain. When the captain saw where we were telling him it was, all of a sudden he just got up, and he charged the machine gun position. He knocked it out. He turned to ask Sergeant Jones for another clip. As he turned, one of the gooks stood up and fired an RPG, a rocket-propelled grenade. They use them to knock out tanks and APCs and bunkers and stuff like that. It caught the captain square in the back, and it just blew him away. He was gone. That was it. Sergeant Jones just went totally ape. Once the gook had fired, he also had to reload, but Sergeant Jones didn't give him a chance. He put twenty rounds out and opened the gook up, the one who killed our captain. When he got hit, he just disintegrated.

By then, it's about four o'clock, and we're calling in for resupplies, and they resupplied us. We wanted ammo, but they gave us two cases of grenades. No ammunition. Two cases of grenades. When we got the grenades, we were low on ammo, but we weren't out. I grabbed five or six grenades. With their machine gun knocked out, I figured we had a better chance of attacking. We did attack again, and they opened up on us again. I saw this one gook running with an AK-47. I cut loose with about fifteen rounds, and I saw him go down. I knew I got him, but I didn't know if I killed him. Then, from where he went down, we started receiving fire, so I knew that he was still alive. He wasn't dead yet. I don't know why, but I was lying there, and I turned to one of the guys next to me and said, "When I count to three, open up. Give me cover fire. Just spray the area." He said, "What are you going to do?" I said, "When I count to three . . . one, two, three," and I jumped up and threw a grenade where he was. I got him. The guy next to me had been over there for about four months, five months, and I was over there for what? Three weeks? He said, "Hey. We don't pull that John Wayne shit over here. You could have easily gotten wasted like that. You could have easily gotten wasted by one of the snipers." It never dawned on me. You know: "That's the way John Wayne did it. Why not me?"

By six o'clock our situation was really critical. I had three rounds left in my 16 and two hand grenades. A lot of guys had only one round left and a hand grenade. One round. We were hurting for ammo. They did not bring any ammo. We were finally ordered to break contact with them when it got dark. We tried to break contact, but they kept up with us, following us, opening up on us, throwing grenades at us. I used my last two grenades, and I saved one round. I figured, "They ain't taking me." We finally broke contact.

While we were making this trek through the woods at night, one of the guys was complaining he had leeches on him. We told him to keep it down. "When we get out of this mess, we'll get the leeches off you. No problem." He said, "Damn, they're bothering me." It turned out he had caught a whole chestful of shrapnel. They weren't leeches; they were shrapnel. Wow. That day. It was October 31, Halloween in 1967. It was my first major firefight with the enemy. About seven o'clock in the morning, they flew the choppers in. We got resupplied with ammo, then we had to go back for our guys that didn't make it: our captain, the guy who was killed next to me, and two other guys. We went back and got their bodies and returned to base camp. From there, we flew eagle flights out every day, searching the boonies.

Eagle flights involve maybe ten, fifteen choppers, helicopters, all loaded down with our guys. They would just fly out to any place in the field and drop you off. That was called "eagle flights." That's all it was, anywhere from five to fifteen helicopters, and they flew in formation. It's really a pretty sight. One of the prettiest sights over there was the eagle flights, especially when they were coming to pick you up and bring you out of there. When they dropped us down, we were just looking to make contact. We pulled search-and-destroy missions and tried to find Charlie.

This one day, we were only going to be out there for half a day. We came across this bunker complex. I said, "We can check it out before we leave." We had a scout dog with us. The dog checked it out. He didn't do anything, so we went ourselves and checked out the bunkers. They were empty. Our new captain looked at his watch and said, "Look, we got about a mile to go. The chopper's going to be here in about a half hour. Let's go." Fine with us. We started going to the area where the chopper was going to pick us up. They were arguing: "Should we take the trail, and get there quicker, or should we do it our regular way, avoid trails?" The captain said, "Look, we ain't got time, man. We're about a mile away. They're going to be here in a half hour. There's no way in hell we'd get there on time. Let's take the trail. Scout dog, go ahead." The dog and the handler went ahead. My squad was put on flank security; there was another squad from another platoon on the right flank. The rest of the company was marching down the trail. It wasn't a full company. There were only about two and a half platoons of us. It was just a morning operation: "Hey, we're going to drop you here, and if you don't make contact, fine. The choppers are going to pick you up here at such-and-such a time." There was no need for having a whole company of guys. All total, there were about sixty of us, which is a pretty good-sized fighting force.

I'm going through the woods and just getting ready to step out in the open when this machine gun opens up. I turned to look at the trail, and I hear the dog yelp. I see the dog handler just spinning down the trail. The machine gun bullets were chewing the shit out of him. He finally falls down. The dog tries to make it to the dog handler, and they shoot the shit out of the dog. All of a sudden, everything just opens up on us. They said we had walked into two battalions of hard-core VC. We had walked into their base camp, and we never even knew it was there.

I just hit the ground and started return fire. We had so much fire power on us, I could hear the bullets just zinging by me. I couldn't get any closer to that ground. I wished I was a piece of dirt, that's how close those bullets were, and, to tell the truth, I more or less froze up. I believed that if I moved, I was going to get hit. I got really scared. My platoon sergeant came up from behind me and said, "Hines, are you hit?" I said, "No." He said, "Let's get out of here." I still couldn't move. He said, "Look, if you don't move, they're going to find you for sure, and then you *will* die." That kind of snapped me back, and I said, "Okay. Let's get out of here." We got back to the bunker complex. We could hear our guys screaming for help, the ones that were caught out in the open, and they said, "We need volunteers to go up and try to get these guys out." I was really surprised at what happened next.

We were all sitting in this bomb crater, and the sergeant says, "We need some volunteers to get these guys, to get the wounded out." I looked around, and everybody is just saying, "Not going back up there, man." The first thought that came to my mind was, "Hey. Goddamn, if I was up there and wounded, I'd want someone to come and get my ass." I said, "Hey, I'm going." There weren't that many volunteers.

Ten guys had been killed outright. That left about fifty of us, and another ten were wounded. We went to the captain, and he said, "Okay, this is the general area where a couple of wounded are. We're going to work it in teams, two riflemen and a medic." It was me, Sergeant Schultz, and this medic. Sergeant Schultz said, "Okay, Hines, lead the way." The next thing I knew, this medic goes shooting by me, crawling into the woods. I said, "Get behind me, man. I'm supposed to be in front." He said, "No. They need our help." I said, "We'll get there, but get behind me." "I can't. I've got to find them." He was crawling, and he went behind a tree, and I was trying to cut him off. Schultz was coming up behind. He started to go to the other side of the tree, so he could cut him off over there. This single shot came out, and the medic caught a bullet. Schultz got to him and grabbed his bag. He wasn't dead at first, because I heard him say, "They're over there." I saw Schultz turn, and he said, "I see them," meaning the wounded. He took off, and I started crawling toward the medic. The next thing I knew, a grenade landed right next to me, and it was smoking. I thought, "Well, I can't run." It was only a matter of seconds, yet all this shit goes through your head: "I can't run, so should I take my helmet off and place it over the grenade? I can't do that. If it goes through the helmet, it's going to get my head," so I turned and started to low-crawl out of there. As I did, my foot got hung up on the branches of a bush or something. No sooner had my foot got caught than the grenade went off. It caught me in the left ankle area, and I thought my ankle was broken, so I figured I'd try to get to the medic again. There was this place where it looked like someone had dug a square hole to start a bunker, and I thought, "If I can get the medic, and we can get in there, we'll have some protection." Then another grenade landed right next to the medic. "Oh, shit." I started crawling toward the hole. A grenade landed in there. That one went off, and I thought, "I ain't got nowhere to go." I couldn't see the soldier, the enemy soldier, but we were really close to each other. I could hear him loading another grenade. I lay there for about twenty minutes, and he just kept throwing grenades at me.

Later I heard about what had happened when another of the guys went to the crater where everyone was saying, "I'm not going up there." This guy told them flat out, "Hey, they're your buddies up there. If you guys don't want to go up there and get them now, I'll empty this clip into you. Right now." That's how they finally got them to move forward. I could hear them. There was a fire-break, I'd say about fifty yards behind me, with wooded area behind the firebreak. It was wooded area, firebreak, wooded area where I was, and I could hear the guys. I heard the lieutenant saying, "All right, get on line. We're going to open up first." I was thinking, "Oh, shit. Here they're trying to kill me with grenades, and our dudes are going to open up, and I'm here in the middle. Fuck that shit." I started yelling, "Hey, I'm up here. Hold your fire." The next thing I knew, that sucker starts heaving those grenades again. I had to move again.

They got across the firebreak, and they were getting closer to me. I heard the sucker getting ready again. I yelled, "Grenade." Everybody got down, and the grenade went off. They finally got up again and got to me: "Where are you hit?" "My left foot." "Anybody else down?" "The medic's over there, but I don't believe he's alive." A couple of guys crawled over and got him. He was dead. They brought his body back, and three of the guys stayed to get me out. We had to go down this little indentation, up this little hill, and then down into the firebreak. They were dragging me over the hill, and there was a thump. One guy turned around. Right there in front of him was the grenade. All he had time to do was scream, "Grenade," and lean backwards. He caught it all in the legs, the chest, the face.

They dragged me off the little hill and just reached over and dragged him over. They dragged me across the firebreak and halfway into the woods and took off my boot and started bandaging my leg. All of a sudden, there's another thump. I'm just lying there, and this guy is kneeling down doing my dressing, and the grenade landed less than a foot away. I thought, "Oh, shit," and this guy just blew my mind. He fell flat on me and covered my body with his. We held our breath, and it turned out it was a dud. Had it gone off, he would have been killed, and I would have lived. He said, "Fuck this shit. Let's go," picked me up, threw me over his shoulder, and ran about seventy-five yards through open area under fire from the enemy. He brought me back to where the wounded were being kept. He went back up and got more, and he did this over and over again. He survived. We ended up with ten killed and twenty-five wounded, out of sixty.

We were low on ammunition again. We had jets doing air strikes that were hitting a hundred yards from our position. The shrapnel from the bombs was falling all around us. That's how close the enemy let us get before they even hit us. Then the medivac choppers came down and took us out. That battle went on all night long.

We put that guy in for the Medal of Honor, every one of us put him in for the Medal of Honor. I told how he had covered my body with his body when a grenade landed next to us, how he picked me up, carried me about seventy-five yards through open area under enemy fire, how he continued to go back and forth bringing back wounded, with only a .45 for a weapon. We put him up for the Medal of Honor. He didn't get the Medal of Honor. I think what he got was a Silver Star or a Bronze Star. I weighed about a hundred and seventy-five pounds then, and six-four, a hundred and seventy-five pounds, that's a lot to carry, especially when you're a little dude. He was a little guy, I think about five-five, five-six, somewhere around there. He did all that, and it really freaked me out. Then I had my doubts about going back in the field. I had superficial grenade wounds. I was in the hospital for a week, then I was discharged from the hospital and put in two weeks light duty. What was going through my head was, "Hey, I finally got wounded." I knew it wasn't a game.

I didn't know it wasn't a game the first time, not the first time we were under fire. The first time we were under fire, we had gone out in the field to join the company, and we were chasing these hard-core VC. We set up base camp, a battalion-size base camp. There was supposed to be an NVA regiment or a battalion in the area, and we were trying to make contact with them. I was put on a listening post. The guy I was with had been over there for three months, and it was my first night in the field. This was before my first major fight. I was just hounded by this John Wayne syndrome early on. I felt I learned from him how to take over. I automatically told this other guy, when they opened up from the tree line, and we were told to come back, "Go back ten yards, and I'll give you cover for it. Let me know when you've gone back that far, then you give me cover fire, and I'll get back to you." That's the way we worked our way back. Even though I was the new kid on the block, I told him what to do. I was doing what was in the movies. That's what I did. It was as if I had been doing it all of my life.

The day after that, our company went in one direction, and the other company went in two other directions. They left just a handful of guys back to guard the perimeter. They put me on an observation post. Me and this other guy went out there. From eight o'clock in the morning until about one o'clock in the afternoon, we were pinned down by this one sniper. I think that's when I began to realize, "Hey, this is real." We could not move. We were lying in the hot sun, and we could not move. It began to affect me then, the realization. It was like, "Hey, I could get killed out here." I was in a bad situation. I was pinned down by a sniper. We didn't know where he was firing from. We had a chopper finally get there around noontime. It was flying around trying to spot this son-of-a-bitch. It finally spotted him and killed him. I realized then that I was in a war zone, but it still didn't affect me that much. When that guy's brains got on me, I thought, "Whoa. This is hitting close to home now. That is an American soldier that's dead."

I could see any Vietnamese body; it never bothered me. It didn't matter how bad it was. It never bothered me. It bothered me when I saw an American body. It bothered me also when I looked into the face of that VC we took prisoner, when I looked into his eyes. He was human then, and I couldn't kill him; but when I got it, that's when it really came home. Before that, it was always someone else, but it just kept getting closer and closer. First it was the sniper pinning us down, but that wasn't close. Then a fellow American fell next to me, and his brains got on me. Then, when I got hit, it finally hit home: "Hey, you can die out here." All the other times, going out, it was: "Well, I hope I don't get hit; oh, so-and-so got killed." I felt bad and everything, but, even then, it was real, but it was not real. I got through without a scratch. When I did get hit, and I actually knew what it felt like to get hit, I got my doubts. I was saying, "God. Do I want to go back out, or don't I?" I don't know if I had a choice. I never tried it.

I got out of the hospital, and we were still flying those eagle flights out every day. Each morning I'd see my buddies saddle up, go to the chopper pads, and fly out. Each time I looked at them, I said to myself, "Is this going to be it? Am I going to see them coming back?" I felt like I was deserting my buddies, so I went to the aid station where I had to go on a regular basis for treatment. I said to the medic, "Hey, I can't take this no more. I got to get back out into the field." He said, "How's your ankle?" "It's good." He started tapping it and said, "I can't, man. You're not fully recovered. Hey, man, you don't have to go out in the field." I said, "But I got my honor. I'm living in the hooch with my buddies, and each morning they're going out, and I'm wondering if they're coming back." He finally said okay and signed papers that I could go back out. When I got out there, our medic knew. He said, "Hey, you ain't fooling nobody. You ain't well enough to be out here." I said, "Look, I need something for the pain. Give it to me, and it's cool." That's what he did.

It was good after that. I had made the decision that I'd rather be there if my buddy was going to get killed than to be sitting back on my rack while he was getting killed. I had determined that my buddies came first. Not even buddies, *brothers.* You could take the closest family back stateside. They do everything together, never argue or anything like that. We were closer. That's how we became. When 'Nam vets get together and they talk about it, they're brothers. That was the tightest-knit family in the world.

Then the Tet offensive of 1968 broke out, and that was hell. That was hell. I mean, Charlie was all over the place. He didn't give a shit anymore. He would come out in the open. A bunch of our gunships caught this one platoon of NVA soldiers marching in broad daylight in an open field. They wasted every one of them. Before the Tet offensive, they would sneak around at nighttime. Now they were saying, "We're bad, and we're going to kick your ass."

We were in a reaction force one time. It was during the first week in January, 1968. Our sister battalion was out in the field, and our company was a reaction force. If they ran into trouble, we'd be flown in first. If more help was needed, platoons from the rest of the battalion would come in. Well, we listened to the radio while we were in the helicopters waiting. Our guys made contact, and they had a spotter plane in the area. We could hear the commander giving the enemy's location. The spotter plane spotted the enemy, fired the rocket, and hit the location with white smoke. Any pilot in 'Nam, no matter what he's flying, who sees white smoke knows that means "enemy." If he has anything, any bombs, ammunition, anything, he hits the location marked by the smoke. At this particular time, the spotter plane had three or four jets circling the area, ready to make a strike. The spotter pilot said, "As soon as you see white smoke, hit that area."

As the jets were making their turn to come around and make the hit, the wind shifted. The wind blew the white smoke over our guys in the field. When that happened, we could hear the observer in the spotter plane. He was screaming to the jets to hold off. They were already committed. They saw the smoke, and they dropped napalm. You could hear the commander screaming to the spotter plane pilot to call off the air strike, and you could hear the spotter plane guys screaming to the guys in the jets to call off the air strike. They were too late. The napalm had already been released. Oh, God. We could hear the screams and explosions.

We jumped on the choppers and flew out. I think it was the 101st Artillery Unit that was giving fire cover. They started logging shells in on the enemy position. We got there and were told to spread out. Whatever was left of the First 27th was just taken the hell out of there. It was our job to secure the area and pick up the bodies. We knew we were going to be there all night, because it was already getting dark, so we started flying in the supply choppers. All this time, the 101st was firing at the enemy position.

I was lying on the ground in an open area. We were lying there, watching the shells blowing over. We could see the artillery rounds going over. I said to the guy next to me, "What would happen if a round fell short?" The next thing I knew, I was flying through the air. My ears were ringing. Three rounds fell short. They landed right amongst our guys. We had three short rounds. As soon as they were told "Short rounds," they stopped firing. As the smoke started to clear, guys were coming out, screaming, and the blood was running down them. There was one guy who had both his legs blown off, one arm, part of one hand, and they took a big chunk out of his side. I held him in my arms for about a minute. He lived that long. I called for a medic. He ran over, took one look, and just kept on going. The guy took one last breath, and that was that. I left him there. I went over to check on some of the other guys in my squad. One, a guy named Hill, had his left foot hanging on by a piece of skin.

So. We're out in the open. We've got medivac choppers coming in. We've got supply choppers coming in. All of a sudden, we saw this jet circling over us. I was bringing the .50-caliber machine gun up to the command post. I had the gun. Someone else had the tripod for it, and someone else had the ammo for it. We had just set it down. The captain and the lieutenant were looking up in the air. I looked up and watched. The captain said, "You don't think . . . you're not thinking what I'm thinking, are you?" The lieutenant said, "I think I am." Then he said, "Oh, my God. Get on the line." The jet started coming in. He strafed and bombed us. We were screaming, "Get him out of here. We're Americans. Hold your fire." He started coming around for a second pass, and everybody locked and loaded. There were 16s, machine guns, and the guys were trying to put the .50 together so they could use that. At the last second, the jet pulled out on the second pass. It turned out he was a Vietnamese pilot. His brother had been with a special forces unit. They had been accidentally bombed by American planes several days before. The pilot's brother was killed. Today was payback time for him. Payback time. We never knew what happened to that pilot.

That night, the captain came over. This was Captain Chicken Shit. He said, "I want you to take your squad to the listening post up there." This was around six-thirty, seven o'clock at night, and you could hear the gooks jabbering away out there. I said, "I ain't taking my men out there." By this time, I was a nervous wreck. I had lost Hill with the short artillery round. Two days before, a guy named Hank and another guy had joined my squad. Both of them were hit. I had lost three of my own guys that day, by my own people. Friendly fire. Friendly fire, and I was shaking like a leaf, and he was saying, "You're going to take your squad out there and listen." I said, "No, I'm not," so he left. Our lieutenant came over and said, "The captain wants us to go over there." I said, "I am not taking my guys out. You can hear them. They're not more than ten yards in front of us." "I know. I'll try to talk to the captain about it." He went back, and I heard them arguing. The lieutenant came back with the captain, and the lieutenant was saying, "I don't want to send them out." The captain said, "I told you to get your squad together and get out there, and you're going to do it right now." I just pulled out my .45, and I pointed it to his head. I said, "Before I go out, sir, I will blow your fucking brains out." He turned beet red and turned around and walked away. The lieutenant said, "Don't worry about it." I said, "I'm not."

I never knew what napalm did to anybody. I thought it just burned the bodies, but it explodes. Bodies explode. I never knew that. When it hits, it explodes, then it spreads around. I don't know if it's really the napalm that does it, or the bombs that are dropped with the napalm. I don't know. The napalm itself is a jelly gasolinelike substance. It burns. To get it to spread out, I guess they must have an explosive device on it, because when it hits, it just explodes and then goes in one direction. What we saw was Americans hit, Americans hit with American napalm. I saw part of a boot with part of a leg. I said, "Oh, God." I looked at a hedgerow. It looked like someone had taken toilet paper or something and just strung it onto the trees. We went over there and looked, and it was intestines. I just threw up right then and there. I said, "Get me out of this crazy scene here." This was in January of 1968, after I was wounded the first time.

The enemy was still in the area. We had an air strike coming in, and we were lying there. We watched the jets come in. They dropped the napalm. We had just finished picking up what was left of the bodies, and we were lying there. We thought the napalm was going to get on us. We froze. It didn't hit us. It went further down. We could feel the heat, but that was all. I thought, "Oh, shit. It's going to happen to us now." I still think about this shit. I still have nightmares.

February 25, 1968. We were in a company-sized operation. I had my squad, and we were walking point. I was in the second platoon, and I had the second squad. The squad leader for the first squad was away on R & R, and our lieutenant took the first squad and went on the other side of a rice paddy. The first squad was walking on one side, and we were walking on the other side. We got word to hold up, and we were sitting down. We were in a wooded area, and we could look across the paddy and see the first squad. We waved to them. The next thing we knew, we heard this AK-47 open up, and the first squad started firing, and we started firing across at whoever they were firing at. The first squad started to pull back, so we were giving cover fire. They came back, and one guy was wounded. The lieutenant's radio man, Brooks, was killed.

The family over there consisted of the lieutenant, Brooks, Joe Weaver, who was the squad leader for the first squad, Kelvin, and me. We were family. When we were together, nothing happened to us. We were invincible. We pulled some crazy-ass stunts and got away with it, somehow. We figured as long as we were together, we were invincible, and, what had happened, one of us was hit. The lieutenant said, "Brooks has been hit." I looked down at Brooks, and he had his shirt off, and it was like he was just . . . you know, when you take a deep breath, and your stomach goes in . . . well, his was in, his mouth was open, his eyes were open. I called the medic over, and the lieutenant said, "Bring Brooks back and get him patched up." I said, "Lieutenant, Brooks is dead." "No, he's not." "Yes, sir, he is." "He was just talking to me." "He's dead." Then the lieutenant said, "I want volunteers." I said, "You got my squad." "Let's go. We're gonna get that motherfucker." We went over to get in position, and the lieutenant turns to me and says, "Give me your bayonet." I gave him my bayonet. He put it in his M-16, then he said, "Set up security. I'm going to get that son-of-a-bitch." I said, "Oh, no, you're not, man, we're in this together. I'm coming with you." "No. Brooks was my radio man."

We set this machine gun up on one of the dykes on the paddies and put a couple of guys out for flank security and one guy in the back to cover our back. All of a sudden, we heard this one shot. Just one. It was quiet after that. We waited for a few minutes. Nothing. Then Martinez said, "What are we going to do?" I said, "Wait here. I'm going to go see." He said, "You can't leave the squad. I'll go." I said, "Okay. Go find out, but get back here." He's gone for about five minutes, and all of a sudden he comes running out. As he came running out, my machine gunner, Jim, starts yelling, "I see him. I see him. Martinez, get down." Instead of falling down, Martinez kept coming. He was in Jim's field of fire. Jim didn't fire. Martinez jumped over the dyke, and, as he did, before Jim could fire, the gook opened up and took the top of Jim's head right off. I said to Martinez, "What the hell happened?" He said, "I found the lieutenant." "Where is he?" "He's dead." "What happened?" He said, "He took one round through the eyes," and I said, "We got to get the body."

We got a call from the captain. He wanted to know what the hell was going on, so I told him what happened. He said, "Pull your ass out of there. We're going to call in an air strike." I said, "Wait a minute. We've got the lieutenant's body and our machine gunner's body." He said, "I said pull your ass out *now*," so I ordered the guys to pull back. I said, "When you get to so-and-so, who's providing the rear coverage, tell them to come on up." I kept one of the other guys in my squad with me, a guy by the name of Joe Lamonica. We were going to at least get Jim's body out. We wait. So-and-so isn't coming. By this time, the gook opened up with the AK-47 again. We know where the fire is coming from, but we can't get the son-of-a-bitch. It's just one guy. We couldn't see him. He started firing that AK like a pro, and Joe said, "If we don't get out of here now, we ain't ever going to get out." I said, "Okay. We'd better go."

The gook opened up again, and we had to go under water and crawl under water, that's how close to the surface those rounds were coming in. He was just skimming them across the surface. The company was on the other side, so we crawled and broke air to put it in our nose and mouth. We were crawling on our backs. That was the only way to get out. Otherwise, we would have had to come up into an almost standing position or a kneeling position to get our heads out of the water. On our backs, all we had to do was break surface long enough to get our mouths and noses clear, take a deep breath, and go right back down. The company saw us go down. They thought we bought the farm, and they opened up on the position. It didn't phase that gook at all. He knew he didn't get us, and he wanted us. He just kept firing at us. The hell with the company. I think if he had turned the AK-47 on them, he could have killed eight or nine guys. They were standing right out in the open. You could see everything that was going on. We went all the way down and around, then we crawled all the way across the paddy. We popped up out of nowhere, and they said, "My God, we thought you guys were dead. We saw you go under." I said, "It's the only way we could get out of there." "We're calling in an air strike, an artillery strike." "You can't. My lieutenant's over there, and my machine gunner's over there."

There was this one guy, Moe. He carried the M-79 grenade launcher. He and Jim grew up together, the same home town, trained together. They went in on the buddy system, the whole works. They were from somewhere down South, I think, North Carolina or South Carolina, something like that. Moe came over and said, "Don, where is Jim?" That was that. That's the part about being a squad leader I didn't like, telling someone else, "Hey, sorry, man. He didn't make it." We called in choppers to get us out. In the meantime, they were just blasting the shit out of this one position. There were three or four jets and maybe a half hour of artillery fire. Just for one gook. God knows whether they ever got him or not. We didn't know. We got in the chopper, and they were still delivering the strikes while we were being flown out. He opened up on us once. After that, we just left the area. We don't know whether he got away, or what.

Usually only three platoons are taken out into the field. One is left back. This was worked on a rotation basis. If nobody in the platoon got hit or anything, then the first platoon would stay back the first day, the second platoon the next day, the third platoon the third day, and the fourth platoon the next day; but if a platoon got hit and lost men, that platoon would stay back the next day. We lost a lieutenant, my machine gunner, a radio operator, and two guys wounded, so five guys out of our platoon were hit. At that time, our platoon was really down. I usually had eight guys in my squad. After that day, I was commanding five guys. Everybody was under strain, and we wanted to get replacements. This was on the twenty-fifth of February. When we got back to our base camp, we were talking about the mission the next day, and we didn't care. We knew that we were the only platoon hit. Then our captain decided our platoon was going on the mission on the twenty-sixth.

There were three villages. Alpha Company had the first village, Bravo the second, and Charlie Company would take the third village. Afterwards, they told me that instead of Bravo hitting the second village, they hit the third village. We landed at the second village by mistake. We got out of the choppers. No fire. Nothing. We walk up, and off in the distance we see these four enemy soldiers taking off. The captain sees them and says, "Let's go. Charge." Just like Custer's last stand. They just showed a few guys, dangled them in front of us, knowing that, "Hey, if the Americans see these men, they're going to come after them." The captain should have known better than that. That's a standard ambush technique. A lot of people should have known better, but, then, it was body count and all of that. It didn't matter. Nothing mattered but body count.

We had one captain for a while who was the type who would say, "Hey, I want you to take your platoon, and you find that sniper. I don't give a shit if he kills thirty of you guys. I want his body." We used to get on the radio and call him "Captain Chicken Shit." He knew who was doing it. It was the family. Every shit detail that came up, every time he thought there was a chance guys weren't going to come back, he would say, "The second platoon, first and second squads, you got a mission. Oh, yeah, you're going to need a lieutenant with you, too, so, Lieutenant, get your gear ready." The captain would always be way behind, safe out of fire.

This was another captain on the twenty-sixth, but we shouldn't have been out there, anyway. It was our turn to pull base security, because of what had happened to us the day before. We were really pissed at that. I was never so mad in my whole life. I went to the captain, and I told him, "Hey, I lost two family members, man. I lost my lieutenant and Brooks, the radio operator. What is this shit, man? We're not supposed to go out on this mission." The first platoon was staying behind that day, and they had stayed behind on the twenty-fifth, too. I said, "Hey, it's the first platoon's turn," and he said, "No. No, you get over it much faster this way." He meant get over the loss, and that's bullshit.

So, anyway, we go charging out there, after these four gooks. It's on this rubber tree plantation. They're staying just far enough ahead of us that we can't effectively fire at them. Then we come to this hedgerow. On the other side of the hedgerow was an open area maybe a football field or two football fields long, about a hundred and fifty or two hundred and fifty yards of open area, then more woods and shrubbery. The captain ordered us to get on line, and we lined up there along the hedgerow. I said, "Okay. Let's go through." We started walking through the open area.

This captain that day was new. I think he was there for about a week. Captains were rotated faster. They came and went faster than the regular grunts. Captain Pitts was my first captain. He was the one who got caught with the RPG. He won the Medal of Honor for that. That was in my first major firefight, back on October 31, 1967. Then we got this other captain, the one we called "Captain Chicken Shit." He came in November and left in the middle of February. He spent about three and a half months with us, then we got this other guy who was with us on February 26. He'd been with us a week or two, or maybe just a few days. I don't even really remember how long.

Anyhow, we're going across this open field. Everybody who's been out in the field very long at all is saying, "This sucks, man." They know enough to recognize an ambush, and we're saying, "It's too quiet. I don't like it." We get almost to the bushes. All of a sudden, we hear the bushes rattle, and we swing to the left. We saw something, and it looked like a bird taking off. That was the impression I had. As soon as I saw it, I relaxed a little. Then it landed, and it was a grenade. We yelled, "Grenade," and everybody just turned and dove to the ground except Moe. He turned and ran, and he got shrapnel in the back of his leg, his back, and the back of his head. A couple of guys grabbed him, and, at the same time the grenade went off, they opened up on us. Oh, God. I never saw so much automatic fire in my whole life. They were really together.

I made it behind this mound of dirt. There were two Puerto Ricans there. I think they were from the first platoon. They had the M-60 machine gun, and I said to them, "Look, I'll give you cover fire. Run back to the hedgerow, set the gun up, and, when you see me wave, open up, and I'll get back there with you." They're just looking at me. I said, "Hey, get moving. I'll give you cover fire. Get moving." All of a sudden, they start talking to me in Puerto Rican. I said, "Whoa. What are you saying? English, guys." They didn't know English. I thought, "Oh, my God. What the hell is going on?" I pointed to the hedgerow behind us, and I pointed to the machine gun. I said, in hand motions, "Go back there. Set up the machine gun. When I wave, like this, open up. Then I'll come running." Yeah, yeah. Sure. Right. Heads nod, all of that, so I say, "Go." They start running, and I opened fire and sprayed the whole area. Then I think, "Well, they should have made it by now," and I turned around and looked. Sure enough, they had made it. They kept right on going. I said, "Ain't this a bitch. Not my day."

I put another magazine in my 16. I just popped up real quick, sprayed the area again, turned around, and booked. I could hear those bullets from machine guns walking up behind me. I never ran so fast in my whole life. The captain and a couple of other guys were in this one position. I could hear them laughing and saying, "Run faster." Laughing. They thought it was a nice big joke. They knew I was being fired at. They could see it. I thought, "I'll fix those motherfuckers." I ran straight toward them, and, at the last moment, I just dove away. They saw the bullets coming toward them, and they stopped laughing. Then they were pissed at me. I said, "Hey, you were laughing, man, and I was running for my life. The least you could have done was give me cover fire."

I went back around to the rubber tree plantation, back to my platoon and my squad. I went over and checked on Moe. I said, "How are you doing?" He said, "I'll be okay." I said, "Let's get him back to the medivac pad." We got him there. We were receiving some sniper fire, and the medivac didn't want to land. We sent out a couple of squads to try to find the sniper. We couldn't find the sniper, so we just waited until they opened up, then we sprayed the area again and told the medivac chopper, "Hey, we got the guy." He dropped in real quick, and we put Moe and a couple of other guys on it. We didn't get the sniper. He was still firing at us, but if we hadn't told the medivac that we got him, Moe would still be waiting for the chopper. The captain said, "Okay. Everybody get back on line. We're going to attack the position again."

This time, we know that they're there. We know that they have machine guns and everything set up, and we're scared now. We attacked again, and ole Charlie threw us right back. We got about three-quarters of the way to his positions. He opened up on us and just put too much fire power on us. We went back to the hedgerow, and the captain said, "All right, we're going to bomb them and call in artillery strikes." We did that for a half hour. When that stopped, the captain said, "Let's go," and we went back up again. Charlie pushed us back again. We called in more air strikes, more artillery. We went back up again. Charlie pushed us back again. We called in more air strikes and artillery.

The captain said, "You got all your guys in the squad?" I

checked around. "Yeah." He said, "Okay. Check the other squads," so I went to the squad leaders, and I said, "You got all your guys?" Looking around, one says, "Wait. I'm missing a man." "Who?" "I don't know. It's the new kid." I said, "Oh, shit. Where did you see him last?" "When we attacked last." I went back to the captain. He said, "Well, we got to try to get him out," so I took what was left of my squad, which by then was three guys. We took part of the first squad, and we went up while the artillery was pounding the positions. We found him up there. He was just totally wasted, his mind. Evidently he didn't hear the orders to pull back, and bombs were going off all around him, artillery shells going off all over the place, and he just flipped out completely. We just brought him back, called in the chopper, and got him out of there. He hadn't been hit. It just snapped his mind.

At one o'clock, they told us to break for chow. We'd been going at this since around eight o'clock, nine o'clock in the morning, and finally they let us break for chow. I can still remember what I had for chow, too. I had chicken noodle soup and a can of peaches. That was my lunch.

The acting lieutenant came over. He was our platoon sergeant. We had lost our lieutenant the day before, the twenty-fifth, so the sergeant became our acting lieutenant. He said, "Put your gas masks on. We're going to gas them." Gas masks? Who carries gas masks? The filters had to be kept dry, and nine times out of ten we were in water, so there was no way. No one carried gas masks. We kept ammunition in the gas mask containers. I just told everybody to take his towel—everybody carried a towel—water it down, and put it over his face. It would filter the gas out.

After the gas attack, we went up there. Charlie let us get right on top of him again and let us have it again. About three o'clock we got on line again. We had hit their position about seven or eight times. Each time, they just threw us back like flies: "Hey, get out of here." About three o'clock we all got on the line to hit their position again, and the captain yelled down, "Move out." No one moved. The captain really got angry: "I said move out." Nobody moved. He started running up and down the line. "Get your men moving." I'm standing there, and I have three guys in my squad. "No. No, it's not worth it."

Finally, the machine gunner from the first squad says, "Fuck it," and started walking through the hedgerow, firing. Then, all along the line, "Fuck it." We went again. Charlie let us get about halfway across that time before he let go on us. We were giving it right back to Charlie. We were tired. We just wanted to call it quits, and the army was saying, "You guys can't quit. Charlie's got to quit." We figured the sooner we got it over, the sooner we would get out. One of the guys from my squad went down. My 16 jammed, and I got behind this mound of dirt and took the clip out. I asked one of the guys if he had a cleaning rod. No one had a cleaning rod. We took a branch, a thin branch, and I rammed it down the barrel to knock out the round in there. I took that out, put in a fresh clip, locked and loaded and started firing again.

We had passed the three-quarter point by now, and we're getting right on top of them. Another dude from my squad caught it, but I didn't see him get hit. I was squatting down, and Sergeant Schultz, who was the acting lieutenant by this time, came over and said, "Did you see Lamonica?" I said no. He said, "He's been hit." I said, "What do you mean?" "He caught a round—two rounds in the leg and one in the shoulder and one in the side." I said, "Where is he?" As I was talking to him, I could hear the bullets walking up to me. I thought to myself, "I'm going to get hit," and I could not move. I was just frozen into position. The next thing I knew, it felt like someone took a sledgehammer and hit me in my right side and drove a hot poker through me. I screamed, "Oh, God, I'm hit," and fell forward. The bullet went through me. It took out three or four vertebrae in my back. I was paralyzed from the waist down.

Our acting lieutenant said, "How bad you hit?" "I can't move my legs." "Can you crawl out?" The ground was like blacktop, that's how hard-packed the dirt was. I said, "No." In the meantime, my buddy Kelvin stood up. Bullets were flying all around him, and he was standing up, shaking his fist, cussing out the VC: "You shot my buddy, you motherfuckers. You'll pay for this." I started laughing. I said, "Kelly, you asshole, get down, or they'll kill you." He got down and came crawling over to me. Schultz said, "Well, we've got to get you out of here." He went down the line to get help. Kelly just reached down, grabbed my arms by the wrist and started dragging me out. I said, "Kelly, what the fuck are you doing?" He said, "Got to get you out of here." I told him, "You got the radio on your back, and I'm going to slow you down. Put me down." He said, "No. What are buddies for?"

We got about halfway across, and Charlie opened up and stitched Kelly right across the chest. We lay there. He was on his back, and I was on my stomach. We just laid there. He asked me how I was doing, and I said, "Hang in there, man. How are you doing?" He said, "I'm okay." I said, "Are you hurt bad?" He said, "I think so." We were quiet for a few seconds. He said, "Don, I love you." I said, "I love you, too, man." Then he died.

We laid out there for about an hour, and no one would come and get us. I remember Schultz came by and yelled out, "Hang in there. I'm trying to find some guys." The machine gunner from the first squad, the one who started it by saying, "Fuck it," was about twenty-five yards away from us behind this mound of dirt and bushes. He and two other guys were there. I turned my head so I could see him. Every now and then Charlie would fire at us, and every time I took a breath, I would hurt. It wasn't always a little breath. It was always a deep breath, and I could feel the blood oozing out. I turned to those guys and begged them to get us out. Pleaded with them. Everything. "Get us the fuck out of here." The other two guys just booked. I was looking at the machine gunner. I was crying, and I was saying, "Come on, man, get me out of here." He just looked at me, and he started crying, too. He said, "I can't, man, I can't. I don't want to die." I said, "I don't want to die, either, man. Get me out of here."

They had to get another platoon. No one in my platoon wanted to come and get us, and I didn't want to die. About twenty minutes later, they got the first platoon. They must have thrown about twenty-five or thirty smoke grenades, and that poor guy, that machine gunner, he came out with some of the first platoon and grabbed Kelly and me and brought us back to the medivac pad. I had to wait another fifteen minutes for the fucking chopper to come in. When the chopper landed, they put me on a stretcher on my stomach. Lying right next to me was Kelly. He was on his side, dead. They flew us in to the hospital at Cu Chi.

I still had grenades on me. I was lying on them, and they were digging into me. They hadn't even taken my boots or clothes off. It felt like my feet were ten times normal size. When they took the shoelaces out of the boots and tried to pull them off me, I couldn't take the pain. They ended up cutting them off me. I told them, "I'm lying on some grenades, and they hurt me." They got them out of there. They brought me into an X-ray room, and put me on an X-ray table. I didn't understand what they were telling me then, that the vertebrae were blown out of my back. All I knew is that I was hurting.

This fucking major came in and sat down and started asking me about what had happened in the field. "Man, I want a doctor, man. I'm hurting." "You'll get a doctor as soon as you answer a few questions. What kind of weapons did they have? What kind of weapon got you?" All this bullshit. I don't know if it was true or not, but before he left he said, "You realize that your company hit the wrong village?" All I could think was, "My God. There was only one guy left in my squad. I don't know how many other guys were killed. Kelly had been like a brother. He died trying to pull me out of that stinkhole, and it was the wrong fucking village."

They took X-rays and brought me into the waiting area for OR. "Don, what the fuck are you doing here?" It was Moe. He still hadn't been operated on. That was four or five hours after we got him out. All I could say was, "Kelly's dead." I started crying, and this nurse came over. She told me to shut up. She said I shouldn't cry. Moe told her, "Hey, man, leave him alone. He's just lost his best buddy." She said, "Don't cry about the dead, think about the living." I wanted to kill that bitch. I told her so: "If I could reach you, I'd kill you."

They found out I had blood in my stomach, and they took

me into OR. About a week later, I came around. The doctors told
me, "You're never going to walk again." "I don't care, man. I'm
alive." I stayed in a hospital in Japan for about a month, then went
to Fort Devins Army Hospital in Massachusetts. My brother John
visited me there. He said, "I know about it, bro. I know you had
it rough. You'll never guess what's going to happen." "What?"
"I'm getting married." We were talking about it, and he said he
wanted me as best man. I said, "I can't even walk." "Don't worry.
We'll take care of that." They asked the doctors if they could take
me to Troy, New York, for the wedding, but the doctors said I
couldn't go that far that soon. He was married during the summer
of 1968. I stayed at Fort Devins until August of 1968, then they
sent me to the VA Hospital in Albany. All this time, John kept
saying, "I'm going back there, man, I'm going back." I said, "Shit,
man, you ain't going back. You're married now."

During the summer of 1969 he and his wife had a baby, a
baby boy, Randolph Scott Hines. He got a two-week leave and
came to Albany, and we went out drinking, bullshitting about the
war and all of that. Out of the clear blue, he said, "Looks like we're
going back to California in a few days." He was stationed at El
Toro, the marine base in California. He asked me to go back with
them, stay a couple of weeks. Those were the best two weeks of
my life. I remember I was twenty years old and it was June, and
I had about two and a half months to go before I would be
twenty-one. One day he said, "I get off duty at such-and-such a
time. I'll swing by the house and pick you up, and we'll go out and
have a few." I was walking by then, with a cane. I have about three
or four plastic vertebrae in my back. I always tell everybody,
"When you tell a Hines he can't do anything, he does it just for
spite." It took me almost a year to get around pretty good walking.
It was freaky. When you think of walking, it's like it's nothing,
but I can tell you that I really learned to appreciate it.

Anyway, on this one day, John came by and picked me up,
and we went to this bar. John was still in uniform. The bartender,
a young guy, came over and asked me, "Are you twenty-one?" I
told him no. "We can't serve you beer here." "What do you mean,

you can't serve me beer?" "California state law says you can't drink unless you're twenty-one." I said, "Hey, motherfucker, I was over in 'Nam, got my ass shot off, and you're telling me I can't drink here now? I fought for this goddamned country." "I'm sorry. It's the law." I couldn't believe it. Wow. John said, "Fuck it. Let's go. I know a few other places where they ain't going to ask questions." We left. When the two weeks were up, I went back home.

During the wintertime of 1969, he came home on a two- or three-week pass. I said, "Wait a minute. You just had your leave." He said, "I've been reassigned. I'm going back to 'Nam." I said, "Man, you got a wife and kid, and you're going back? John, we did our time over there. What the hell are you going back for?" "I need the money." "Bullshit you do. You're going back for revenge, aren't you?" "Yeah. Nobody fucks with a Hines." His exact words were, "Nobody fucks with a Hines." He went back over during the beginning of 1970, February or March, something like that. Not too long after that, we got a telegram saying my brother had been wounded in action, just slightly, nothing to worry about. When we got the telegram, I sat down and started writing him a letter: "You dumb shit. Don't you marines know how to duck?" I got about halfway through the letter, and it just popped into my mind: "He's going to die." Just like that. I got scared. I wrote and told him I had that feeling, that it's not going to turn out all right. I told him not to volunteer for anything.

August 24, 1970. My sister from Connecticut was staying with us. About seven o'clock, the telephone rang. I looked at her, and she said, "Aren't you going to answer the phone?" I picked it up, said "Hello," and it was my mother. I said, "He's dead, isn't he?" She said, "Yeah." I said, "Here. Talk to Jeannie." My oldest brother was living about four or five blocks away. I rang the doorbell, and his wife came to the door and said, "What's wrong?" I said, "Is Bill here?" "He's lying down." "Wake him up." She went and woke him, and he told her, "Hey, tell him to come back tomorrow." I said, "Would you tell him it's important?" I heard him yell, "What?" I said, "John's dead." No response. I said, "Did you hear me? My brother's dead." Then I got mad and said, "Well, fuck it. You don't care."

As I was walking back to my apartment, I was going by this church and this little park where all the hippies hung out. There were a bunch of guys standing there, and this girl came up to me and said, "Would you sign this, please?" I said, "What is it?" "It's a petition to end the war in Vietnam." "I'm not signing that. It's too late." "What happened to your leg?" "I got shot up in Vietnam." "Then you ought to sign it. It's a senseless war." "Girl, not more than an hour ago I got word that my brother was killed over there." "That's all the more reason you should sign it." I said, "Get out of my way, or I'm going to hurt you." She made the mistake of standing there and saying, "Well, you're a warmonger and a baby killer," and she spat on me. I grabbed her, and I threw her, and the dudes started coming toward me. I said, "If any of you want to die, keep coming." They didn't do anything. They just stood there and looked. She picked herself up off the ground yelling, "Baby killer," and I just went home.

I got the telegram. I read the telegram. It said, "John *G.* Hines." His name was John *Charles* Hines. I thought, "It could be a mistake. There's more than one 'Hines' around." It was a closed casket. He had stepped on a bouncing betty, a little mine where a grenade pops up in the air behind you, reaches a certain height, and explodes. It caught him in the back of the head. We finally got the body back. We had wake services, and I still had this doubt, maybe a little hope, that it wasn't John, because of the telegram. After the funeral home closed, my brother Bill and I went to the funeral home director and said, "We want to view the body." The doubt was gone. I did see him. The doubt was gone. It seemed so unreal: "This isn't happening." I was good at the funeral. I was good until they gave the salute, and taps, then I knew it was final.

After the burial, we went back to his in-laws' house. Our family always fought. It was always, "Either be on Dad's side or on Mother's side." You couldn't be on both sides. During all of this, I had been neutral: "Leave me the fuck out of this. I want no part in this." Like a dummy, I thought that John's death would bring us closer as a family. It didn't. Everybody was still at everybody's throat. You were either on Mom's side or Dad's side. At his in-laws' house, I couldn't understand it. Everybody was laughing, joking. I was sitting there and thinking, "God. We just buried our brother. What is going on?" Mrs. Reynolds, his mother-in-law, was standing by the coffee pot. Ole Mr. and Mrs. Reynolds treated me like a son. They loved John as their own son. So, I said, "Ma, can I have a cup of coffee?" Out of nowhere, my mother was there. She said, "Sure." I said, "I'm not talking to you. I'm talking to her," which didn't help matters much, but at that point, *I didn't care anymore.* I thought about suicide. That was it.

No one wanted to talk about Vietnam. I remember one time, before John died, we were sitting around my mother's kitchen. Something was said about war, and I started talking about Vietnam. My mother said, "I don't want to hear it." Okay. I didn't bother with it. I'm more or less the loner in the family now.

In order to talk about the war, I just hung out with guys that were over there. I met most of them at the VA. There were about ten of us. We must have made a comical sight. Every one of us was disabled. We either walked with crutches or with canes. We hung out in a group, and, as the years went on, everybody just went his own separate way. I had joined the Disabled American Veterans when I first got to the VA. I never went to their meetings, just paid my life membership, and that was it. I never bothered with organizations. Most of them were made up of World War I and World War II and Korean vets, and they never bothered with us, either.

I just kind of bummed around here and there for jobs, tried to get on the Albany Police Force in Narcotics as one of their undercover cops because I knew some of them, and they were saying they were really backlogged with paperwork. I figured I had a shot at the job, because I was a disabled Vietnam veteran. They told me to fill out an application and go to be interviewed. The interviewer said, "Well, I see that you were in the army. Wounded twice in action. Honorable discharge. Several of the guys on the narcotics force spoke highly of you, but we can't use you." I asked why.

"Because you're disabled. Every member of the Albany Police Force might have to go out in the field at least once on a call, and you have to be in shape." "Wait a minute, you said *every* member?" "Yeah." "The ones at the courthouse, too?" "Yeah." "What's required for going out in the field?" "Well, due to your injuries, you can't run. That's one of the requirements. Suppose you have to chase a suspect?" I said, "Wait a minute. Wait a minute. I'm applying to do the *paperwork* for Narcotics. I would also be doing some undercover work. I'm not supposed to be chasing anybody. They wanted me for the paperwork." "Well, in order to do the paperwork, you've got to become a cop." I said, "Because I can't run, I can't have a job. You mean to tell me that in the courthouse, your two courtroom guards there, they're about sixty-some-odd years old and about three hundred pounds overweight, and they're going to chase someone down the street? My God, they doze off in court." "Just got to go by the rules." That was shot. I took a job with the labor department, the New York State Labor Department. I took the beginning office worker's test, passed it, and was offered a job as a file clerk in the liability determination unit. When I got there, they did a number on me.

I had files in the office where I worked, but the file room was down the hallway a bit. If anyone needed information, I'd go to the file room and get it. One of my main jobs was to open the mail. It came in at nine o'clock every morning. I would open it, determine who got what, distribute it on the desks. The rest of the morning, I would be working in the file room. At one o'clock, the next batch of mail would come in, and I'd go through the same routine again. Then one day they started running the number on me. I had finished distributing the mail and was going to the files. "Where are you going?" "I'm going to the file room to get some files." "Oh, no, no. Sit down. Take it easy." "Why?" "Oh, come on. We don't want you to hurt yourself." I said, "What am I supposed to do?" "Don't worry about it."

After a while, I'd punch in at eight-thirty, the nine o'clock mail would come, I'd open the mail, distribute it, and just go walking around, or I'd bring a book. This went on for about two months, and I said, "Hey, I can't take this. I'm not a cripple. I'm getting out. I'm resigning." "Why?" "Because you're treating me like a cripple, that's why. You won't let me do the job I'm supposed to do, so the hell with it. I'm resigning. I don't need this." I resigned. I was a short-order cook, bartender, laborer, painter, security guard. Oh, God, I think from the beginning of 1971 to '77, I must have had about thirty or forty jobs. Worked a little bit here and a little bit there. I kept running across the same thing: "We don't want you to hurt yourself."

One day I got fed up with this and went over to the State Division of Veterans' Affairs. I said, "It's your job to find me some decent work." They said, "Hey, that's not our job. You got a problem, we try to help you with it. That's our job." I ran down what was going on, and they said, "Okay. We can send you down to Job Service." I said, "It doesn't do any good. I've been down there. They asked me what my skills are."

When I first got back from 'Nam, I went down to Job Service. They gave me this orange veterans' application card to fill out. You have to put your work history and previous duties on the back. I didn't have a work history, other than the army, so I put down "squad leader," "demolition man," "sniper," "tunnel rat." They said, "There's nothing we can do with this. What exactly can you do?" I told them they should tell me what I could do. I said, "I can blow up any building. I can shoot anybody. You're supposed to be here to help me. Find me a training program or something."

Then I went to the hospital again. I was in and out of there a number of times, but this time my leg had started acting up on me again, and I had to go back because they were planning to take off my right foot. That was at the time that I had a job as a shipping and receiving clerk. I had seen an ad in the newspaper about a manpower training center, so I went down and applied. I got into the school and took their clerical training. They found jobs for you, and I got the job as a shipping and receiving clerk.

I was in charge of about six or eight guys. I didn't mind that job.
I liked that job. I got along good with the boss, and I was more
or less back in a position I could do. I was also in charge of guys
again, and this time I knew there was no way they were going to
die. That made it even better.

Then I had to go back to the hospital. While I was there, this
counseling psychologist came by and said, "What are your plans?"
I said, "I've got a job now, but I don't know if I'll still have it by
the time I get out of the hospital." He said, "Have you ever
thought about going to school?" I said, "I can't afford it." In 1969
I had gone back to night school and got my high school equiva-
lency diploma, so he said, "How would you like to go to college
and have everything all paid for, and get money while you're going
to school?" I liked that. That sounded good. It ended up that they
didn't take my foot off, and I started going to Junior College of
Albany in September, on the VA's vocational rehabilitation program.

The first semester was good, then there was a one-month
thing for January. That was good, too. I completed the first year,
then I ended up back in the hospital in September of 1973. I made
it back for the one-month term in January, made it through the
spring semester, then I was back in the hospital again. I had
completed a year and a half of junior college and was enrolled in
my last semester, but I ended up in the hospital again by November. Then I just lost interest. Going to school meant being with
teenagers who went from high school to college because mommy
and daddy were paying for it. It just didn't work out for me. I just
started bumming around again. That went on for about six
months, then I received a cablegram from the New York State Job
Service. They wanted to interview me for a job as a veterans' aide.
I went there, saw the office manager, and he went over my work
experience. I got the job. It started on January 20. At that time,
the job title was "Disabled Veterans' Outreach Program Aide."
We were called "DVOPs." Now we're called "Veterans' Outreach
Specialists." It's a federal program, but I'm a state employee. I've
been with it for six years now.

I joined the local chapter of Vietnam Veterans of America some time back, and now I'm a local board member. When there's a function or meeting relating to veterans going on, some of us guys are always there. At the Gold Star Mothers' Luncheon, I represented our chapter. We don't march in parades. That's not our bag in this particular local chapter. Some guys in other chapters like to march in parades. Fine. We don't try to stop them. But, for me, for instance, Memorial Day is the day for mourning the dead, those who died in a war. To get up early in the morning and march down Central Avenue and Washington Avenue and then finish with the parade and march up to Sears and Macy's to get their Memorial Day sales or Veterans Day sales, to me, that's not patriotic. I would rather just go visit my brother's grave. That's it.

You know, before I went into the service, I wasn't that much of a fighter. Now I don't take shit from nobody. I can't stand the people of the United States. I hate them with a passion. We could have fought in Vietnam, and we could have won, no doubt about it. We had too much fire superiority, but they said, "You can bomb here, but you can't bomb there. You can shoot anything that moves in this area, but, right next to it, in that area, you can't shoot unless you're shot at first." When you start putting restrictions on a war, it's crazy. Nothing was thought of losing a bunch of guys taking a hill, only to be taken off that hill the very next day, then turning around three weeks later and retaking that same hill all over again and losing more guys in the process. There were no lines in Vietnam. We could have gone from one end all the way up, right on through North Vietnam, and demolished them completely, but they wouldn't let us do it.

My hatred is for the people who protested the war. They put the pressure on the politicians. I'm not just blaming the people, I'm blaming the politicians, too. The politicians and the generals. They're the ones who said, "This is what you do, and this is what you don't do." The generals were rewarded with higher rank. The politicians made a mint off the war. They got rich off it. They made money so bad off of American soldiers, with the arms factories that were in full production. That's how it is. You got money, you got power. You got position, you got power. When you got both, you're God. A lot of politicians put themselves in the role of God and decided what was best for the Vietnam soldier when he was slugging it out in the rice paddy or up in the jungle. They made these decisions back in Washington, where it was nice and safe, and the people went right along with it. Then when they started calling up more people, they started saying, "Whoa. I don't want to go to Vietnam and get killed. Shit. I'm going to run off to Canada or Sweden." Carter had the audacity to pardon them.

Carter said, "You can come home," and they were welcomed home. Guys that deserted the country of their birth to go to another country to avoid a war, and they came home as heroes. Guys that were stuck in 'Nam, hell, they were snuck out of there in the middle of the night. No matter where you landed, it always seemed vets landed in the nighttime. There was no family there to meet them. No one wanted to talk to them about the war. There were little kids, little brothers and sisters, coming up to you and saying, "Did you kill any people? How many babies did you kill?" I said all along that I went to Vietnam to fight for my country. Not the people that are in my country, but to fight for the ideas that the country is based upon, like freedom of speech for everybody in the world. Vietnam was a country that was being denied that.

We would see all the stuff on the news at night. A village after we'd gone through it. They'd show a bunch of Vietnamese children in hospitals, all bandaged up, but they never showed a village after the VC went through it. They never took the cameras into the hospital wards and showed American GIs. What should have been said was, "End the war now, or declare war." One way or the other. That didn't happen, and they portrayed us as drug-crazed baby and women killers. When we got back, it was bad. "Mod Squad": "Vietnam vet flips out." "Hawaii Five-O": "Vietnam vet flips out." On any police program it was always a Vietnam vet flipping out and shooting people. Flashback to Vietnam: "He thinks he's in the war. Shoot him." No one dealt with that realistically. They came out with *Coming Home.* I loved the movie, but I hated Jane Fonda. To this day, I can't for the life of me understand why they had her portray a marine officer's wife. She was so gung-ho for Vietnam. When Vietnam was really going on, she was up north preaching for us to throw down our rifles and go back home. Nothing happened to her, because it wasn't a declared war. It was a police action.

The Deer Hunter. I had people ask me, "Did that really happen over there? Did you guys really do that?" They meant the Russian roulette game. I got to the point where I was so fed up with it that when another kid asked me, I said, "Yeah, and you know something, I lost three times." It never dawned on him. How can anyone lose three times? You'd be dead the first time. All those movies that portrayed the Vietnam vet as a psycho. People believed it. If it's a horror story, they believe it. They actually believe it. I think it's time the American people started straightening their act out.

In the past few years, some better things have been coming out, articles about the war, delayed stress, agent orange. More books are coming out about Vietnam. More seminars are being held about Vietnam. People may finally be realizing the Vietnam vet is here to stay. We're not going to go away. We're saying to them, more or less, "Fuck it. We've had it. We're here, and it's time we got recognized." That's what I believe.

My brother was up north during early 1967, up around Khe Sanh, at Hill 881. In the book *The End of the Line,* they talk about the siege of Khe Sanh. That was in 1968, but my brother described things that sounded just like that book in one of his letters. He described this one battle where the VC let them get right up on them before they opened up on the marines. A lot of the marines' weapons weren't working right, and a lot of them didn't even have a chance to turn a weapon to shoot. They were just cut right down. My brother wrote a letter about it, and it was really bad. He said there were guys dropping all over the place. He doesn't know how the hell he ever made it up that hill. They were really dug in on that hill.

I got sick this past November or December with a kidney and bladder infection. I was in the hospital and running temperatures of 102.4, 103.6 for six or seven days. I was out of it most of the time. I didn't know where I was, and I had nightmares about 'Nam. I relived the day I got shot. I could feel the impact of the bullet, and I could hear the impact of the bullets on Kelly.

I have a very understanding wife. There are times I feel really out of it. I've got to talk, and she'll listen. She'll say, "Well, I don't really understand all the things you've gone through, but I'm here. I'll listen." She'll say, "I don't know what I can do for you," and I say, "You're listening. That's the main thing, listening. If you're willing to listen, that's all I need." At that time, I just need someone who can listen. I've had people tell me, "You should forget the war, leave it behind you." Like I told my wife, "I'll never leave this war behind me. It's going to be right alongside me." I can rationalize the war. I cannot say it never happened. How can I forget something that permanently changed my life? If you forget it, if you try to forget it, you're only hurting yourself more, because you're holding it all in. People don't understand that.

Something to do with Kelly brought on the nightmares this last time. I had a thing in my squad. When we got a new guy, and he was introduced to me, I said, "What's your nickname?" We went by nicknames. I heard his name only once. He said, "Call me Kelly." From then on, it was always Kelly. When I got back to the States, I tried to find out: "Kelly who?" I wrote the army, wrote to congressmen, my lieutenant colonel. I gave them the whole story, and they said, "No. There's nobody by that name." Now, I've found out. I found out with the Vet Center's help. I've talked to his folks.

I was having these nightmares last winter, and the guys at the Albany Vet Center said, "Well, the Chicago Vet Center has this one Kelly who was killed." I said, "What date?" They said February 16, or something like that. I told them no. It was Kelly from Illinois, that's all I knew. They called the Chicago Vet Center again and told them the first Kelly wasn't the right one. They said,

"Oh, we got this other Kelly." "When was he killed?" "February twenty-sixth." "What outfit?" "Charlie Company. Wolfhounds." The guys here told me, and I said, "That's the one. What's his name?" "Kelvin Bigger." I thought, "Wow. I'm free."

This happened right after I got out of the hospital, in January. I wanted to get in touch with his parents, but I was afraid they wouldn't want to remember, so I didn't say anything about that. I just said, "Oh, God. Thanks." Then: "We have even better news for you. Here's his parents' name, address, and phone number. They'd like to talk to you." Wow. I got up the courage to call. I told them who I was, and the first five or ten minutes we just talked about the weather, then everything just opened up. For another forty-five minutes, we just talked about everything. I said, "I'm not going to tell you how Kelly died over the phone. That's too personal a thing for me to do. I want to stop by and see you and sit down and talk to you, face-to-face." They said, "You're welcome." I said, "Oh, God. You don't know how good this makes me feel." I was really scared. I was thinking, "Oh, my God. They'll probably say they don't want to have anything to do with me, because he's dead, and I'm alive."

I'm going to go see them this springtime.

ILLIAM A PERKINS Jr ·
STANDEFORD · THO
NCENT J ANASTASIO ·
JONATHAN BROWN ·
OND W TYMESON Jr
RANCE L LOVE · JOHN
D ROBINSON · THO
· GEORGE H STAMPS
E VAN BARRIGER · WI

RAYMOND WILLIAM TYMESON

Born: March 31, 1948
Troy, New York
Killed: December 2, 1968
Quang Nam Province, Republic of South Vietnam

WILLIAM J McATEE · M

Raymond Tymeson

RAYMOND J. TYMESON

Born: May 24, 1918
Troy, New York
Father of Raymond William Tymeson

A Dreadful Age to Die

My son wanted to get into the marines because a couple of his friends had spoken about joining, but Ray got disappointed when he first went down to join. He had sort of a back injury, and they told him, "Look, you're going to have to be operated on before we can take you in the marines." He had a fistula down at the bottom, all the way down the bottom of his back, and once in a while it would break and run. There was not too much pain with it, but it would spread like a spider web if it wasn't taken care of. It wouldn't do for him to be in a combat situation with a problem like that, so they told him he had to get it fixed. He wanted to get in the marines so bad that he went over and got operated on. Three months after he was operated on, he went back and told them what he'd done. The marines looked at him again, and they said he could join.

They sent him down to Parris Island, then he went to Camp Lejeune. That was in the winter of '67 and '68, when it was ten and fifteen and twenty below zero there every day. And they were training for the jungles of Vietnam in that weather. Well, they finished up there, and they were sent out to Camp Pendleton in California for training that entailed climbing mountains like in Vietnam. This required tremendous stamina and was done to put them in good shape. They finished that, and every weekend they would get off. They would go down to Oceanside, California, swimming and so on. Then one day the captain said, "You're all confined to quarters now. We'll be leaving tomorrow. We're leaving for Vietnam, for what you've been training for." Their platoon left the next day, the next morning at five-thirty. They flew to Hawaii, then they just refueled and took off. They landed in DaNang.

When they landed in DaNang, they came under mortar and artillery fire, so they were ordered right to their stations. They were hit with mortars all night long. I guess it's a baptism of fire that most new men get. Then they were moved up to Phu Bai up in zone one, up in I Corps. Well, that was around the end of February, and I think the Tet offensive was beginning to dwindle down. It was still going, but the main thrust of it was . . . not gone . . . but the main thrust, the deadly fire, was pretty nearly . . . not over, but starting to simmer down.

Khe Sanh had already come into being by then. Nobody knew what it was all about, I don't think, including the marines. Nobody knows what it was, what it was there for, what it was intended to do. Ray's group thought they were going to Khe Sanh, but they didn't. They were stationed at Phu Bai, and they went on several operations or missions. He was promoted in the field in Operation Arizona, and he was probably in Vietnam about ten months when he went on Operation Mead River. That was an operation that was supposed to clear out the NVA from the Da-Nang area. The captain of his company wrote and told me that they killed over two thousand of the enemy, which seemed like an awful lot to be around DaNang.

The Cong stuck with the jungles. If you were in the jungles, you were in trouble with the Cong. The NVA, they were hard, tough soldiers, but a little different than the Cong, more disciplined in every respect. So, when they went out on Operation Mead River, they ran into heavy stuff all the while, heavy fire I mean. Machine gun fire and things like that. Ray liked to be on the flank. A boy named Bob who lives in Bridgewater—I've been down to see him, and we correspond, and he sends a Christmas card every year—Bob was on the right flank. Another boy always wanted to be on the point. He was a Mexican boy, so he had the point, and Ray and Bob were on the flanks. It wasn't that they didn't want to go on the point, but they just wanted this other lad to be on the point, and he wanted to be there. But this day, the enemy let the point man go through. They let him go through by a hundred feet, and they waited for the main body, which would be nine plus the two flankers, eleven in all, to get in the kill zone. Then they opened fire on them. It was sort of an ambush, and I guess five or six of them got killed right away. I learned all the details of this from Bob.

Anyway, they went down. They hit the ground, and Ray said that he was going to go in and try to silence the machine guns. He wasn't killed right at first. No. He went in and tried to silence the machine gun, and there was a couple of others who went in and offered covering fire, but a machine gun opened up from another direction. It was two machine guns firing from one way, and one firing from another way, and Ray and another boy went in, and they were killed from this fire. That is exactly how he died. That's what he got the Bronze Star for. When Ray had gone forward like that, he got killed. He got hit in the neck, and two wounds in the leg. The wounds in the leg he would have survived, but the bullet he got in the neck severed the carotid artery. An aid man went to help him, and the aid man got killed. That medic got killed, and another medic was called in, but it was too late. Ray was gone, and a couple of others were gone.

This is what it says in his citation for the Bronze Star:

On 2 December during Operation Mead River, Company B came under intense fire from a well-fortified hostile unit. Reacting instantly, Corporal Tymeson fearlessly maneuvered his force forward in an attempt to suppress the enemy fire. While boldly leading the attack, he was mortally wounded. Corporal Tymeson's superb leadership, professional ability, and unwavering devotion to duty contributed significantly to the accomplishment of his unit's mission and were in keeping with the highest traditions of the Marine Corps and of the United States Navy.

That's what the Bronze Star is for. That's why he got it. It was awarded in the field.

Ray was killed December 2, 1968. We didn't get his body back until December 23, 1968, and we buried him on Christmas Eve. Stop and think of that for a minute. The cemetery is behind our house. Since the tree leaves were all down, we could pretty nearly see the filthy clay and earth and everything that was thrown up. A twenty-year-old boy. Ray was twenty. Paul Baker was twenty. Peter Guenette was twenty. It seemed like they were all twenty. It's a dreadful age to die. I mean, if we're seventy or eighty, what the hell. We're all going to die, right? You don't pay much attention to it. But when a young man like these men, and I call them men, they ceased to be boys the minute they got over there; when they go, and they go violently, as in any war, you don't forget as easy as you do when an older person dies, like when your mother dies or your father dies. The older ones have lived their lives, but when a young person, nineteen or twenty or twenty-one, is cut off, you say, "Gee whiz, it's terrible," and you never get over it. The memories come flooding back to you. You can't help it. You should throw those things off, and people do try to throw them off. I try to think in a positive manner and throw the negative things away, but it's kind of difficult to do that when a young person gets killed violently in a war.

We buried Ray, and all the other boys were buried, and it sort of faded, but never entirely. It never faded entirely. The class of 1966 at Catholic Central High School took up a two-thousand-dollar collection, and they started a scholarship. They called it the Tymeson-Baker Memorial Scholarship.

I can remember the last letter I got from Ray. It was just a short one, because, I'll tell you, they were out in the field all the time. They never had time to do anything, get anything, or write anything. They ate field rations probably for six months. They never got a hot meal because they were always on sweeps or operations. They'd start at five-thirty in the morning and make a sweep and climb to the top of a mountain and find out there was nobody there. I think the Cong were smarter than they were. The

Cong went underground in the daytime to play cards and drink and have a good time. Then they would come out at night. They were deadly at night, and they terrorized the whole country, but in the daytime you'd never see them. The marines worked just the opposite. The marines would be going down from heat stroke and prostration while there was no Cong around for them to get.

Anyway, we got Ray home, and he was buried. Then we got his clothes back, got his clothes back all laundered from the Marine Corps. I don't know why the hell they send his clothes back. What were we going to do with them? I called up the Marine Corps down in Albany, and they came up and got them. His personal stuff, like . . . oh, different items he had . . . he had a prayerbook from when he was an altar boy . . . some personal stuff we kept, but we didn't want the clothes and things. The officers in the Marine Corps, the battalion commander and the platoon commander and the company commander—all nice guys, all killers, but you've got to expect the marines to be killers, when you know they were trained for that—they were sending nice letters. If they didn't call, you'd get a nice letter. They'd tell me, you know, that he was a good marine, and how he died.

The people here were quite upset when so many boys from here got killed. There was a lot for such a small town. The people gave a monument to the boys who got killed. It was made by Allegheny Steel. It was donated by ever so many people. My God. The whole thing cost nine thousand dollars, and the gas and electric company said they would leave the flame on perpetually. Forever. Yes. Then it was vandalized. Everything was stolen about a year after it was put up. The whole thing was vandalized, and they never found out who did it.

You know, I think the amount of casualties from the Vietnam War is pretty close to sixty thousand. I think there's probably more than that that got mained and are emotionally crippled and mentally injured. If you added the family members and friends, the people that were indirectly affected by the Vietnam War, psychologically, emotionally, and mentally, I'd say that altogether there's nearly a million and a half people who had their lives disrupted. Some of them died; some of them just took off. Some families were disrupted, and some families are not all together anymore. It seems to have an adverse effect on a lot of families that were not in the war or wounded or maimed or killed. They were injured psychologically, emotionally, and their lives have disintegrated. Well, maybe not disintegrated, but pretty nearly so in several instances. There's many a boy that just started drifting after this war. I knew one of those pretty good. The last time I could trace him was in a rooming house in Virginia, but after he left that rooming house, nobody seems to know where he went. He was a casualty of the Vietnam War. Whether he's out on the road, whether he's a drug addict, whether he's an alcoholic or something else, I don't know, but that war took its toll in other ways besides death and wounded.

People don't like to think about that a lot, but they have to think about it now, because they're reminded of it because of the monument that they put in down in Washington. That brought a lot of things back, caused a lot of people to feel bad, but what we want to remember is those fifty-eight thousand names down there of men who died for their country—not that they were in a war that wasn't supposed to be fought, but that they died and gave their lives for their country. But it's something you don't get over. It's something you don't get over, you know?

Well, the boy who escorted Ray back seemed like a nice boy. I said to him, "I want to see my son." "Well," he said, "I'm not allowed to let you see your son. I'm the escort of the Marine Corps. I'm afraid that they might send me back." He said, "I've only got seven weeks to go, Mr. Tymeson. I'm afraid that they might send me back, and I couldn't stand it." He was a combat veteran, and he was afraid they might send him back to Vietnam. Nice boy. I said, "I'm his father. I've got a right to open that casket." "No, you haven't," he said, "I'll have to stop you." I went to the undertaker, and I said, "Why can't I open that casket?" He said, "He's got the key. You have to ask him." I said, "Well, I already did ask him, and he wouldn't let me open the casket," but

I was assured that it was him, and I know he got killed, because of talking with boys who were with him.

His mother never got over his death. Oh, no. Never got over it. It killed her. She was a good, strong woman. I could see her failing. She'd sit over there crying, and I'd go over and pat her and put my arms around her. She just couldn't control herself. That would happen, I'd say, every so often. Not every day.

I had a picture of Ray up, and I was going to take it down, but she said, "No. Don't take it down." I said, "Well, I don't think it should be up there." I was going to take it down, but no, she wanted to leave it up. I said, "I don't think it's a good idea to leave it up there," but, well, we kept it up. She wrote this on the front leaf of the family Bible, in the front of the Bible. It says, "My dearly beloved son, Raymond, died in Vietnam December 2, 1968, and I think every part of me died." She signed it, "His mother, Marie J. Tymeson." Then she wrote, "He was born on a Monday, died on a Monday, and was buried on a Monday."

She died three years ago. Three years ago last month. She never got over Ray's death, never got over it. She died at noontime. My daughter, Noreen, was here when she took the attack. I said, "Marie, you think we'd better go over and sit down?" "Yes," she says, "I want to go over and sit in the new chair I bought." We managed to get her over, but she couldn't straighten up. I said, "Is the pain in the back?" "Yes," she says. "It's from the front to the back." I said to call up the hospital right away and to get the paramedics. The hospital came, but they stopped a block down the street. I got out in the middle of the road and yelled, "Right here." They came and they took her out. They took her into the emergency room and put her in intensive care and she died. You just never know. There was nothing wrong with her, nothing physically.

Personally, I'd like to throw all this stuff out, all of Ray's stuff. All of it. It just reminds me of something terrible. But I'm probably just saying that. I probably won't.

When Ray's clothes came back in a couple of packages, the

marines came and took them in a car, a nice car, and I said, "What are you going to do with them?" They said, "Don't worry about them. They're not going to the Salvation Army or in any trash dump." This was a major talking, and he said, "I'll take care of them properly, the way the marines take care of their own." I felt like saying, "Yeah, with a coffin." He was going to take the dress suit, and he was going to bring me up a little box to put the medals in, but he got transferred, so I still have the suit.

TYMESON: These were his dress shoes. I kept them. They're a little big for me, you know, but see what I have done. I've put that filler inside, and now they just fit me. The poor boy, he only wore them a couple of times, and why the hell should I give them away? What do you think? No. I'm not going to give them away. And these here, the other ones. I know a fellow that's down on his luck. Nice guy. He just went downhill. He lives in a hotel down in North Troy, and he wears this size. I wonder if it would be proper for me to give him these?

BRANDON: I think it would be proper if you want to.

TYMESON: I want to.

BRANDON: Then do.

TYMESON: All right. Thank you for telling me that.

BRAD D CHRIS
KENROAD · KENNETH R EYP
E GROOMS Jr · LEE T HAM
RY L HOSKO · JOE S HUSTO
NCARNACION-BETENCOUR
AN L MOON · JAMES H MO
ESUS C OLETA Jr · DONALD
HTER · ELLIS A ROBERTSON
ATTERTHWAITE · GENE W S
LIAM W UTTS · JOSEPH R V
· DANIEL G WESSLER ·

JESUS ENCARNACION
BETANCOURT

Born: December 21, 1944
       Hato Rey, Puerto Rico
Killed: March 19, 1969
       Chu Lai, Republic of South Vietnam

ROGER L PHILLIPS · NIG
FILEMON SERRANO · CLA

Jesus Betancourt

BELEN BETANCOURT

Born: February 7, 1923
Trujillo Alto, Puerto Rico
Mother of Jesus Encarnacion Betancourt

A War Is a War

My son signed a six-year contract with the national guard, then he went to New York on a vacation, and he stayed longer than he should have stayed. If I recall, he was in Puerto Rico on January third, then he went to the States. He got stuck with the idea to go outside and know the world. This was while he was still with the national guard, but in February, as a punishment, they sent him to South Vietnam. There, he took care of an ambulance. By February third, he was in South Vietnam. I didn't receive the letter he wrote on March nineteenth. His sister received it, but she never read it to me. He gave her orders in the letter to not show the letter, as he seemed to be unhappy.

I do not know much about this. As much as I know, he was in a battle, or maybe many. The point is that he took care for all the soldiers there, apparently very well. What I don't understand is how he joined the army. I think it was a punishment. A mess! Maybe the punishment was because he stayed in New York and missed his national guard exercises. What I think happened is when he was in New York, the army found him, and they re-cruited him. If I recall, it was at the same time that four men came to see me, asking for him. I don't remember all this. My mind fails me! Maybe he was not supposed to go on vacation, and, in the States, he was drafted. I gave his address to the four men who came. They must have found him and sent him to South Vietnam.

I really didn't want him to go, as I heard a lot of people were dying in Vietnam. He was scared, so much that he had a premonition. He said, "I'm going to die. I'll never come back. Nevertheless, I go." His brothers said to him, "Nothing is going to happen to you," but neither his father nor me wanted him to go. I worried. I didn't know where he was.

Going back to the tragedy, I had to leave the job for a while, as my nerves were shattered. He had wanted to get into the Puerto Rican State Police, and I said no, but I am sure they would have killed him the same, in one place or another. I believe in fate. It is written some place. He received an official recognition. When I remember that fatal day, it is so upsetting. For his father, it was worse. We resign ourselves when we consider that the body was intact. His father stated to me there was no part missing. I had no heart to see the body. At times I go to the Catholic chapel. I am a Catholic. I pray, and then I feel his presence, and I believe he still is alive. We all felt very deeply his death, but time cures, and one grows accustomed to it. He had many friends. He was well loved. After his death, no one around here wanted to go into the army.

He was buried in the cemetery close to home. His mausoleum is in white marble. We invested three thousand dollars in it. Today it would cost six thousand dollars. His father wanted to spend every penny from the army insurance for the mausoleum. He was deeply affected by the death. We are divorced now. After my son's death, we divorced. My husband went a little bit crazy. We just started to talk to each other again. His father first became terribly nervous when he found out that he was going to South Vietnam.

I have reacted against violence. I cannot stand war films or violent ones. He bled to death. The medical communication said that he died because he lost all the blood. He was young. I loved him, but there is a certain thing: A war is a war.

AM L HILL · ROBER
NETH E ISER · CHA
HEL · LARRY D KE
THOMAS K LYONS
N · EARNEST L M
GOMERY · TERRY
GEORGE C OLSEN
DWIGHT C REIG
PH T ANDERSON

GEORGE CHARLES OLSEN

Born: June 9, 1947
      The Bronx, New York
Died: May 1, 1968
      The Philippines

George Olsen *(right)* and Lennie Wilson

LEONARD C. WILSON

Born: January 4, 1947
The Bronx, New York
Brother of George Charles Olsen

Something's Gotta Be Said

There's something about Vietnam, even today. It seems like yesterday, and then it seems so far away. I guess it all began before Vietnam.

I grew up in the Bronx. I was adopted when I was three years old. I had a brother who was my stepbrother, and I had a real sister. I guess I had a pretty normal life. In no way were we rich. We were building superintendents, sort of a middle-class upbringing. Maybe because I was adopted, I was basically a quiet person. The people I was really close with were my friends. That's how it's always been in my life. My brother and I got along pretty good as brothers. We had times when we would fight, but, basically, we didn't hang around together too much until we got older, until we were around thirteen or so, then we all hung around in the same crowd, including my sister. We got into a couple of troubles here and there, the normal things that kids do, drinking and smoking. Marijuana wasn't big at that time. Sniffing glue was the big thing then. A lot of people tried it, and cough medicine, stuff like that. We had our good times. A couple of times we got into trouble with the cops. Nothing serious.

My brother seemed to be the one who was unfortunate in that regard, because he was so tall. He always seemed to be the one who stood out in the crowd somehow. Other people were able to escape trouble, but with my brother, it just seemed to come to him. He was six-foot-three, and he was always tall for his age. He was really one of the tallest in the crowd. He got in trouble with the cops one night bad. I wasn't there that night. A lot of my friends had been in trouble, robbing or something like that, and they were sent to children's homes. Anyway. This one night, one of the guys they were with was on probation, and they brought him downtown to the halfway house. That's where they started carrying on, making a lot of noise. I don't know exactly what happened, but a taxi driver started yelling or something, and they got into an argument with him. Before they knew it, the cops came down, and they got into a real battle with the cops. It was in the papers, as a matter of fact, the next day, in the *Daily News*. My mother was wondering what the hell was going on. She got a call that he was down in the precinct. She had to go pick him up and take him out. The whole thing went to trial. He got off. It was a first offense, and the cops were a little bit lenient that time.

By that age, say sixteen or so, my brother and I were closer than we were when we were younger. I could never get a full understanding of my family, or they never understood me, but somehow my brother and I seemed to know each other well. If I could say that I really loved a person, it would have to be my brother. I never thought of it like I was his adopted brother or anything like that, and even though I wasn't his big brother in terms of size, somehow I felt caring for him and protective of him. He was six months younger than I was. We were all three within a year of each other. He and I were close. There was a cloud, though. We were having a good time, but somehow getting into a lot of trouble. If it wasn't a gang that was coming up to look for us, it was the cops chasing us.

It was about that time that I ran into Roseann, who eventually became my wife. It was almost like love at first sight, or it seemed that way. I didn't get along with my parents at the time, mainly my mother. I felt she had too much control over my life, and I just couldn't handle it. One of my friends, Willie, had the same kind of situation, so he asked me if I wanted to move out.

That's what we did. We moved into Roseann's mother's house, in an apartment there. This is when I'm nineteen. I'd just turned nineteen when I met Roseann, and this is March. This is March of 1966. I moved out, and that whole period, from March until August, those are still the best five months of my life, because I was free, able to do the sorts of things that I liked. I guess I was independent all of my life, and now I was out on my own. I had a job. I had no problem holding onto a job. Some of my friends did. They would work and just pick up a couple of bucks, but I was able to hold down a job.

Roseann and I got more and more involved. Before you knew it, we were talking "love" and "getting married," and all that. We were even thinking about just going down to Maryland, just running away. It was such a great thing to think about. It was something we were really serious about. What was so different about it was that I felt so much love there that for the most part I was able to give up most of my friends. I didn't spend all that much time just hanging around and getting into trouble. I spent those months just being with Roseann. We became involved sexually, but it wasn't only the sex. It was just the ability to sit there and talk to her and to enjoy ourselves. Being with each other for hours and not really doing much. Stuff like that. It was great.

At the same time, my brother had met this other girl. He was feeling strongly about her, and my sister met Tony, who she eventually married. She's still married to him to this day. We were all attached to somebody. My sister and my brother hung around together a little bit more then, because Tony and George were very close. It was my brother who brought Tony around. They were good friends, so my brother and sister double-dated a lot. I stood basically with Roseann. We'd occasionally join my brother and sister, but not that often.

We didn't know anything about Vietnam. I don't think there was a word even said about it. Nobody even thought about it. It's a funny thing. We just hung around every day, did whatever we did, going to the beaches, whatever. This was the summer before I got drafted. We were doing all sorts of crazy things. Most of it was innocent. Occasionally we were in a little bit of trouble, but most of it was really good times. Looking back at it, I think that's what I was so bitter about. Right in the middle there, in the prime of my life, everything was taken away. The only thing we were aware of was the word, "Vietnam." We had heard that, and we understood that more and more people were getting drafted. My friend Andy was a couple of months older than I was. He went down to the draft board, and he said, "Lennie, I'm going to get drafted in September. Why don't you go down and find out when you're going to get drafted?" This was around May or June. I said, "No. I don't want to know about it." We continued the summer along, and it was great. It was the greatest summer of my life. It just seemed like the summer of light and sun. The sun was always shining. That's the best way to describe it. It was just getting up and going to meet her. It was a really good feeling.

Then, August comes. I had the job and everything like that, and my friend Tom got his draft notice. Tom was twelve days younger than I am. He got his draft notice. August tenth, he was leaving. We were having a party for him. That was a Thursday, or that's when we had the party. The following Saturday, August twelfth, I went over to my mother's house for my weekly visit. I got along with my family better with that kind of space. I would just sit and talk. This was one of those Saturday mornings that I came over about eleven o'clock. My brother and sister were there. We were all sitting down, probably doing something stupid, like watching cartoons, whatever, having a little breakfast. My brother was always the one to go out and get the mail. He came back, and he was whistling something: "Over there, over there . . ." I knew what had happened. I knew this was it. I looked at the letter. I didn't know much about what to think at that time. I didn't go into shock. I think one of the first things I did, within five or ten minutes, was that I ran out of the house and started looking for this guy Andy. I ran around looking for him, and, lo and behold, he was looking for me, and, yes, he got drafted the same day I did. We were drafted August twenty-fifth. It turns out my friend Michael, who I hung around with when I was younger, and who lived two houses away, also got drafted the same day. That was it. That was it.

The crazy thing was that my girl friend had gone away just like she did every summer. She had just left to go away with her parents. She was somewhere in the Catskills for a month. For some reason, I couldn't go upstate to her, but one of my friends knew exactly where she was, so they went up and told her: "Roseann, Roseann, Lennie got drafted." I guess her father understood that we were really serious, and he allowed her to come back home and stay in the house with the grandmother and the grandfather. We spent the last ten days just having a good time, trying to rush everything in. Somehow the army seemed the end of the world. The army seemed the end of the world because I was happy for the first time in my life. I mean really, really happy, and my feeling was, "What right do they have to take this away?" I never even considered running, or anything like that. That just didn't seem like a good solution, so I went into the service.

My friends Frankie and Terry and Roseann and I went down to the draft board on Whitehall Street at some kind of crazy time in the morning, seven o'clock in the morning or something like that, and I'm kissing Roseann good-bye, you know: "Don't worry. I'll be home in eight weeks." All of that. Her standing there crying. It was hard. I just remember giving her my handkerchief, crossing the street, and getting on this line with everybody else and just looking at her still standing there. Then I just went into the building. That was it.

The army. I went into basic training. There was nothing really hard physically about basic training. I had no problems there. It was just the harassment of somebody else running your life that was the hardest thing to face. The lack of emotion. That's the best way to describe it. You're by yourself, even though everybody else is in the same boat. Eight weeks. All you look forward to is getting home. But the eight weeks passed, then they told us we couldn't go home. We had to go into advanced infantry training before we would get to go home. I remember how depressed I was about that, that I wouldn't get home. I had to write the letter and tell Roseann I had to take another eight weeks. Roseann was the only thing that seemed to keep me going. Nothing else did. Anyway, finally the advanced infantry training was over. It was around Christmas, December seventeenth or something like that, and I went home for a two-week leave.

I don't know. I went home, and I had the army uniform on, and I stood out. Everybody was paying attention to me, at least my friends were. I was at one party after another, and I was with my girl friend. My family were all home for Christmas, and everybody was sort of close. We had the Christmas tree and everything like that. I remember the pictures we took. My girl friend came, and we all took pictures around the Christmas tree. My brother and my sister, my father and mother and my grandfather and grandmother, Roseann and myself. Then, before I knew it, of course, as always happens, that fifteen-day leave was gone. Quicker than I could imagine.

After my leave I was supposed to go to officers' candidate school in Missouri. The only reason I got mixed up in that was that the rumor was at that time that all officers were stationed at Fort Dix. You always hear all these crazy rumors. I don't know how they come about, but that's the reason I went to OCS. Anyhow, I went to OCS at Fort Leonard Wood. Right away the harassment started, as soon as I got off the bus. I thought, "No. There's no way I'm going to put up with this." As soon as I got off the bus, in my dress uniform and everything—and it's raining —right away I'm in a push-up position, just lying there, thinking that as soon as I got off the bus I knew I was back in the army. OCS was like a green beret-type thing. They really put you through harassment. That was the whole idea, to see if you "had it." You were supposed to be better than anybody else. You were supposed to be a leader of men, so what they were trying to do was break you, to see if you could be broken. It would have been worse than boot camp. Definitely. No doubt about it. They laid out the program, and it was continuous, with hardly any leave and all the study programs, and running here, and push-ups there, and harassment, spit-shined boots, and all this other stuff. Anyway, I didn't quit officers' candidate school because of being worried about that kind of stuff. One of the reasons I quit was a logical thing. Number one, I didn't get closer to home. I had no intention of becoming an officer. In fact, it was my idea to get to Fort Dix for the six months' training program and get thrown out of there in five months, because once you became an officer, you had two more years to serve. I knew that I wasn't going to do that, because I hated the army from the word go. It was just the idea to be closer to Roseann so that I could get home on leave. Once I learned that wasn't going to happen, three days later I just handed in my paper and I said, "No. I don't want to be in this." That was it. But within the week, I guess the army said, "I'll teach you for not going through this officers' candidate school." I think every draftee who went to officers' candidate school and didn't become an officer went to Vietnam. Within a week, I had my orders cut. I was going to Vietnam. February twenty-fifth. That was it.

So I knew I was going to Vietnam. I wrote home to everybody, and the crazy thing about it is that it doesn't sink in at that time. At least it didn't with me for some reason. It should have depressed me, but it was like: "Ahh, it's happening. It's going to happen. Okay." So I wrote home nonchalantly, in a way, just wrote home to everybody and told them. No big thing. But then, when I got home, on February tenth or eleventh, for another two-week leave, then I think that's when it sunk in. Just getting back home and realizing, "This is what you're going to leave." For the first time I realized, "This is possibly what you're going to leave forever." I couldn't believe it, because I was walking down the street, and everything was normal. Everybody's normal. All the neighbors, the old tenants I always said hello to. I'd tell them I was going to Vietnam, and it's "Good luck," and everything like that. Talking. All that stuff. Everybody wishing me well, but, as the days through that leave started passing, I couldn't put the brakes on. I wanted to put the brakes on. It was fourteen days. It just left. They just disappeared.

The worst day in my life—and I still say this, even as bad as some of the days I had in my marriage and everything else were—the worst day in my life was leaving for Vietnam. I remember just sitting in the room with my girl friend, maybe from ten o'clock in the morning until whatever time my plane left. I think I had a seven-thirty flight on the twenty-fifth. I had a seven-thirty flight, and we just spent the whole day together. Really spent the whole night together, being out until five o'clock in the morning, then she went home, had a couple of hours' rest, then she came back over, and we just spent the whole day together. My family was there, and it was like a morgue. Listening to records. It was weird, just sitting there. There were so many different feelings that I had. I had a morbid thing. You know, you're supposed to go over there with confidence and say, "Hey, I'm going to come back." Somehow I didn't go over that way. I guess I was always a pessimistic-type person. I loved Roseann, and I wanted her to stay with me and be with me, and I wanted her to wait. The other part was that I wanted to break up with her and not have to worry about anything, like her being home and leaving me while I'm over there in Vietnam. I thought, "God knows what's going to go on in Vietnam." I didn't want to have to worry about that. A couple of times I said, "Maybe we should break up." We didn't, though. We just stood there crying. We ended up staying with each other.

It came to the time we had to leave. I had to leave my parents. I kissed my mother good-bye and my sister good-bye, and my brother was saying good-bye. I was hugging him. My brother always had a crazy sense of humor. He said, "Don't worry about it, Pee Wee. You'll make it. You'll be back within no time. Everybody will be here. Don't worry about the home front. Everything will be all right." I walked out of the house. I felt really bad. I was walking up the block, because my friend had his car up the block, and Roseann wanted to be with me all the way to the end. In a way I wanted her to be with me all the way to the end, even though I knew the emotional state we were going to be in. But I was walking up to the car, and my father—I still remember this—he wasn't saying anything, just staying a couple of steps behind me, just following me and Roseann up the block. He just walked up to the end of that long block, and I crossed the street and turned around and waved good-bye to him.

We got to the airport. We were just standing there at the airport. I guess we had a drink or something, maybe we had enough time for that. Then it was just time to leave. God. Kissing her good-bye. One more kiss. Just letting go of her and looking at her. It was the worst thing in my life, just letting her go, just looking at her face and knowing I had to get on the plane, just sitting there, and I'm just looking out the window, and I'm holding back the tears, and I can't believe it. I couldn't believe what was happening here. Stupid. Then, lo and behold, on top of everything else, the plane is not going to leave for another half hour. I remember just getting off the plane and running and running to get there. They're gone. They left. I ran outside. For some stupid reason, I just wanted to be there with her for another fifteen or twenty minutes. That was it. I got back on the plane.

I flew to California. Then I was in Oakland, waiting for orders to be cut. I guess that was for about a day, then we flew overseas. I took out a Bible, and I was reading a Bible in between playing cards. It was the longest flight. Trying to sleep. I don't think I slept. I spent most of the time reading the Bible. That was it. I just landed in Vietnam, and there I was.

It was a funny feeling, landing in Vietnam, because you land there, and you can see it, and you think, "Wow. It looks like a pretty place." You don't understand what it is. You can't understand what the big deal is, or anything like that. I landed in Bien Hoa, stayed overnight; then in the morning we stood in formation and waited for orders to get cut as to where we were going. I must have gone through a day and a half of that, just waiting for my name to be called. In between standing in line waiting for your name to be called, they had you doing these stupid details, picking up weeds, butts. One of the first experiences I had when I was there . . . if there's two things about Vietnam that stand out in my mind out of everything else, it's the smell of shit burning . . . and that's one of the first details that I got put on . . . and the sound of helicopters. When I think about Vietnam, those two things for some reason come to mind. Anyway, I got my orders cut, and they said, "Pleiku." I didn't know where the hell Pleiku was. Central Highlands. I guess the sergeant knew, and he said, "Play it cool, Central Highlands." From what I understood, it was supposed to be a bad area. Anyway, I got stationed with the engineers, with C Company, 20th Engineer Battalion.

My company was out in the field when I arrived, and I was just hanging around in the base camp. It's hard to describe. The anguish that you . . . the loneliness of being there, especially those first couple of days, is unbelievable, because you really weren't doing anything. You didn't know what to expect. You didn't know what Vietnam was, whether the people were going to start running all over the place, or what. You didn't know what to think about Vietnam. All I did is spend time in the tent. Of course I had my gear and everything like that, and I talked to these other people who also knew nothing. They were just as new. I hated being there. I hated the people who were there with me for some reason. At the beginning, anyway, I hated them. I don't know. One guy was from Texas, and I hated his accent. There's this guy from Mississippi, and he's an asshole because of the way he talks. I'm in a foreign land, and I'm with my own people, and they're just as foreign to me as anyone else. I remember thinking about home: "Yeah. People are actually living a normal life back home, and here I am." Anyway, that was it.

In Vietnam, I spent most of my time out in the field. I went from Pleiku to a hundred and twenty-five miles south of Pleiku, where we built an airstrip. Then seventy-five miles north to Dak To, where we kept a road open, QL19, during the monsoon season. We built bridges and all this other kind of stuff, policing the roads for mines so that nobody would blow themselves up. I don't know. The best thing I can say for myself for the year I spent in Vietnam is that I didn't see a lotta, lotta action, definitely not as much as an infantryman, but definitely more than somebody who's stationed back in base camp. A lot of it was harassment. A lot of mortar attacks. A lot of threats of ground attacks. There were a couple of ground attacks. Scary moments, definitely.

There were a couple of times I thought it was all over. Mortar rounds landing pretty close to where I was. The scariest time, really, was within a month after I got there. We were building a bridge, and we always had someone protecting us, because the enemy always wanted to destroy what we were doing, so we needed protection while we were going about our business. I guess that was the crazy part about engineers. Or the insecurity about being in the engineers. You're standing there, building things. You don't have a rifle in your hand, and at any one moment somebody could take a shot at you, or drop a round in on you, and all you're doing is just standing there, with a shovel in your hand or carrying a piece of metal from a bridge and putting pieces together. That was the uncomfortable thing about being an engineer. The other thing, of course, was that they worked you to death. Always being tired.

Anyway, there was one night that we came home after building part of a bridge, and we're sitting there eating our food. I guess it was around seven o'clock. It was still light out. I remember just sitting there and hearing a thud, then another thud, and all of a sudden people were screaming, "Incoming rounds!" I really didn't know what to make of it, but just the screaming made me know something was wrong. Everybody was running around trying to find their rifles. I guess that's the whole thing. It was a disorganized war. Nobody knew what the hell was going on. Everybody was always running, scrambling for everything. One of the worst things was that those of us who were in the engineers didn't have anything to scramble to. The stupid sergeant that we had, or lieutenant or whatever, didn't have enough common sense to think that we should build foxholes, which is one of the first things you do for protection when you get into a new compound. We were here for about a week and a half, and that was it. We didn't have anything to run to. All we were doing, just like dopes, was just lying on the ground, just hoping that a round wouldn't land on us. We didn't have nothing. We didn't have anything to protect ourselves. We formed sort of a perimeter, and we could see rounds coming in. Everybody was yelling and firing. We were just firing. I didn't know what the hell I was firing at, except these little green lights. Green tracers, which we found out later were Czechoslovakian communist rounds. At least somebody said that. As quickly as it started, before we knew it, we had the helicopters. The helicopters were the greatest sight in the world to see. The gunships were coming down. They blasted them with the machine guns. It was a pretty sight to see, sort of like a relief that we weren't going to get overrun. Then, all of a sudden, tanks blasted through and went through the village. They must have leveled that village, because they saw the tracer rounds. I imagine no matter who was there: women, children, whatever. The whole thing was blasted, between the helicopters and the tanks. They had "Puff," the gunship. "Puff the Magic Dragon." That was the first time I ever saw that. All I could see was a line of bullets coming right down. That was it. It was hectic. It was a crazy experience. A scary experience. That was one of the scariest experiences we had. There were a couple of other cases that were like it, but that was it.

What made up Vietnam, though, besides the action, was when there wasn't any action. The frustration. They couldn't keep you busy enough, even though they worked you to hell. The constant thinking of going home. That's what I did, listening to everybody, every day. "Short." That was the famous expression. "How many days do you have left?" Boy, I used to hate it when I would hear of a guy who had just twenty-five days left, or something like that. "How many days do you have left, Lennie?" "I don't know. About two hundred and seventy-six days." Then, he'd say, "If I had that many days left, I'd dribble a basketball through a mine field." Saying those kinds of crazy things. The frustration used to build up inside me, but I would act crazy. I used to have this crazy sense of humor. I guess out in the field it was like a brotherly love sort of thing. There wasn't any racism or anything like that. We didn't think about it. We were all buddies. We had one thing in common: to get through Vietnam. We really helped each other through acting stupid, doing crazy singing, everything like that.

I used to do a crazy imitation of "California Dreamin'." I'd make believe I had a guitar in my hands, and I'd really get into it, into "California Dreamin'." I knew the words, and I'd get down on my knees. I'd imitate and really act it out. Crazy things like that. I guess that was my way of getting through it. I was more of a comical-type person. I was really the one. Me and maybe one other guy. We were the ones who kept spirits alive by doing crazy things. Acting crazy. Acting stupid. Whatever. Making people laugh. I was able to maintain my sense of humor a lot of times, and that was good.

I guess the worst time for me was the first three months. You talk to any Vietnam vet, and I think they'll say, too, the first three months you're scared shitless. Next six to seven months: "If it's going to happen, let it happen now." That's really what it was like. When I first went over there, I was so scared that something was going to happen to me, and I was bitter, so I used to write all these letters. I was bitter at everybody, and I would let them know the hell that was going on, because I was frustrated at being there, wanting to be home. I don't know. Wanting to be with Roseann. I missed her so much. I was really in love, and it was torture waiting for the days to go by. Anyway. That was the first three months. After that, I just stopped. It just didn't matter. No more bitter letters. It was like: "Ahh. If it's gonna happen, let it happen." I continued to write, of course, and the most important person to write to was Roseann. I would say I wrote Roseann 80 percent of the letters.

Now I'm into October, the end of October. I went on an R & R to Hong Kong. I guess that was the biggest mistake, because R & R brought me into a real world, even though it was oriental. Hong Kong was almost like New York, if you take away the oriental-type of feeling. Of course, there were women, and I had a chance to touch a woman, a real woman. That's all we did. Spent the whole five days . . . they call it "I & I," and that's really what it was. "Intercourse and intoxication." That's all we did, but we enjoyed ourselves. I went with my friend from Kentucky, and we had a great time. Then we came back. Ouch! At that time, I had seventy-eight days left. I said to myself, "God, no. We've come this far, had a taste of life again, and now it's here. There's the possibility I can get home." The possibility of making it home was beginning to become a reality.

My friend and I were back in base camp, and the fortunate thing—and this is crazy—the fortunate thing is that we both came back with the clap. As crazy as it sounds, we were happy, because we had a little more time to collect our thoughts, write some letters, and feel clean a little longer and not worry about being killed. This was the 4th Infantry Division base camp. There were jets all over the place. We always thought that base camp was safe. But the time was up, and that was it. We had to go back out in the field. What the funny thing is, what changes, is people with nine months or so left. They're now the gung-ho people. They're the ones who are saying, "Hey, I hope this happens, or that happens," which is exactly what I was feeling for a time: "I hope something happens now." I didn't care. I *wanted* things to happen. But now, hearing these people saying this, I'm saying to myself, "Okay, shut up. Shut up." In fact, I did say that. I said it to them: "No. You *don't* want this or that to happen. You're imagining these bastards running over the fences and you whipping them off, John Wayne-style. You don't want that to happen."

For some reason, we did have that killer in us. No doubt about it. It was so easy to do. Your knees shook like hell before something happened, but I think once you pulled the trigger, something happened, and that was it. You could do it, although I never knew myself whether I killed anybody or not. I definitely fired the rifle, and fired into an area where somebody was firing at me, but I never knew what was happening. I don't know. Listening to the new people talk like that, I didn't want them to. I didn't want to hear it. That the days would go, that's what I wanted. It just seemed long, those last days. What was bad was that as I got shorter, Vietnam got worse.

The last days in Vietnam, I was the most insecure. We were stuck near a Montagnard [Vietnamese mountain people] village. A Special Forces camp was nearby, but we were a company of about one hundred and fifty engineers, and the most we had was rifles, maybe some mortars. For some stupid reason, our captain refused to go in with the Special Forces people. We were supposed to go into their compound. The Special Forces captain asked if we wanted to do that. Anyway, our captain decided he didn't want to do it, and that was that. During that time period, though, there was a lot of . . . not action, but I guess what you would call "scares" going on. We were out there when the Tet offensive broke out, and we heard radio reports of all kinds of things happening all around us. For all we knew, the North Vietnamese were going to be marching right through our campsite. Anyway, it was a very edgy time. People were all edgy.

A lot of us were getting ready to go home around this time. About forty of us in the company itself were going home sometime in February, so a lot of people were getting nervous, and every night we would have these alerts. Alerts were going on. Flares were going up. You would hear noises in the bushes. There'd be firing in the bushes. Anyway, there was one night that it was really bad in the sense that we thought this was it for sure. We ran into our areas, the ditches, and my friend and I went into one area. I was manning the machine gun, and my friend just sort of panicked. The words I think he said were, "I can't take this anymore . . . this shit." It looked like he was ready to go. He was supposed to load the machine gun for me. He couldn't do that, and I loaded it. I don't know. We talked, and I guess we were both nervous, but I calmed him down a little bit, and, as it turned out, it wasn't the end of the world. It was just another one of those alerts that was going on constantly. That's pretty much how it went my last thirty days in Vietnam. Just a lot of harassment. We were building the airstrip down there, and there were sniper attacks and stuff like that, but, other than that, it was just constant on guard for nothing. Not for nothing, I guess, but lifting you up. The adrenalin was pumping and everything like that, and you were waiting for something to happen, and the big battle never came.

I think the real sickness of Vietnam, forget the action or whatever, the real sickness . . . well, for example, when I had about thirty days left, I was out in the field. I was cutting down trees. This Vietnamese walked by, and, I don't know, they have this stupid smile on their faces. I don't know. Whether I thought they were Viet Cong or not didn't matter. It was just that stupid smile that they always had on their face. Anyway, the one time that I came close to doing something that I guess was morally wrong, and *very* close to doing it, was . . . for some reason this guy got to me that day, and I went for my rifle. He was just walking by. I had this strong urge just to walk up to him . . . and just kill him. I don't know. It's weird. I don't know what stopped me, because it was . . . maybe getting caught. I guess that's the only thing that stopped me. I don't know. Maybe. I don't know. There was no-body around. I guess I could have done it. I had the urge just to kill this guy, and maybe the urge was just because there was so much frustration, in a sense, that you kept on firing, even though you didn't know what the hell you were firing at, because you never saw who it was. There was no scoreboard you could keep, so that you could say to yourself, "Okay. I wiped out thirty Viet Cong, because I actually saw my rifle kill them." Maybe that was part of it. The idea of seeing somebody drop in front of your rifle.

There's one thing about the army—the army, the marines, whatever. They do make killers out of you. It's easy to do. But I didn't do it. I just let him go by. I think what it was, though, was maybe the morbid excitement that would have come out of him fearing, knowing that I was going to kill him, knowing that I . . . yeah. There was a certain power there, I guess. I guess a lot of people over there experienced it, probably a lot of infantrymen did. The thrill of somebody falling in front of you from your rifle. Like I say, I never saw that happen, because it was always crazy, but that one time . . . maybe it was just the frustration that just kept on building up, and the idea of getting out of there. It was getting close, and maybe I wanted to pay somebody back for having me over there: "I didn't want to be in your country," and all that.

One of the things that would happen is that you would go through the villages, and you learned right away that you weren't loved in Vietnam. Okay? Right from the start. I think that was the crazy part. We would go through the villages, riding on the truck or whatever, and these little kids would stand there and stick their —you know, the old American symbol, they learned that right away—they'd stick their finger up at you. These were little kids. I couldn't believe it. It was a weird feeling to first see it. After a while, I got used to it. What we used to do is throw things at them. They were always sticking their finger out or begging for food, or whatever, and I hated them. Okay? I mean, I *understand* . . . I understand, without a doubt, My Lai. I understand it, because after a while it got to me to see these people every day, knowing they hated me, and knowing that they're the cause of a lot of American people dying. We used to sit, and we'd talk. We'd talk to our buddies. We'd say, "Yeah. I could kill these kids." I don't care how young they were. There was such a hate buildup, seeing some kid, little kid, sticking his finger up you. I think . . . I don't know. I think that was the real craziness of Vietnam.

So. Lo and behold, I got out of the field. You know, you always hope to get out of the field a little early. Some people get out of the field with fifteen days left. Not our crew. Not our lieutenant. They kept me out there until I had four days left. Then I went back to base camp, and, lo and behold, that place got hit. That was right after Tet began, and the whole country was going crazy. There wasn't a safe place in Vietnam. What happened was that I was in the Quonset hut, and all of a sudden Chinese rockets were coming in. You knew Chinese rockets, because they had a different sound. You just knew the difference between them and the regular mortar rounds. No doubt about it. All of a sudden, everybody was screaming and running, and all we did was run into a ditch along the highway. Without any rifle. I had already given up my rifle. We were just sitting there, the whole base camp, all along the perimeter, and the helicopters were flying around and everything like that. From what I understood, the base camp was getting hit from different angles. Fortunately, where we were, there wasn't anything major that was happening, although everybody was scared. I don't know. It just kept on following me, it seems. I went over to Cam Ranh Bay. I spent a couple of days there. Cam Ranh Bay got hit, too, and that was it. I finally got out of the country.

The last thing I remember about Vietnam is watching "Mission Impossible." This was while I was waiting for my orders to be cut to go home. That's the last thing I actually remember. I think the greatest feeling was sitting on the plane, with all the soldiers there. As the plane was taking off, we're all screaming and yelling, "Go, go," or whatever. I forget exactly what we yelled, but everybody joined in this joyous celebration as the plane took off. There were goose pimples on me. It was a great feeling. Everybody felt good. I got out of Vietnam, and that was it. A fifteen-minute celebration. It was quiet after that. Everybody was reflecting, I guess. I know that's what I was doing, and I was hoping, "Jesus, after going through Vietnam, I hope to hell the plane don't crash!" That's what it was like: "Wow. I got out of Vietnam, now something's going to happen to me." I guess that's what it is always. After getting out of Vietnam, I was so insecure that I thought of so many things that happen, that can happen, and I continue to worry about them in life.

So. I got home from Vietnam, and I met my girl friend. The last two months she didn't write as much, and I was wondering what the hell was going on. Well, what I quickly found out was that she was mad because I went on R & R. She knew what I was doing over there. One minute she was saying, "You should go," but the next she would be jealous. I don't think she did anything, really, except start going out a little bit with this guy, but as soon as I got home she broke up with him, and she came back with me. There was no problem there. I spent thirty days with her and with my family.

The unfortunate part of this whole time while I was in 'Nam

was that my brother had gotten into more trouble. He was doing a lot of fighting, I guess. He'd drink; he'd go into bars; he'd fight and all this other kind of crazy stuff; and he got into trouble, I guess, a couple of times more while I was in Vietnam. Nothing big, but it was the kind of thing where a judge said, "Listen, George," and I guess that's what they did in those days, "Look, you either do this, or I'm going to lock you up." That's what happened. He could either go into the service or be locked up. Lo and behold, my brother joined the marines. I knew about it while I was in Vietnam. He wrote me a letter, and I remember trying to talk him out of it. I remember writing my mother a letter, too, trying to talk him out of it: "Don't go into the marines." Not that they were a bad outfit or anything like that, but somehow it seemed the marines got themselves into a lot of trouble all the time. Anyway, that was my thing: "George, don't go into the marines. Don't even go into the army. Go into the navy. There's nothing over here that you like, that you want to like."

Like I said, before you went into the service, to Vietnam or anything, you had the goose pimples, and you could picture yourself as John Wayne and all this other stuff, as a kid, not understanding. But, okay, I was there, and I realized what was going on, so I tried to talk my brother out of going into the service, period, but definitely the marines. I remember my mother saying it was something he wanted and that she couldn't talk him out of it, that he wanted to do it. So then he was in the marines. He was in California, and he was writing me letters, and I knew he was getting ready to be shipped out. This was sometime in January. I tried to work it out so that we could see each other. Anyway, I found out that wasn't going to work out, that his outfit was going to leave before I would get back into California. To this day, I think I missed him by a week at the most.

One of the bitter things I have about Vietnam, not just about Vietnam, but about the service, the emotional feeling, is that I had gone up to my captain, and I had told him, "Look, I haven't seen my brother for a year, and he's the only person I won't see. He's coming over to Vietnam. I'm requesting that I leave Vietnam a week early." I think that's what it was. It wasn't any big deal. I remember the captain saying something like, "Life is hard. We can't have everything the way we want it. I can understand your feelings for your brother, but we all have a job to do." That was it. He was going over as I was on my way home. I must have hit Seattle February twenty-second, because I got home the twenty-third, and my brother must have left California maybe the eighteenth, something like that. Like I say, within the week. I don't know exactly, but I remember calling my mother. She said, "No. He left already. He left the other day." That was it. He was in Vietnam.

He was in the 1st Marine Division, C Company. He was stationed first in Hue. That's where he first landed. It was getting to be holy hell then, and when he got there it was the worst possible time. He had written me a letter, and I had written him back and said Roseann and I were getting married: "I want you to be my best man. You're going to be back a year from now. We'll have a wedding then."

I went through the leave and I guess basically had a good time, although Roseann and I started fighting. I was insecure, definitely an insecure bastard. When you're in Vietnam, you figure the worst: "She's fooling around on me." I didn't trust anybody, and, somehow, no matter how many times she told me that she didn't do anything, I *wanted* her to say she had. I wanted to believe she was bad. She wasn't. I know that, but in between the kissing, there was a lot of crying, and there was a lot of fighting. The first time I ever hit her was on my thirty-day leave. I remember feeling really bad about that. Anyway, we got through that thirty-day leave. We were still intact, and we went through the same old crying routine when I left to go back to Fort Campbell, Kentucky. I still felt miserable, but somehow not quite as miserable.

At Fort Campbell, I was lucky enough to be in a full company, so we had all these stupid formations, stupid police calls and all this other kind of stuff. During that period we were doing riot training. There wasn't much about Kentucky I liked, except that my friend Andy was there with me. We went out some, went into town. Got drunk, whatever. There wasn't anything much else to do. As usual, most of the towns that we were stationed in in the service were worthless as far as any kind of entertainment went.

One day, after lunch, somebody came up to me and said, "The first sergeant wants to see you." I walked over, and he said I should call my mother at home. I did. I called my mother, and that's when I found out that my brother was wounded in Vietnam. The only thing I knew at the time was that he wasn't dead, but he was wounded seriously. My mother was upset. I could hear my father in the background, and he was upset. I had a friend drive me to the airport, and I went home. I got home and found out what was going on. My brother was in the Hue area. He was on an ambush patrol. Apparently, although you never really get the full story, they were walking in this area with bushes all around, then they walked into an open area. All of a sudden, all hell broke loose. My brother got hit twice, once in the wrist, and another round hit him in the stomach area. I know this because my brother wrote about it. Anyway, I spent about a week at home. We were all together, the whole family, Roseann and everybody. We were waiting for reports. We knew he was in the Philippines and that he was on intravenous feeding. We got the letter from a Red Cross person. My mother couldn't read it. Everybody was nervous, so I read it. They gave me the letter to read. It was basically good news. He couldn't write, but a Red Cross volunteer was writing everything that he said. My brother, with his typical dumb sense of humor, said, "Tell Pop I didn't duck, but I'm all right." That's how I knew that he took a bullet in the arm and in the stomach. He said, "Don't worry. I'll be getting out of this place and I'll be going over to St. Albans (Hospital)." So everything was rosy. Everything was great. We all sighed in relief. Everybody felt good. We took out a bottle, drank it, then I went out with my father. We had a couple of beers in the bar and celebrated with Tony. Then my sister and I left my mother and father together. I'm sure they wanted to be alone. My sister, Tony, Roseann, and I went over to Tony's house. We celebrated, continued celebrating and drinking. Everything was great. We were going to see my brother: "In a little while he'll be home, and everything will be good."

I went back to Fort Campbell after about ten days, and everything looked good. Then I got another one of those stupid calls. Somebody told me to call home. I called. My mother was on the phone. She said, "Georgie's dead." I don't know. I said something like, "Just like that?" She said, "Yes, he's dead," and I remember hearing my father crying. I guess it's my father that I remember the most. He said, "It's all over," and just the way he said it sent a chill down my spine. I think that's when it sunk in, because when he said that, that's when I burst into tears. I said, "Okay. I'll be home. I'll be home as soon as I can," and hung up the phone. I walked back. It was at night, and there was a sergeant on duty. I said, "I gotta leave." He said, "Why don't you wait until morning?" "No. I can't stay here another second." It was about nine o'clock. "I have to leave right now." There was this guy, Kenny Baker, I remember him. He was one of my friends in Vietnam. Another crazy guy. He volunteered to drive me to the airport, which was about a hundred and twenty miles away in St. Louis, Missouri. That was it. The sergeant said, "Okay, son." That was probably one of the only times I was shown any compassion by one of those bastards. He was a black sergeant. He was a nice guy, and he understood it. He said, "Okay. I understand." They did whatever they do, drew up orders for compassionate leave or whatever. I don't even know if they gave me any papers or not. I just left. I took the trip to the airport and got on the plane.

I remember sitting on the plane and not really talking to anyone. It didn't seem real. It didn't really seem real. It's the same old story, I guess, that you always hear, that you think that there's a mistake or something like that. You refuse to believe that it's true. So I flew home and took a cab to the house. It was early in the morning. I think I must have got to the house about seven o'clock in the morning. I remember getting home. I must have had the keys with me. I opened the door, and it was weird, because there was the dog, Spot, and everything seemed so normal. I petted the dog, and I walked into the house, and everybody was sleeping. For some reason, that seemed so weird, that everybody was sleeping. I guess that made it unrealistic. There was a certain kind of crazy quietness in the whole house, and I remember going into my room and just sitting on the bed. I looked at my brother's pictures. That was it. I didn't fall asleep or anything like that. I guess I just waited for everybody to get up. My mother came up, and she saw me, and she burst into tears. I hugged her. I didn't know what else to do. My father was there, and that was it.

The whole period was crazy. We went over and over the story of how it happened. I think the unkindest cut of all, the bitter part of it all, is the fact that he was alive. You say to yourself: "Okay, die, and die quickly. Okay. I can accept that," but "Don't do this to us. Not when we think he's all right. I thought he was coming home. Here's a letter. I know that it was dictated, and I know that it's him because of the expressions." That was the shock, and I think that's what put everybody through hell. We all believed he was coming home alive.

What seems to have happened is that he somehow couldn't survive on the intravenous feeding. He became very weak, and infection set in. That's the story that we got. All of a sudden, when he looked so good, he took a turn for the worse. That's what helped to make it so unacceptable to everybody.

We waited for his body to come home. It took a couple of days. We were notifying relatives, and going through the same story over and over again, how he died, and all the tears and the breaking down and regaining composure quickly. Somehow, the biggest pity of it all is that you feel you've got to act proper and all that. You think, "He wouldn't have wanted it this way, not the tears." You have to go for a walk, you have to do the right things. You have to be brave and all those other stupid things, keep your chin up. That was basically how it was, but it hit home when he finally arrived. For some reason, I didn't go. My father and my uncle went to view his body. My father said, "No. I don't want you to go." I agreed, I guess. I didn't go. They went and viewed the body. They did whatever they had to do. They said it was him. I talked to my uncle, who I was pretty close with, and he tried to assure me that it was the best thing that could have happened to my brother, in a sense, that he died, because he wouldn't have been a man, in a sense. I guess that the bullet hit him in the stomach and traveled downward. Sexually he would have never been able to do anything. I think that's what my uncle was trying to tell me.

Then we had the body. My brother's body was there. It was a long ceremony, and, for some reason, we wanted it. In a way, you know, we didn't want to bury him quickly. It hurts. It hurts, but you don't want it to end. I think it was three long nights. It was crazy, the agony that we had to go through, but for some reason we didn't want those three days to end. I don't know. It was a big funeral. There were so many flowers there. My brother was one of the few around the neighborhood to die, and this is in a large area of the Bronx. The Fordham/Kingsbridge Road area. Everyone came. All these people came. The whole room was filled with flowers. One after another, people would come in and view the body. My one friend, Jody, he was a good guy. He was the one who was in the halfway house the time they got into all the trouble. Anyway, Jody came, and I walked him up to view the coffin. That was my job, to make sure that nobody went crazy on me. Jody was just standing there, and all of a sudden he fell. I grabbed him. He had turned white as a ghost. That's what it was about. It was unbelievable to view a person who would have been twenty-one soon. He would have been twenty-one that June. He died May 1, 1968. June ninth he would have been twenty-one. I don't know. It was crazy.

Then came the morning that we had to view the coffin for the last time. People say crazy things. You try to get close to him. My mother. I'll never forget this. My brother was always a comic book reader, I don't care how old he was. There was something about him. He always had a comic book in his back pocket, and my mother—one of the times that we went up and viewed him—she broke down and said, "I can't believe he's gone. I can just see him sitting there with a comic book." You say to yourself, "Why did this have to happen?" That's what it's like. You remember all the stupid little nice things that happened in your life, and the reality of this comes home, and it's crazy.

In between the crying, you laugh. You remember all the good times you had, and you laugh: "Remember, we got in trouble here." We thought it was the end of the world when we were kids, running away from other kids, running away from the cops when we were in trouble. We thought that was the worst thing. We laughed now, because it was nothing. It was nothing. That was it. Just my brother, lying there.

My sister. My sister really took it bad. She had a bad heart, too, and we were all concerned about her, that she wouldn't be able to handle it. I guess we all handled it. The bad thing about it is that we all handle it. The bitter thing about it, though, the bitter thing inside of me, was saying: "Hold up. Hold up. There's something wrong here. There's something . . . no. Wait a minute. Let's stop. Let's hold this thing up here. The world has got to stop. My brother's dead. Something's got to be said. We're not going to just put him in the ground and just forget about him. Something's got to be said." That's what I wanted to do. I wanted to put the brakes on, maybe get up on top of a building and say, "Hey! Look what happened." I didn't know what I wanted to say. I really didn't, but I didn't want life to continue. It's mean. It's mean. It's mean to go out in the street and actually see people walking around, and they're normal. They don't know what's going on. Their life is continuing, and somehow . . . it was weird. I guess that's the only way to say it. It was weird that in here is death, and outside the sun is shining. Somehow, that's wrong. Somehow, the sun. "No. No. It can't be shining." It should be raining, or whatever, but it shouldn't be sunshiney or anything like that, and there shouldn't be people smiling.

Everybody got through that three-day period the best way they could. My mother talked to her friends. I talked to my friends. Somehow, though . . . you go into a bar. When it got to be too much, I'd go and have a couple of extra drinks. I was with my uncle, and we went and had a couple of drinks with my father.

We knew the bartender. We'd lived in the area for twenty years, and we knew everybody. My father would express himself to the bartenders, and you know what my feeling was? See, this is the thing that I didn't like. I didn't want them to say anything. My father would say something about how my brother died. He was getting it off his chest, and my feeling was, "These people don't care." I didn't want him to say anything. For some reason, it was like, "What do these people care?" I guess that was one of my first reactions out of this whole thing. I didn't trust people anymore. I felt people were laughing, for some crazy reason. Maybe this was the way Vietnam hit home, with the hippies and everything like that. For the first time, I understood that I was alone, so I shuddered every time my father would say something to somebody. I don't know if I ever said anything to him, but I know I wanted to say, "These people don't give a shit. They don't care." In my morbid way, I almost felt people were laughing: "Good. Good. Okay. We told you. You shouldn't *be* in Vietnam. We told you that. Okay. So you all deserve to die, all of you that went to Vietnam. That's the kind of feeling I had. That was the kind of anger. That's the hatred I built up inside of me. I wanted to beat a hippie up. That was the thing to do, and it ended up that I did that a couple of times, purposefully just walked up to some long-haired freak. At the time, I didn't want to admit it, or maybe I was too young to realize why I got into those fights. I just said, "These people don't care. Nobody cares."

Then the next morning came. That was a scene in itself. You say your last good-byes. Everybody went up to the coffin. My uncle was telling me, "You're the one who's got to hold up. You can't break down. You've got to take care of your mother, your father, your sister." I don't know. I remember sitting down and looking over my brother's face. There was no problem with that. We were able to have an open coffin. I remember I started crying, then my body started shuddering, and everybody said, "Oh, wow! You can't do that. That's the worst thing in the world. You can't cry. Come on. Hold up." They pulled me away, and I wiped the tears away. "Okay. I'm all right. I'm all right." My mother and my sister were both crying. My father. Somehow I felt the most sorry for him, because he took it . . . men somehow don't express emotion, or they can't, so I understood him. He was holding back the tears, and the last thing he did . . . I still remember it to this day . . . the last thing he did is that he saluted him.

We closed the coffin. We got the limousine. We dragged it out, because we wanted to. We tortured ourselves. Somehow, that's what we wanted to do, torture ourselves. We took a trip. First we went down to the church for blessings, then we got out of the church and we got back into the car. Before we went to the cemetery, we took the trip to all the different places that had affected our lives, where we grew up. We went around the park. We passed the corner candy store. Then we went to the cemetery. We stood there. The priest said his prayers, and there was a twenty-one-gun salute. My mother broke down, and my father broke down, and my sister broke down. I broke partly down. I wanted to break down, but I guess I was kept too busy, watching all the others. I don't know. Then it was over, and he was in the ground. We went and had the dinner that you normally have, whatever you do to try to forget it. We were with all our relatives and friends. Some friends who are never there during your normal life, but who are there when funerals come. We talked the normal bullshit: "Hey, we'll have to get together. We haven't seen each other in a long time." You know it'll never happen. You won't see them again, and maybe you don't even really want to see them again until the next funeral.

It was crazy during that time. My father and mother were arguing. We thought of so many stupid little things, and we picked on ourselves. We were afraid we did something wrong. My mother was Catholic, my father was Protestant, and my brother was Catholic, and . . . I don't know. I don't know. I was Protestant, but there was something my mother and father were arguing about. "Why didn't you become Catholic?" my mother was saying, because something in the church that could have been done wasn't done, or whatever. I didn't think it was a big deal, and I remember screaming, "What the hell are you two people arguing about?" I was so mad at my mother and father, but I think they were . . . you know, there were periods when people were out of control. We were doing stupid things, and saying stupid things. I think I brought them back in line, you know: "*This* is what he doesn't want." I almost saw the family crumbling. That was a scary part. There were all kinds of things like that going on. Somehow, though, we got through it.

I wrote to the army for compassionate reassignment. I wanted to take care of my mother and my father, because I knew they needed it. I really felt at that time that they needed me and that I needed them, so I wrote away to the sergeant major or something, and then I went back to Fort Campbell, Kentucky, which was probably the worst thing that I had to do. It killed me.

Then, when I was back in the army, Roseann called me. She didn't tell me what was happening during the funeral, but she told me now that she had missed her period and that she was going to the doctor. She was going to the doctor four days later, and I called her back. Sure enough, she was pregnant. My first reaction was to be happy, because I was so insecure about losing her. Even though we were fighting like cats and dogs, there was love there, and I was happy. I thought, "Yeah. Now we're going to be together." Then, gradually, it began to sink in, the bastard that I was, or that I thought I was. The compassionate reassignment had come about, and I was going to Fort Hamilton sometime during the beginning of July. I thought, "Here I am, supposed to help my mother, and I have to tell my mother, 'Look, Roseann's pregnant, and I can't help you out. I got my own problems.' " That's what happened.

·I came home, and I had to spend a lot of time talking to Roseann. We were in a bad state. We didn't know what the hell was going on because everything had changed. What was love was now two frightened people, arguing constantly: "What are we gonna do? What are we gonna do? How are we going to tell the parents?" Anyway, we did. We told them. I don't think any of the parents were very happy about it, although my father was more understanding. My father was really a quiet man. He didn't say much. He didn't make it into an end-of-the-world type thing. We got married two days before I got out of the army.

We continued along, and we had Laura, and I still say the best thing about it is that Laura brought a lot of happiness into our lives. Definitely to my father's life. He was very excited about her. You know that old expression, "One person dies, another person takes his place." She brought a lot of happiness to all of us, but it just seemed like everything happened at once. We got married, and I went back to work and carried on what I guess you would call a normal life, no problems with the job or anything like that. Laura brought a lot of happiness to the family, my father and my mother, Roseann's parents, but, somehow, Roseann and I just couldn't get along.

I saw it as her fault. She saw it as my fault. I was cold. She was cold. We fought each other. The battles just got worse, I guess. There was a lot of physical fighting in it. I don't know. I had a temper. I . . . you know, one minute I'd be arguing . . . I don't know. I guess I wasn't good at arguing. She was better at it. She had words, and somehow when I argued, I would only get up to a certain point, and anger would get to me. Before I knew it, I would be hitting her. We'd go back and forth: "I'm not going to do it again. I'm sorry." But, somehow, we just didn't understand each other. I don't know. In a way I felt alone, because everybody was against us, against me, or . . . I don't know . . . against Vietnam, or whatever. I was so bitter. Maybe that's why I wasn't affectionate. I look back at it now, and I *knew* Roseann was right. I was cold. A lot of times I should have been more understanding of her. I knew I was being stubborn, and I knew . . . but, somehow, I don't know . . . except for sex, and I guess I was just greedy there, I knew I was being cold. I knew I should have reached out and held her, but the hands just never came. I couldn't hold her in my arms like I used to. That just stopped, and the marriage just crumbled. But Laura. Laura brought a lot of happiness, and we struggled to maintain our relationship because of Laura. No doubt about it. Because we did love her. She was a beautiful baby, and we got a kick out of her and everything like that, and my father loved her, but, somehow, that wasn't enough.

My father died at the age of fifty-eight. I knew my father wasn't going to live long. I knew he had always had a respiratory problem, but, somehow, when he went to the doctors, the doctors would say, "Look, you're not going to live much longer than ten years," so we were figuring he'd live until he was around sixty-five. I guess ten years seemed like a long time then, especially when my brother had died before he had lived twenty-one years. But he died, and I *know* he died because of my brother. I mean, my brother's death caused something to go out of him. He carried on at work and everything like that, and I know my daughter made him happy, but something left him, his will to go on, maybe. I don't know. I don't want to say that he gave up, but I'm sure he thought about my brother every day, and it hurt him. Every day of his life. He could never get over it. He'd go to the cemetery and just stand there and look at the grave. There was something about my father. I just looked at him and would just see him, by himself, like there was nobody else around him, and nobody else could do anything for him. Somehow all of the rest of us had something to go on with. My mother was stronger, or whatever, but my father was not.

They went on a stupid two-week vacation to Florida. Everybody felt good for them. They were going down to Florida to meet my mother's brother, and they spent the first week there having a good time, going out, doing whatever you do in Florida, eating out and everything else, and the second week my mother called up and said, "He's sick. He's in the hospital." My father tried to get back to New York, I guess to his roots. He didn't want to die in Florida. I guess he knew he was going to die. I think he wanted to die. My mother got him on a train, because he couldn't get on a plane, and he died before he got to Jacksonville. That was it. My mother called me up and said, "Your father died." I said, "Just like that?" I couldn't believe it. It was hard to believe it.

It sometimes seems like August twenty-fifth, the day I was drafted, my life ended. Not "my life ended," but it just got worse, it just kept on going downhill. Nothing seemed to jell right. One thing after another. There's something about Vietnam. Even the word, the word, "Vietnam." 'Nam. Vietnam. Something about it that will live on for the rest of my life. Some power in that word. Something weird, something crazy. At certain times there's a deadly fascination with going back there. I don't know. To somehow find out what happened, to try to fit all the pieces back together again.

I think of my brother all the time, even to this day. Not daily, but often. I think of him often, and I always think: "How would my brother have reacted to this? How would my brother have liked my daughter? How would it have been to have him as an uncle? What would he have been doing now? Would he be married and how many kids would he have?" All that kind of normal stuff that's supposed to happen in a person's life.

I hung around with my friends after the service. We did a lot of crazy things. There were a lot of us who went to Vietnam, and we hung around together, formed a softball team. We used to carouse around, drink kegs of beer. I guess we did a lot of drinking to try and relieve all of the frustration, yelling and screaming, getting into our share of trouble and fights. At that time, we were all right wingers: "The U.S., love it or leave it," all of that. That's a long time ago now. And we had our march, our protest march, our own protest march. I can remember us walking down the street like a bunch of nuts, marching down the street, holding up traffic, twelve of us. We went marching down the tunnel, the Kingsbridge Tunnel. It went under the Grand Concourse, and there was a lot of traffic, but we just decided to demonstrate. We started marching, and we had our own thing. We were all "pro–United States," and the cars were beeping at us. This one taxi beeped the horn at my brother-in-law, and he jumped on top of the hood, screaming at him. Oh, wow. We were just looking for trouble. I guess it's good that we didn't run into any left wingers, or whatever. I don't know. Whatever you called them at that time. That was that.

Then, slowly but surely, it came. I started listening to people talk. I had a lot of arguments, not so much in my neighborhood, but at work. There were different people there: "The war was wrong." All this, and I remember yelling, getting into arguments: "No. It's not wrong. You son-of-a-bitch. My brother died there." I wanted to take somebody and punch him out, because I didn't want to think it was wrong, but it gradually sunk in. Some of Roseann's family thought it was wrong. They were "educated," I guess you would say. I guess when I became educated, I guess that's when I started to learn that it was wrong, but, in the meantime, learning that it was wrong was like feeling that everybody was against you. That's the thing. The scary part is that I did go over there, and that, number one, my brother's life was lost, and that I did miss the best part of my life, that so much happened to ruin my life. The realization that it was wrong, that the United States carried on, for whatever reason, this madness, hit home so badly. And the ending came when we just got out of there, and the whole place just folded, and Vietnam was lost, and that was it. The end of an era, supposedly.

My father died in 1974, in December of 1974, and maybe that's another reason he died. Maybe he didn't want to be around because maybe there was a realization there, too, that his son's life was taken for something that it shouldn't have been taken for. I don't know. My mother knows. I know she knows. That's something that we talk about, and I don't want to say that concretely to her, but she knows. And I know. And somehow your feelings about the country are not the same anymore. I mean, I don't hate this country, but I'm very bitter about it.

A certain kind of screaming . . . something's gotta be said. You know, I want it to be said, but I don't know what to say. I don't know what should be said, but it just can't end like that, you know: "The book's closed." Maybe it's as simple as . . . I don't know. I don't know even if this is done. Maybe it's as simple as a politician, the president of the United States, saying that we were wrong, and "I apologize to the American people. I apologize to all those people who went there." Something was lost. Some of them lost their arms, their legs, their lives, whatever. Maybe. Maybe something like that, just to have the guts to admit it and to come out with some sort of apology. Somebody needs to say, "I'm sorry." Somebody does. Somebody needs to say that it'll never happen again, that "I'll never let these kids go like that again." Maybe something like that.

A lot has got to be said about Vietnam, and it's not to brainwash people, but there's so much to be learned from it, and maybe next time . . . or with what's going on now . . . the parents . . . the parents who in those days were called "right wingers" . . . maybe those kinds of parents will speak out and won't let their sons or daughters just leave without some kind of mass, mass, mass protest going on. Maybe that's the biggest thing to be learned. Unfortunately, in the kind of world we live in, there's a "right war," but, hopefully, that will never come. A "right war" is somebody coming over here and getting on our shores. Other than that, though, we've got to learn from Vietnam. That's it.

There definitely is still a deadly fascination about Vietnam. Somehow I wish there weren't. I wish I were back there, just to remember how it was, and to try to put all the pieces back together. Somehow, that country unraveled it for a lot of people. I know it did for me. I don't know. There's nothing else I can say. The thing is, I'm just starting to understand everything that happened to me, all the hate and anger and everything else that has built up inside, and I'm finally able to talk about it and get a little bit more understanding of these feelings that I have. I don't know how many times a year I've had this same dream, and it's such a real, real dream. It's that I'm getting drafted again, and all through this dream I'm trying to convince whoever it is, I'm trying to convince them: "Wait a minute. I've been drafted before. You've made a mistake. You've made a mistake. Look, I'm thirty-five. I've already been drafted, and I've served. I've served my time. You're wrong." I keep on hoping, through this dream, that somehow the mistake will be found. I'm telling my family, and I'm telling the people. I'm worried about losing them. I don't know. Somehow it doesn't . . . I'm not able to convince them that I was drafted, and I think I wake up knowing that I'm going to get drafted, and it's weird enough to realize: "Oh, wow. It's a dream."

Yet it is so real. It's amazing how many times that has happened since I left the army. That's the effect of Vietnam on my life.

Roseann and I, every now and then . . . well, we don't talk like that now, but before we were breaking up, we would say, "If only Vietnam hadn't come between us." This was in between the tears. There would be the hate and the anger, okay, but I know we didn't mean it. I know I didn't mean it. And in between the tears, we'd say, "If only Vietnam hadn't happened. It would have been different." You could never believe that we loved each other so much at one time, and that eventually it turned to hate, or maybe it was still love, but we knew it would never be the same again. I think Roseann understands that now. I think I understand now that a lot more of it was my fault than it was her fault. At the time, though, I didn't think that way.

• JOSEPH R BACHUS • WAYNE A McC
EDWARD R STANTON II • DAVID E T
EDWARD G BLACKMON • LEWIS E BC
WILLIAM L CYR • DAVID B DANN • AR
RRY LEE HAPPEL • CLABE HERALD Jr
BERNARD F KISTLER • RANDALL W MC
NFROE • EURIPIDES RUBIO Jr • WALTE
H III • JAMES W WASHKUHN • FRED J
FF • GEORGE E BRYANT • DAVID K DE
N • ROBERT E HARRIS • CARL D HOFF
ANN • PATRICK T McDERMOTT • HAR
PE • JOSEPH BACZALSKI • SYLVAN K B
ER • LLOYD S SMITH • DENNIS L DOO
• DAIN W MILLIMAN • JOHN E MITC
N • ERIC L SCHODERER • LOWELL E SC

EURIPEDES RUBIO, JR.

Born: March 1, 1938
        Ponce, Puerto Rico
Killed: November 8, 1966
        Tay Ninh, Republic of South Vietnam

LARRY D DE FILIPPIS • HEROLD T DE
HOMAS G FITZGIBBON • GEORGE

The Rubio family attending
the dedication ceremony
of Rubio Hall at Fort Bragg,
North Carolina,
on June 12, 1976.

Euripides Rubio

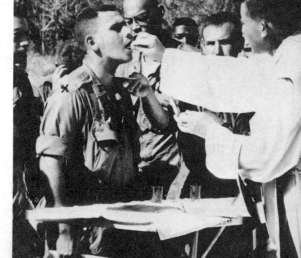

EURIPEDES RUBIO, SR.

Born: July 27, 1910
    Yauco, Puerto Rico
Father of Euripedes Rubio, Jr.

LUISA V. DE RUBIO

Born: June 21, 1911
    Peneulas, Puerto Rico
Mother of Euripedes Rubio, Jr.

A Privilege

FATHER: I am pensive. I am thinking of the Congressional Medal of Honor. He was the second recipient of the Congressional Medal of Honor in Puerto Rico, and the first Puerto Rican to win it in Vietnam. We attended a ceremony awarding him the medal at the office of the Secretary of State at the Pentagon, and we have just returned from a ceremony in New Jersey. These things are great honors, but they are difficult. They bring back the old feelings again. I somehow liked his soldier's cap. I always looked at the soldiers' caps.

MOTHER: We think of him still.

FATHER: Let me put my thoughts together. He was in the army some years. He was stationed at several places in the U.S.A., and in Germany for four years. But while he was in Germany he complained that he was not going to sit at a desk while the war was going on.

MOTHER: Still, we look at it as a privilege for him. I refer to the fact that they gave him a choice and he chose Vietnam. But I must be honest. We tried to dissuade him. I talked to him, as I usually had influence with him, but it was to no avail. He answered me, "You're not going to convince me, nor I convince you, either, so let's leave it alone."

FATHER: Going back in time, I recall that he said to me, "I want to go to Vietnam and defend democracy." I think he was born for this. Since he went to Germany, he was planning it. He always said he wanted to see a battle. Before he went to South Vietnam, he took vacations, to be with us. He spent one week with us and one week with his wife and two children. His oldest child was one year and ten months old, and the baby girl was seven months old by that time. He liked the peace of our home.

The day that he died, he was serving as the communications officer of his battalion, the 1st Battalion, 28th Infantry, 1st Infantry Division. A numerically superior force attacked them on that day. He had been in South Vietnam five months. He went there in July. When he saw that the enemy force was so large and was outnumbering the U.S. troops, he calmly called the air force and told them where the enemy was located. As you know, it was not easy to locate them. In order to direct our planes better, he took a smoke grenade and threw it toward the enemy troops to pinpoint them exactly. With bad luck, it fell in U.S. territory. He was worried, as the air force was coming to bomb the place where the smoke was. He went to reposition the grenade in the midst of tremendous bullet fire. He got the grenade and advanced, crawling, to throw it in the midst of the enemy territory. He was wounded four times. Soon the planes came and bombed the enemy troops. He fell for the last time, but his action turned the tide of battle. He was twenty-eight years old when he went to Vietnam, and five months later he died there.

MOTHER: They gave us the news and explained that he died as a real hero. I remember vividly that grim day.

FATHER: My wife, by the way, was very sick. When one of my sons returned home that day, he took the news very hard. He went crazy and burned the pot on the stove.

MOTHER: As I was so terribly sick, I was not told the news at first. My family let me sleep quietly. They were very protective and let me sleep in peace the whole night. But, of course, the next day came, and they had to tell me. After they gave me the bad news, the doctor came and gave me a shot. Our neighbors were very nice. They took care of me, and they all wanted to do something. I always said *no* to that. They enclosed me in my room, as everybody on our street was very moved and wanted to come and see me, and, of course, I was not up to that.

My husband and sons went to wait for our son's body at the airport. What an anguish! I barely knew what was going on. It was good for me that a friend of ours was a doctor, and his wife also was our friend, because they took care of me all the time. I was really so off and depressed that when we all went to my daughter-in-law's house, I didn't even recognize the place.

FATHER: When my wife went to the burial, she screamed and cried. She was in shock. After the burial, we returned to Ponce. Some weeks later my wife began to recover, but very slowly. It took all of us a long time to get away from our grief and sadness.

Later on, there were homages in his honor. The people in our city are proud of him, and we are also, because he died for what he believed in, democracy.

It was difficult to resign myself, but finally I did it, thinking that, after all, he went ahead to accomplish what he wanted and liked, although I get sad when I realize it cost him his life. He was a good leader and was always very secure of himself. He was never fooled. He knew that probably he could not get out alive from Vietnam. He also knew he could contribute to a victory for the U.S.A. there. When I think about this last point, it's good for me. It serves as a consolation. The truth is that he had a choice, and he volunteered to go to Vietnam.

MOTHER: I read the citation for the Medal of Honor, and it says he was wounded four times before he fell to the ground for the last time. The father of another soldier that was killed in Vietnam came to visit us. He tried to console me, as I was close to fainting. Everybody was scared about me.

FATHER: If my son were alive, he would be forty-four years old. I have always hoped that my grandson would decide on a military career, but he is closer and closer to being in show business.

MOTHER: I would like war to stop, and we must do something about it. I am sad for his death, but I hope it has not been in vain. I am proud he died defending our democracy.

FATHER: I think that all of those young men that refused to enter the army did so because they lacked courage. They think more of themselves than of our country and the future of our sons.

REGINALD A WATKINS · ALEXANDER
RON · CALVIN BOUKNIGHT · RICHAR
JOHN C ELZY III · LUTHER V GILREATH
ETON · BILLY M KNIGHT · REAVIS A M
OSVALDO AMODIAS · CHARLIE AND
D A BARNES · JIMMIE W BARTON · RO
BRY · CLARENCE V BEVERHOUDT · D
· ROY H BOWLING · THOMAS G BRA
E · WILLIAM R BURTON Jr · EMMETT L
EZ · MELVIN E COOKS · FRANCISCO
OX · MACK C COX · DONALD E CRAN
ROBERT L DAVIS · TOMMY A DOAK ·
RLES L ELLER · RALPH H ERNST · JAMES
RDEN D FORRESTER · MELVIN F FORT
N · MELVIN W GUNTER · OTIS J HAM

CLARENCE VERENO BEVERHOUDT
(FAMILY NAME:
VAN BEVERHOUDT)

Born: September 1, 1929
Williamslect, Curaçao,
Dutch West Indies
Killed: November 17, 1965
Republic of South Vietnam

· PALMER B MILES · MICHAEL J MILLE
WICZ · ARTHUR R MOODY III · CHAR

CLEONE J. BEVERHOUDT

Born: July 13, 1932
    St. Thomas, Virgin Islands
Widow of Clarence Vereno Beverhoudt

HYACINTH E. JAMES

Born: November 9, 1913
    St. Thomas, Virgin Islands
Mother-in-law of Clarence Vereno Beverhoudt

Let the White Men Kill

WIDOW: My husband was in the service for fifteen or sixteen years. He was in the army. I met him in the ninth grade, and we graduated from high school together here in St. Thomas. I decided that I was going into nursing, and he enlisted in the army. After four years he reenlisted, and he was in the Korean conflict. We got married in 1958 in Germany. He was stationed in Germany at the time. He was a sergeant then. We moved a lot. I have traveled. I love traveling. I had my son in 1959 in Germany, then we came back to Philadelphia.

Philadelphia is like my second home. I was trained in nursing in Philadelphia. I finished that in 1954. I graduated from Charlotte Amalie High School in 1951, and then I went into nursing. I graduated in June of 1954 from nursing. I worked at Cornell Medical Center in New York, and then I didn't like New York. I had been there a year, and I went back to Philadelphia. It was then that I decided I would go to Germany and get married. I traveled by boat, then I got to see several of the different areas in Europe. I had a brother stationed in Germany with the air force at the time. My first child was born in September of 1959, and we came back to the U.S. in November. We came into port in New York, and I relocated in Philadelphia. In February of 1960 I came home to St. Thomas, and I stayed until 1962, November of 1962, then I went to Hawaii. My husband was stationed in Hawaii.

For two years I was in Hawaii, and my daughter was born in Hawaii in 1963, in June of 1963. My daughter was also one of those hyaline membrane babies, like the Kennedy baby, but my daughter pulled through. She was very sick. Oh, I tell you. She was born in a private hospital, then she was so sick that she had to be hospitalized in the military hospital. We didn't have that kind of money to spend, so she was transferred to a military hospital and spent about thirteen or fifteen days there. Then she came home. People told me if I was not a nurse, she would not have lived, because she went through quite a lot. When she turned black and blue, I had to do mouth-to-mouth resuscitation, call the doctor, because I lived in Swofield Barracks, which was on the island of Oahu, and it took us an hour, back and forth. After Hawaii, I came back to Philadelphia, then visited him in Georgia. He was in Georgia from 1964 to 1965, August of 1965, when he was sent to Vietnam. He was killed in November of 1965, the seventeenth of November. I think he was sent off to Vietnam the twenty-third of August of 1965.

In November, my mother called me. I had a cousin who delivered me. She was a midwife here in St. Thomas. My mother called me and told me my cousin was sick. When my mother told me what was happening to her, I said, "Mommy, that's cancer. I'm coming home." She said, "Why not wait until December?" "No, Mommy. When my mind tells me to move, it's now," so I already had my trip planned to come home when the cable about my husband came. I was leaving the next day. The cable for my husband's death arrived the night before I left from Philadelphia, but I did not know anything about it. When the message came, my sister received it, and she kept it away from me. I had heard about this ambush in Vietnam on the news, and when I came home, I wrote to ask him if he was caught in the massacre. I didn't know he had been killed.

My father met me at the airport in Puerto Rico, and a priest that I had gone to school with. Nobody said anything until they got me in the right place. They had gone to the doctor, and the doctor had medication prepared, knowing that I was coming in. But I, being a nurse, didn't know how I was going to find my cousin, so I had traveled with some tranquilizers to calm me down. They took me to this cousin. She was in the hospital at the time. Then, they told me, "Come," so I said, "Aren't all of you going to let me spend even five minutes with my cousin?" Then they told me. My father-in-law told me of my husband's death. I couldn't believe it. I went up to my mother, and I asked her about what my father-in-law had told me, and I still couldn't believe it.

When my sister had received the telegram in Philadelphia, she had called my mother and father. I was already packed, because usually when I traveled with the kids I would be packed for two weeks, because I traveled a great deal. My sister enclosed other things in the suitcase, and I didn't know it until I unpacked. She enclosed black clothes and stuff. I had recently gone out and bought a black outfit. When I bought it, I said to myself, "I don't know why I'm doing this. I'm not going home for anyone." But the dress was a hundred and twenty dollars, and it came down to thirty dollars, so I thought it was a good buy, and I bought it. That's what I used when I came home. My sister had done all of this through the advice of my mother and my father.

MOTHER: We advised her to do this. We told her to go ahead and throw on top in the suitcase the things she would need. When she got here, we told her and took her over to her husband's mother and father. The mother said to her, "Look at this," and showed her a little book of prayers that she said every morning. The text for that morning was, "The Lord has given, and the Lord has taken away."

WIDOW: My husband died when he was leading the group. They had gone on a search-and-destroy mission and were returning. On returning, they were ambushed. The whole group was wiped out. He was killed, from what they say, from repeated bullets in his chest, and I do believe it, because the watch that he had on was busted, and it was loaded with blood. Apparently when he got shot, he must have put his hand to his chest. They sent everything, the chain with the blood that he wore, a chain of St. Christopher . . . a medal . . . and the watch, the busted watch, with the blood. I got that back after he was buried.

MOTHER: Remember, this is the time at which they were telling the United States that the Russians had a black eye, so that they could see things, whatever it is. The United States knew this, but they didn't believe it. It was some kind of instrument that the Russians had, and they could see in the dark. It was some dark box. There's some scientific name for it that I don't remember, but I've read about it, and the Vietnamese were seeing everything, they were knowing what our men were doing there. The Vietnamese knew, and our men were not aware of it. It seems that our men thought they were doing a secret affair, but the enemy was aware of what they were doing, and our men didn't know this. So the Vietnamese picked out the leaders, all the leaders. When they picked them off, the others were upset, you know, the confusion. They said that was the first major massacre that they had in Vietnam. The first major massacre.

WIDOW: I didn't know there was so much unhappiness in this world until my husband was killed. That's when I became unhappy. I had always been happy. My family had always been happy. I'm the oldest of six children, four girls and two boys. In his family, he was the oldest of eight, but the father had an outside child, so there were nine children for his father, and he was the oldest son. His mother had four boys and four girls. My husband was always very much admired, and he was really a gentleman. As many people say, I put him on a pedestal, because he was a good husband. He respected my ideas and where I stood, and he tried to please me and to keep me happy. As I say, things were much better then. It's rough here in these Virgin Islands.

In Philadelphia, we had the Veterans Administration to go

to. We had the PX that we could go to. We could go to any PX in any of the states. In St. Thomas, the nearest one is in Puerto Rico. You have to have transportation. You have to fly in a plane. You have to pay seventy dollars round trip, and then about twenty or twenty-five dollars by taxi if you do not know how to travel by bus, so it makes no sense to travel, to go there to shop. To get my ID renewed, I must pay that seventy dollars to go down there. I have to go to Puerto Rico to get my ID renewed. There's no facilities, no arrangements made here on St. Thomas. I was told about a VA office out in the Haversight area, but they are more geared for the men, the living veterans themselves, not dependents. This is what I find. The dependents are like an outcast. No one has done anything for them. I myself have been saying I would like to get involved in that, but I just don't have the time, because I'm involved in other things, plus my housework. I have a full-time job working for the government, for the Virgin Islands government, two children who are in college, and I have to work extra to keep them going, because they do not have scholarships.

When my husband died, I got the ten thousand dollars' insurance. My daughter was two years old. She was two years, five months, and my son was six years old. My son will be twenty-four this year. He's completed his pre-med, but he wants to go on to medical school, so now he's working. He graduated in May from Howard University. He graduated May 14. He's trying to see where he can get the financing for medical school now. He lives in the state of Maryland, so he's hoping that he would be able to get some kind of educational benefits there, and he's working at the capital at the present time with our representative from the Virgin Islands. He's working in his office for the time being. When I got married, I planned my life out, my education for the kids, everything, so this is very frustrating for me.

When my husband was killed, this was when I realized I was unhappy. The first thing people would say was, "Oh, that's a lot of money you're going to get." Ten thousand dollars is nothing for two growing children when you have to buy shoes every three months. They were growing, and I had to buy clothes. I had a sick child, and I was always running to the doctor. Sometimes at two or three o'clock in the morning she would start with these temperatures. I would have to leave my job in the city of Philadelphia and go to her. That means I had to take two to three transfers before I could get to the navy hospital. As a nurse, thank god, I knew what to do. With the hyaline membrane disease, she had underdeveloped lungs. She was also allergic to milk products. She was vomiting all the time, and she had dental problems. I mean, it was hard.

While I was in the States, the people at my job were considerate. I was working at Jefferson Hospital at the time, at the time my husband was killed. From the time my husband left to go to Fort Benning, Georgia, I realized the danger he was in. We knew he was going to Vietnam, and I was not myself from the time I knew he was going to Vietnam. My co-workers were very good during all of this time. After he was killed, and after I went back to work, that's when it really hit. My memory was terrible. The doctors would give me orders, and I had to make notes. If I didn't read the note, I was lost. It was a psychological effect that his death had on me, that I just couldn't believe it, that this was it. I think he felt, too, before he left . . . I don't think he thought he was going to die . . . he tried to reassure me of that, but he said he might get it in the arm or leg. When he wrote to my father, he told him that after he got to Vietnam, he felt . . .

MOTHER: Clarence used to write to my husband. I remember the last letter he got. He said, "This is terrible. You don't know anywhere you can go to get me out of this? This is terrible." We didn't know where to go, so we started praying. We were praying to get him out, but not *how*. It's after he died that we said, "You know, we were praying. We should be more careful how we pray." We didn't think about that. We asked that he come out, but we didn't specify *how*. He did come out, but *how*. After he got to Vietnam, when he saw what was happening, I guess when things got so terrible, he wanted out. I remember when his body came home. Hubert Humphrey came to the funeral, him and the governor of the Virgin Islands at that time.

My grandson, he was only six years old at the time, and one visitor noticed him and said, "Why are you looking so sad?" He said, "Why did they have to kill him?" He and his father were very close. He used to march around like him, to copy his father. Somebody had explained that he wouldn't see his daddy again, so he said, "Why did they have to kill him?" He said to me, "You see, St. Anthony didn't answer our prayers." I was just left without words. My mind was full of sadness, and I couldn't think of how to answer him. I didn't expect him to come out with something like that. We had prayed to St. Anthony for him to come home, but we failed to say, "alive," and he didn't come home alive. I could answer that now, but then it just hit me like a bombshell.

WIDOW: They gave me a choice about whether to open the coffin or not. They said that their advice would be not to. Since there was so much disease in Vietnam, they would be exposing the community if they were to open it. I said, "Well, let me remember him the way he was in life." I think this way is better, because if I had opened it and seen it just looking like some body or parts looking like a body, it would have been very bad. I wanted to remember him like he was.

If there is another war, I will get out, and I will tell those mothers and wives to keep their sons out. Let the white man fight that war, because in the Virgin Islands, we have no recognition. We are supposed to be a territory of the United States, and we don't have commissary benefits. We have no commissary here. We have no VA hospital here. We have no benefits. We must leave St. Thomas to get our benefits. Like I say, I don't see why we were fighting. For what?

A lot of people in this world suffer. A lot of people need help, and that is why I went into nursing. I don't only nurse the poor. I have a garden, so I nurse the plants. I have animals around me. I always have a dog around. I have raised goats. When we were growing up, I would raise chickens. I take care of things. I don't see why people should suffer more because of war.

MOTHER: As regards the Vietnam War, I think it was an unnecessary war. Those people have been fighting for numbers and numbers of years, and they were satisfied to go on fighting, so it was an unnecessary war. What has the United States gotten out of it? I thought it was an unnecessary war.

WIDOW: I have very close white friends, and I get along with all of them, and people are predicting there is going to be another war pretty soon. From yesterday's observation, I am afraid this is going to happen. Yesterday these guys from Kentucky were on maneuver in Puerto Rico, and the military gave them a trip to St. Thomas. Free. The military plane flew them over for the day. One of the boys is a fraternity buddy of my son's. He is a lieutenant, a first lieutenant, in the army, and two of his friends were with him. They came, because, you know, this was a million-dollar treat. I didn't tell them that I understand the next war is supposed to be fought in the Caribbean. There have just been maneuvers in Puerto Rico.

MOTHER: Yes. You can see it. You can feel it. In Central America, they are angry with the United States. They are close to us here in St. Thomas. I guess the United States is trying to help them, but I don't know if we know, really, what's going on in those countries, if we are helping the right group. You don't know, really, if we are doing the right thing, helping one faction. You never know what will be the outcome. If the United States sends in help, it would be the same thing they were doing in Vietnam, and, then, instead of helping, they might do just the opposite, like in Vietnam, where things got out of control.

There are a lot of jealousies toward the United States, but . . . it's just human. . . . the people in other nations who have jealousies in them, they want to be like the United States, but yet they have jealousies because they can't have this, and they can't have that, like the United States. With all these things going on in these countries, it's hard to know what's going on. The people are so poor, and you would say you would want to help them, the poor people, but there are other people in those countries who are keeping the poor people in that position. They want to keep them in that position.

If you would look around, you would see how these people

are so poor. And these poor people see that the people in the United States had a revolution when they wanted to get out of something, so they say, "I guess I'll have a revolution, too." Then they say, "Those people who had a revolution in the United States, they don't want us to have a revolution to be like them." It's a terrible thing going on all over. But then, in these Central American countries, and in many other countries, too, even in some European countries, everybody wants to go to the United States, because that means you have a chance to make a future if you want to. Then all this dope comes in, and you have a bigger problem, you know. I don't know. I don't know where we're going.

WIDOW: Well, I have only to tell myself that I would like to be prepared. I have food. This is why I'm into gardening, and I try to plan the things I know we can use, like the fruits and vegetables. I don't have to have meat. Mainly fruits and vegetables, and some meat if I can get it, or some other kind of protein. But I can see it coming. The main thing I'm worrying about is the future of my children and grandchildren.

You can see things going on here now. You can feel the tension. When I say the next war is going to be in this area, I was at a dinner, and this general or colonel, he said for the years he had been in the service, he had never been in this part of the world, and he was thinking that the next war would be fought here. This was at a big banquet we had for the veterans. This was in January 1980. This was so far back. This was when there was a lot of tension in Cuba and Panama, and in Venezuela, where they're killing all these priests and nuns, all these religious people. I mean, it's really sad around here, and when you see the drug influx . . . even the soldiers. When they come, they know the spots on this island where to go and get the drugs. You can see them. It's really sad.

I can sit by myself—I don't live too far from the airport, and, after the airport, it's just ocean—I can sit and watch military maneuvers. This is the Americans in Puerto Rico. I can see parts of Puerto Rico from my porch. Every year the Puerto Rican National Guard has its maneuvers, but that's not it this time.

These guys that came the other day, they were from Kentucky, and they are in the army there. They flew from Kentucky to Puerto Rico, and they came over here to visit me, and they flew them free on the military transport. I say this is only an appetizer. I have also been told that the Puerto Rican National Guard maneuvers this year are different, because they are not only bringing the army in from the United States, but they are bringing them in from Central American countries, also. Yesterday a week ago, there were about ten military transports here. They came in about six-thirty and they left about three-thirty. They had a navy boat in here, and the navy transports were in here. It was here all weekend, but it's not unusual for them to be here. They have their winter and summer maneuvers here.

MOTHER: When you hear the stories of what's happening in Central America, you wonder. You worry about it.

WIDOW: The United States always seems to have to go in with guns, not with other things, like food, like education. No. It's always kill, kill, kill. Kill or be killed. This is why you have all these maniacs going around killing when they have problems, and they can't take care of their families. What do they do? Kill everybody, and then turn around on themselves. You see? Instead of killing when you have a problem, you should talk. This is what I tell the teenagers: "If you can't speak to your mother, your father, your sisters or brothers, your teachers, go to somebody who can help you." I say to these kids, "Your friends are just as dumb as you are, so try to get the confidence of someone that you can rely on." Or write it. If you cannot talk, write it to somebody, because some of them, they do not know how to talk, but they can do better by putting it on paper. These countries should do the same.

We haven't experienced war in this part of the world. I have lived in Hawaii, and I have talked to the Hawaiians, and many of them have told us about the bullets that they heard and how war sounded. And then the experience in Germany. My landlady there told me things. But we in the Caribbean, and even in the United States, have not experienced war, and this, apparently, is where the next war is going to be, because it's only a stepping stone from the Panama Canal Zone to here, and then into the United States, because there is Florida.

MOTHER: You can see the buildup, and you say, "Why are they doing this, and why are they doing this?" It's because they are planning something. At best, the United States has been so good, so willing to help other people with food and medicine. I was in Santo Domingo after a disaster. They had two hurricanes there, and it was devastated. An American boat came in that day, and you should have seen the crowds of people that just went to look at this boat, and they wouldn't let any of the soldiers onto the land. The boat was just in the harbor, but the people were so happy just to look at this boat. They saw that the Americans were the only country that came to their aid and dropped by helicopter food and medicine to them that they couldn't get otherwise. And just to see the boat out there, the people gathered, and they were just looking, you know. I mean, just crowds of people, whatever could press around the waterfront, just watching a boat. They couldn't even see the people on the boat. They were just looking at the boat. This was when I was in Santo Domingo about three, four years ago. So . . . but yet, although they are grateful, underneath they are resentful in some way that this nation is so powerful. So I don't know. The United States isn't really beloved by too many people.

I've traveled a lot. I've been in Europe, and I've seen some of our people . . . because I see myself as an American, too . . . but they don't treat the European people nice. The people in Europe, they are so courteous and polite, and, although the Americans treat them like that, they are still polite. You could see it's the American dollar, just the American dollar. They think that since these people are from the United States that they may have money. Things like that are not good. You see, each of us could be an ambassador for the United States. The people in Europe are probably wrong, anyway, because most Americans are not rich. Maybe they have just enough money to take a trip.

SAMMIE GRIFFIN · DANIEL J GUILMET ·
· STEPHEN J LUKASIEWSKI · PAUL L GOR·
·ON · RONALD W PORTER · GEORGE W
THOMPSON · FRED A TRYON Jr ·
·SEPH P YATSKO Jr · LOUIS J CUNNINGHA·
·R · ERNEST F LOSOYA · BENNIE ROMERO
· RUSSELL VIVEIROS ALMEIDA · LEE E NOR·
·ATTERHENRY · GEORGE I MIMS Jr ·
·RVIN L SHIPMAN · DONALD C SMITH ·
·MPBELL · GEORGE S COSTELLO ·
·LD E MULLINAX · RONALD W NICKERSO·
·GHT · EDWARD F GOLD · MAX D LUKEN·
· JAMES C WISE Jr · JAMES A GRUEZKE ·
· WILLIAM K COLWELL · EARL L CROMW·
·ELL B JEFFORDS · GEORGE E JOHNSTON
·HOVITZ · LYNN C RENNER · FERNANDO

DONALD CLAYTON SMITH

Born: **August 27, 1937**
          San Angelo, Texas
Killed: **December 20, 1965**
          Tuy Hoa, Republic of South Vietnam

·BERT L KRAUS · JACK D McCLURE ·
·IN R WOODS Jr · CHARLES R ALLEN ·
·HAEL L McKINSON · VERNON L SHELLMAN

1. Don Smith and Heather Brandon.
2. Quentin and Errol Smith. 3. Christi Gryder.
4. Larry and Sue Gryder.
5. Rovie Mae Gunnels.
6. Don Smith. 7. Tommye Baldwin.

PEGGY CHRISTINA "CHRISTI" GRYDER

Born: June 21, 1971
     Odessa, Texas
Niece of Donald Clayton Smith

SUZANNE SMITH "SUE" GRYDER

Born: February 24, 1945
     McCamey, Texas
Sister of Donald Clayton Smith, mother of Christi

HEATHER PATRICIA BRANDON

Born: December 9, 1939
     San Angelo, Texas
Cousin of Donald Clayton Smith

Questions at Eleven

CHRISTI: Well, I know that Don died in a plane crash. I know he is my uncle. I know that he is a good man and all that. I don't know a lot about him, but I know he is a good man.

Sometimes my mother talks about him. She tells about when they were younger and Granddad took them hunting or something like that. I think she feels bad about it sometimes, because I see her thinking, you know, and that's when I feel that sometimes she's thinking about it.

My mother said it was a terrible war and a lot of people died in it, and that's all I know. I don't know what cities fought in it, or who ever fought in it, or where all the people came from.

HEATHER: What do you want to know about it?

CHRISTI: Who fought in it.

HEATHER: It was a war that all America fought in. There were sixty thousand American men killed in Vietnam. Some women died over there, too.

CHRISTI: How did women die? I mean, *women* were killed?

HEATHER: Some women who were over there, like nurses, died. As far as I know, there were about nine women who died in Vietnam. One of them was killed by enemy action, I think, and one died in a plane crash, helping to get children out of Vietnam. It was mostly men, though, who were killed, men like your Uncle Don. They were from every state in the United States, from big cities, from little towns, all over there fighting, in Vietnam.

CHRISTI: What were they fighting for?

HEATHER: Well, at the time, I think, many of them thought . . . do you know about communism?

CHRISTI: No.

HEATHER: Okay. Communism is a different form of government than we have in America. In America, we call our form of government a "democracy," and countries that call themselves "communist" are countries like Russia and Cuba. In Vietnam, there were two parts. The top part was called "North Vietnam," and the bottom part was called "South Vietnam." The country was divided across the middle. The north part wanted to be communist, and the south part didn't, and there was a civil war. Do you know about the American Civil War?

CHRISTI: Yeah.

HEATHER: Okay. Well, there was a civil war over there, like the North and the South in America years ago were fighting against each other. In Vietnam, the North and South were fighting against each other, and America decided to get involved in that war. Some American politicians said they wanted to get involved because they wanted to help the South Vietnamese people. Many of the men who went over to fight felt they were going to help the

South Vietnamese people to be free, to be able to choose their own form of government. Now, later, people thought we should not have been over there, because it was a civil war, and they should have settled their own problems, like we settled our own problems in the American civil war. One of the things a lot of people feel sad about now is that so many Americans died or got hurt over there, and maybe they shouldn't have been over there in the first place.

Do they ever talk to you about Vietnam in school?

CHRISTI: Well, they don't really talk about that. They talk about some wars, but they never really talked about Vietnam.

HEATHER: Most teachers don't. Most history books don't have a lot about Vietnam in them, either, so that kids your age have a hard time knowing what it was all about.

CHRISTI: I don't even know when it got started.

HEATHER: Well, different dates are given. We had people over there in the forties, but you hear people say the first part of the war for us was around 1962 or 1964, and that it ended in 1973 or 1975. It was the longest war America was ever involved in. It went on for years and years. Have you ever asked your mom much about the war?

CHRISTI: No . . .

HEATHER: Why's that?

CHRISTI: Well, I think it makes her feel sad to talk about it.

HEATHER: Would you like for her to talk to you about it?

CHRISTI: Yeah, but I don't blame her. I wouldn't want to talk about it either. It'd make me sad, and I would just break out in tears, and . . . I'd sort of get mad at my kid, if something like that happened to me. Well, I mean, if she didn't want to talk to me about it . . . I mean, I can't force her or anything.

HEATHER: Have you ever asked her to?

CHRISTI: Well, I asked her some things about it, but I never asked her to really talk to me about it.

SUE: What do you want to know, Christi?

CHRISTI: How did Don get started in the war?

SUE: Don went into the air force because he expected to be drafted. He didn't want to be drafted, so he finished college and he got a commission in the air force because he wanted to fly.

CHRISTI: How do they draft people? I mean, if you don't want to go, do you have to, or what?

SUE: It's hard not to. There are people who do it, that fight it on grounds of religious convictions, you know. They say they don't believe in killing, they don't believe in war, they just don't believe in warfare. They believe in peace.

CHRISTI: Could Don have done that?

SUE: Yes, but he didn't want to do it. He didn't want to make the air force a career, but he went because he wanted to fly. He wanted to fly well. He had the best instruction that's available in the world, as far as flying goes, and he knew that when he got out he'd have a real good job flying airplanes. He wanted to be an airline pilot.

CHRISTI: Did someone ever order Errol [Don's brother] to be drafted?

SUE: No, Errol never had to be drafted, because he married real young, and he was in school, and they had a baby.

HEATHER: There are rules about being drafted. They are called "laws." They change from time to time, but a lot of the time, or most of the time, if you are eighteen years old, and you're a man, you have to go down to a place called the "draft board," and you have to register . . . give them your name and where you live, how old you are, and everything like that. And now that puts your name in a computer, and they have the names of all the eighteen-year-old men in the country. If they wanted to draft, if they wanted to call up some of these people whose names they have in the computer, it is by law that they would have to go. Now, some people don't want to go. They do have choices to make, but they are hard choices, Christi. During Vietnam, some people who were drafted didn't go. One way people can not go is to say they are "conscientious objectors." That means they are religiously or morally opposed to war or killing. But you have to prove that.

CHRISTI: How do you do that?

HEATHER: Well, you have to go before the draft board, and it can be hard. It might not be easy. You cannot just all of a sudden say, "I'm a conscientious objector." You have to prove it. Some churches don't believe in wars, like the Quaker Church. It doesn't believe in war or killing. So, if you have been a Quaker all your life, that can help you, you know, for the draft board to say, "Okay, you are really a conscientious objector, and you do not have to go to war." They wouldn't make a Quaker go, perhaps, but he might have to do some other kind of service for the country instead, like work in a hospital or something.

CHRISTI: Like Hawkeye on *M*A*S*H*?

HEATHER: Well, Hawkeye was in Korea. That was another war. That war was somewhat similar to Vietnam. Hawkeye might have been a conscientious objector, but I don't think he was.

Another way that people didn't go, who were drafted, is that they ran away. They ran away from America. They ran to places like Canada, and they are called "deserters." Some of them still live in other countries. So you can run away and not go. Some people also got arrested instead of going.

CHRISTI: Did they get in trouble like . . . try to rob a bank?

HEATHER: No, all they did is say, "No, I am not going to go to war," and they got arrested for that.

CHRISTI: How old was Don when he died?

SUE: Twenty-eight. Almost ten years younger than I am now. And when I think of him, I still think of him as my big brother, because he would be, if he were here.

HEATHER: I remember getting really mad when I was thirty, and I was angry because I was older than Don ever got to be.

SUE: That's what Mother said: "When we see him again, he will still be twenty-eight, and we'll all be old and wrinkled." He never got old.

HEATHER: Do you know how long Don had been dead when you were born?

CHRISTI: No.

HEATHER: Do you know when he was killed? He was killed in 1965, so by the time you were born, he had been dead nearly six years.

CHRISTI: You're kidding!

HEATHER: No. It's the truth.

CHRISTI: Gollee. Did he know my brother was going to be born? Did he know you were married to Dad?

SUE: He knew Larry and I were married. He would have come to the wedding, but he was flying cross-country and couldn't come, but we saw him on our honeymoon. Then he came to McCamey at Thanksgiving, and we all saw him then. He didn't know your brother was going to be born.

CHRISTI: Did you name my brother after him?

SUE: Yes. "Don Smith Gryder." I just take things like that for granted, that you knew that.

CHRISTI: I had an idea he was, but I didn't really know for sure. I want to look at the things you have in there, in that trunk.

SUE: There's nothing in there, just a bunch of letters.

CHRISTI: I don't care.

SUE: Do you want to look in the trunk like we did last night? Did you know that's what we were doing?

CHRISTI: Well, I had an idea, because I looked in the bedroom.

SUE: You should have come in.

CHRISTI: Yeah, but I didn't want to disturb you. I was afraid you would get mad at me, but I want to look at the things you have in there, in that trunk. I want to look at it. I want to see the letter that said that Uncle Don is dead. That's what I want to see, really. This isn't to be cruel, but I thought it would be neat, because no one's uncle or relative has ever gotten killed in the Vietnam War that I know of in school or anything. It doesn't make me feel good or anything. I just felt like I needed to look at it. Not need to, but I wanted to.

HEATHER: Would it make you feel special?

CHRISTI: Yeah. But I don't mean that to be weird, or anything.

HEATHER: I don't think that's weird. How would you feel special?

CHRISTI: That I would feel proud of Don.

SUE: Okay, Christi. I will show it to you later. Now, what else do you want to know about Don?

CHRISTI: Well, I'd like to know how they found Don after his plane crashed.

SUE: Christi, I really don't even know the answer to that. It was just on the ground, and when the soldiers could get in, I guess they just went and found the body, or whatever was left of the body. Do you know how his plane crashed?

CHRISTI: No. I think I was told once, but I don't remember.

SUE: He was shot down. He was flying troops and supplies into Vietnam from Okinawa, from an air base in Okinawa to an air base at Tuy Hoa in Vietnam.

CHRISTI: The supplies, what were they?

SUE: Well, he had been carrying troops most of the time, but the day he was killed, he was carrying supplies. I don't know for sure what it was, but I think we heard from someone that when his plane went down there was a red glow or something in the sky, and I've just always guessed that he was carrying gasoline or fuel, and ammunition, maybe.

CHRISTI: That was easy to blow up?

SUE: Right. Tuy Hoa was the place in Vietnam where he was killed. There was an airport, a military airport, a landing strip, for planes to come in, but his plane didn't get in. There were people, you know, the enemy, shooting. The enemy was trying to shoot the planes down from the ground, and they hit his plane, and I've always guessed he had gasoline in it, and that it all exploded.

CHRISTI: Why did he have to be in it, be the one in the gasoline plane?

SUE: He didn't have to be. He didn't have to fly that day.

CHRISTI: He didn't?

SUE: He volunteered. He was doing that kind of flying, but it wasn't his turn to fly that day. He volunteered for someone else.

CHRISTI: Oh. How many years was he in the war already before he died?

SUE: Well, he had been on Okinawa just about a month. Remember, I told you he was home for Thanksgiving?

CHRISTI: Yes.

SUE: Well, a month later he was dead. Thanksgiving. And by Christmastime, he was dead. He came home to McCamey Thanksgiving. He had been on Okinawa a month when he died.

CHRISTI: The boys in my class, they all talk about war. The kids that talk about war are the boys. There's two boys in my class, and they think they're superheroes. They have all these guns and everything, and talk about it all the time.

HEATHER: Do you think they know anything about war?

CHRISTI: No, not really. Well, they know pretty much about it. They know how the Civil War and others got started. You know boys. They like to know about that stuff.

SUZANNE SMITH GRYDER

**Born: February 24, 1945
McCamey, Texas
Sister of Donald Clayton Smith**

I Didn't Know

When we first heard that Don was missing, Larry and I were living in Andrews. We didn't have a phone, but we were both home. The lady we were renting from had a telephone, and we got a call. She came over to get us and said the call was for *"Mary* Gryder," but I just thought she forgot my name, and I went to answer the phone. The operator said, "No. This call is for *Larry* Gryder." I knew then that something was wrong, because it was Mother calling. We got Larry. Mother talked to him, and he came out and told me that Don was missing in action.

It was something I never expected. I couldn't believe it. I never worried about him. I was just too stupid to know there was any danger, I guess. Anyway, we packed up and went to Odessa. Mother and Daddy were at Aunt Tommye's house. All of us went on down to McCamey then. We hung around for two or three days there and then went back to Andrews. Finally, I just couldn't stand it anymore, so Larry quit his job, and we went to McCamey and moved in with Mother and Daddy. Larry was tired of oil field work, anyway, so he started looking for a job in Odessa during this time.

We waited and waited and waited. Don's wife, Louise, called different people. She wrote letters with Mother, trying to see if they could get somebody to do something, find out what happened, what his status was. They kept telling us that the enemy fire was so bad where he went down that they just couldn't get in, but that they were going to. They kept saying, "We will, as soon as we can," which didn't help us much. It was just a waiting game. Errol called often, came home as often as he could. The waiting was really hard, waiting and worrying.

Mother told me what it was like when they got the telegram saying he was missing. Daddy got it at the shop while she was at home. He came home at about the time he usually did for lunch, but she said that when she saw his face she knew something was wrong. He had the telegram in his hand, and she had to pry his fingers open to get it out. He hadn't said a word, but she knew what it was before she even saw it.

I remember the day the second telegram came. Daddy was out playing golf, and Mother and I had been out. We had just driven up to the house when ole Ernie Reeves brought the telegram. He was the operator at Western Union. He didn't want to give it to us. He wanted daddy. He said, "Where is Olin?" We both knew exactly what it said when he did that. Mother said, "He's not here," and Ernie said, "Well, where is he? I'll take it to him." My mother said, "No. I want it. Give it to me." He did, and that was that. Don was dead. We went on into the house.

Mother was very calm. I said, "I'm going to get Daddy." She said, "No. There's no reason to get him now. Let him finish playing golf." She didn't want to tell him, I guess, but I couldn't stand it. I said, "You stay right here and don't do anything. I'm going to get him." And I did. I drove up, and he was there with four or five of his friends. I remember exactly where they were, right across the street from C. W. Brown's house, getting ready to putt. I just drove up right next to the fence. I waited there for him, and, of course, he knew. I said, "We got the telegram, Daddy," and . . . oh, shit . . . it's so hard . . . his face just . . . I can't describe it. He came home. I don't know if he told those guys he was with or not. I think he just got in the car with me and came home. He walked in and started crying. I think that was part of Mother's problem. She held back so hard. Daddy at least got a little of it out.

We started making phone calls, called Errol. They sent us further communications, when his remains would be sent back, stuff like that. I don't remember how long it took. Yes, I do. It was February the sixth when we got the second telegram, and we buried him on February 14, Valentine's Day.

Louise didn't want to bury him in McCamey, because she said that every time he came back to McCamey he was a little depressed about the changes in McCamey, the way everything was so run down. It was just a boom town, and everybody started moving out, and it looked dead. Louise didn't want him buried in Tyler, because if we buried him there, she would be passing where he was buried every day. She didn't want that. It was just a flukey decision to bury him at Fort Sam Houston. I don't know why we did it. I think everybody was trying to pretend it didn't happen.

You know, some funny things do happen at funerals. You know how everybody always gathers together? At Granddaddy's funeral, Uncle Clayton and Uncle Shorty were on the front porch arguing about who they'd all be gathering for next. They were about three sheets to the wind. Shorty would say, "It'll be me," and Clayton would say, "No. It'll be me." They're both dead now, but no one ever thought that Don would be dead before he was thirty.

Mother flew to Tyler and went with Louise to San Antonio for the funeral. Daddy and Errol and his wife and Larry and I drove down together. It's strange, the things you remember. I remember the moon, the man in the moon, looking as if he had a sad face that night. We were driving at night down that long, empty road, and the man in the moon looked sad. One of my big fears was that Mother would get there and insist on having the casket opened. It was supposed to be a closed-casket service, and I knew she better not do that. Had he been dead a short time, it would have been all right, to check it out, but I didn't want her to do that. I told Daddy, and he said, "No, I don't think so. I don't think she'll do that."

The funeral home was close to the base. We went there after we checked into the motel. Louise had said she didn't want any flowers, but somebody had already put some flowers out. Louise just became overwrought. She ran out and kept saying things like, "Don's too big. They couldn't put him in that little box. That just couldn't be Don."

The funeral was the next day. Very simple. We had a ceremony in the chapel and then went out to the cemetery and had the salute, and they played taps. Everybody got through that very well. But that wasn't the hard part. It never is. I stayed with Louise most of the time. She had a harder time at that point than the rest of us did. We suffered later.

Part of it was shock, and part of it was just pretense: "We'll go home, and things will get back to normal." Just trying to pretend it didn't happen. That's what I did when Mother died. I just put it out of my mind. I just thought that if I didn't acknowledge it and grieve that things would go on like they always had. I wasn't consciously thinking any of this. Part of it was the shock, in both cases. I'm sure with mother it just took a little while to set in. Nobody wanted to talk about it. I wanted to cry, but I didn't even know how. We were all worried about each other. Everybody thought that nobody wanted to talk about it. Nobody wanted to upset anybody, so, as a result, none of us really did much comforting of each other.

I don't even remember how long we stayed in San Antone when we buried Don. Probably two nights. I don't remember anything about the ride back home. This was in February, and I was three months pregnant. My son Don was born August twenty-ninth. My brother Don was born August twenty-seventh. I had labor induced. I thought later, "Well, hell, I should have had it induced two days earlier." I don't know why that would have made a difference to me, but it's pretty ironic, really, that my Don was born that close to Don's birthday. He didn't even know I was pregnant. I found out after he was missing.

Mother died as a direct result of losing Don. Cause and effect. Direct. She didn't change immediately. She came back and tried to act as if everything was all right. She did this for a while, but the summer after Don died she went into a pretty bad depression. She layed around a lot. I remember we had a barbecue at the house. My Aunt Opal and Uncle Grover came. Mother was tired all the time; she was in a reclining lawn chair. Opal got pretty frank with her and said, "Look, you know you're going to have to do something, or you're going to die. You're wasting away. I'm just real worried about you. You have to do something." After that, she did get better for a while. She was fun again, but her moods would change. She really didn't care about anything, and she felt guilty about it. Like my kids. She cared about them, but she turned me down on baby-sitting them a couple of times when we wanted to go somewhere on weekends. She said, "I just don't feel like it." But she did get some better. She was playful again sometimes.

I don't know. Maybe if she'd had some kind of help. I didn't even see it at the time, though. I didn't recognize what was going on. I didn't even consider some kind of counseling. Errol said he did, and that he even talked to her about it, but I didn't. I was just stupid. You know how people are about that sort of thing: "God, you're crazy to talk to a psychiatrist." Even I felt that for a long time, that it means you're crazy. People don't see it that way anymore. I don't think they do. The ones I know don't. I think about that, and I feel guilty about that. But then I think, "Well, hell, you were just twenty years old." I knew that she was having problems, but I didn't know what to do about it. I urged her to go to the doctor and get a checkup. She did that, and everything was fine. The electrocardiogram was fine. The whole bit. This was not very long before she died.

She died of a heart attack. Massive. I forgot what they called it. Just a massive heart attack. I used to know the language, but I don't remember it anymore. The doctor said it was instant. Something burst, I guess. I don't know. Dr. Cooper didn't autopsy her. Nobody wanted him to. He said, "It's not fair to you and your kids if you don't have one done." That is bullshit, but at everyone's insistence, we did finally decide to have an autopsy done. I just don't believe that whatever she died of I'm going to die of, unless I bring it on myself. No one else in the family has ever died of heart problems.

She was fifty-five when she died. The twenty-second of December. Almost eight years to the day after Don was killed. She had ups and downs, but I think she knew. She knew what was coming. I remember that at the very end she had Dad in there, trying to teach him how to run the washing machine. There are little things like that I can look back on now and remember. He must have thought that was odd. All those years, and Daddy had never touched that washing machine. He was so dependent on her. She and I would be talking, just talking about things in general, and she'd stop and say, "Now, Sue, when I die, don't you grieve over me." She said that several times. I'd say, "Oh, Mother, you're not going to die," which was a stupid thing to say.

The day she died, the twenty-second, we were planning to get up in the morning and go to McCamey. It was time to go home for Christmas. Larry answered the phone at five-thirty in the morning. That's the first time in my life a call at that time didn't scare me. I thought it was the plant calling for Larry to come to work or something. I can remember it so clearly. Larry was listening, and he started breathing hard. I never dreamed it would be Mother, even at that point. Larry wanted to call Errol, and I said, "No. I'll call him." He answered the telephone, and he knew something was wrong. I just said, "Errol?" He said, "Sue, what is it?" I said, "It's Mother," and he said, "I'll be there as soon as I can get there."

There were times, you know, when it was real hard when Don was missing. Mother did a lot of crying by herself. I went in her bedroom one night. She was in bed, and she was crying. I don't know why we all thought we had to keep our hurt to ourselves. We were trying not to upset each other. That night, though, she said, "Sue, he's just got to come home. He's just got to." I said, "He will, Mother, he will." I knew he wouldn't. I don't know when I gave up, but I gave up at some point. I knew in my mind by then that he was dead. She said, "I'm sorry. I shouldn't be putting you through this." She went through a lot of pain. If she had been able to let it out a little better, she might have been all right.

Errol had a hard time. I think we all probably would have had a much easier time if we'd just sat down and talked and cried. I cried a lot with Larry, especially after Mother died. I accepted Don's death better then than I would now, because I was young, and I didn't question the war in Vietnam at that point. I really wasn't interested in anything about that. I was just trying to have a good time before it happened. It wasn't until later that I started thinking about the war itself, but I do know that Don believed in what he was doing at the time, because he told me he did. He said, "We're going to help them achieve the right of self-determination," or something like that, and I don't think he had any fear. I asked him one time, "Don, aren't you ever afraid of crashing when you're flying?" I wasn't talking about Vietnam, just about flying. He said, "Hell, no. I love flying. If I ever crash, at least it'll be quick," so I don't think he had any fears in that direction. Errol said one time, "I worry about Don from the time he was hit until the time he was dead. From the time he knew he was going to die. I worry about those seconds." Errol wouldn't even say anything like that to me for a long time.

I used to have dreams. Someone would be knocking on the window, trying to get in, and it'd be Don. I haven't had those in a long time. In the dreams, I kept trying to let him in, and I couldn't let him in. There was no way I could get a door or a window open to let him in. I had a lot of dreams like that. I even had good dreams, that he was back, that he was home, and everything was okay. But I miss him. I still miss him. I don't miss him actively like I used to. For a long time, there wasn't a day that went by that I didn't think about him. There's probably not a day goes by now that I don't think about him a little bit, but I really missed him, really missed him, for a long time. I miss Christmas at home, and Christmas will never, ever be the same again. I dread it every year, and that's something I've done to myself. I mean, hell, what if it had happened in June or July? The date doesn't make any difference.

I remember one long, drawn-out conversation we had after we got the telegram that Don was dead. Aaron Cranford came by, and he and Daddy and Errol and I were out in the guest house one night. For some reason we did a lot of talking out in that little guest house. They were all drinking, and I remember Aaron saying things like, "Fucking politicians. They're taking the cream of the crop and getting them all killed in a useless war." That was the first time I ever heard anybody say, "a useless war," or anything to that effect, but I was pretty unconscious about a lot of things that were going on at that time.

Daddy gets more upset sometimes now than he did right after it happened. Not very long ago, in the "Back in the Good Old Days" section of the McCamey paper, it had a paragraph about Don's marriage twenty years ago. Daddy picked that up, and it really upset him. And Louise. That hurt Mother and Daddy a whole lot, more than anybody ever knew, when she remarried and wouldn't let Don's kids come to McCamey to visit them anymore. I wonder if at times they think we don't care. I sent them our new address. For years I sent presents every Christmas, and I wrote a little bit. That was really a big blow to Mother. She was crazy about those kids.

You know, at the time, I think that because she hid her grief, we all thought Mother was handling it well, but in fact she wasn't. I truly believe if she'd had some kind of professional help, she'd have been all right. I could feel guilty about that, but I don't so much now. I did for a while, but you can't change the way you are at the time something happens. I had no idea. I'm very honest about that, even with myself. I had no idea that she needed help.

After Mother died, I had a lot of problems. I was scared, and I had heart palpitations. I lost a lot of weight, and I was afraid to go anywhere. For a while, it was a real effort to even get the kids back and forth to school. I would go into a panic while I was in the car, driving. Then I got some help, and I finally admitted to myself that I had a death wish, an unconscious death wish. I didn't know it before I got help, but I remember clearly thinking, when Mother died, "Okay. I'll go on. I'll accept it, but I'll never be happy again." I remember thinking that, but I didn't realize then that I was deliberately planning to be unhappy. I know now that what you feed into yourself is going to come out one way or another. I didn't know it then. I think that's what Mother did, unconsciously. She did the same thing I did. When Don died, she probably thought, "I'll go on living, but . . ."

I feel bitterness about it sometimes. I really do think it was a politician's war, and that thousands of people died for nothing. I really don't believe in predestination too much. I think we make our own destiny. With Don, I kept thinking, "If he'd waited and gone later, maybe he wouldn't have been killed." Who knows? I remember feeling really cheated when he was killed, because I was pregnant, and I knew my kids were going to really miss something by not knowing my brother and his kids, Don's kids. Even now, I'll be reading the paper, and I'll say, "Look at all this happening, and Don doesn't even know about it. All the changes going on, and he doesn't know it." But then again, maybe he does.

TOMMYE GUNNELS BALDWIN

Born: April 5, 1912
Lawrence Town, Illinois
Aunt of Donald Clayton Smith

Never the Same

The first I knew of Don being missing was one day when the doorbell rang and I went to the door. His mom and dad were standing there. I knew something was wrong because of the look on Peg's face. They came in with the telegram, and they called Sue and Larry. After they called, Peg just went into the bedroom by herself and sat there. She didn't cry. When Sue and Larry got here, they all went back to McCamey.

I accepted that Don was dead. I felt from the first that he was probably dead. My feelings were more for Peggy, what she was going through. She changed a lot, and it was hard to see that. She was drinking more, and she started taking tranquilizers after they heard Don was missing. She could go to the drugstore in Mc-Camey and get tranquilizers without even having a prescription. I can remember her sending me down there to get them some of the time. She was taking Equanil. It got worse after they found his body. She was too calm, and I worried about her not crying. I never saw her cry, and I guess Mother never did either. Mom must have said something to Olin about it, because he said, "Well, don't worry about her not crying, because at nighttime she makes up for not crying in the daytime." So she did cry, I guess. She really was never the same, after he died. She was in pretty bad shape for a long time.

I should have had sense enough to know that something was

seriously wrong with her about two or three weeks before she died. She was over at Sue's. She had had some pictures made of Don, and I went over to look at the pictures. When I went in, Peg got up off the couch, and it looked as if she was going to fall down, as if she were weak or something and couldn't stand up. She had already told me she was going to give herself six months, then she was going to see a psychiatrist. She didn't tell me what was wrong, but she was always going to the chiropractor and getting those adjustments. They made her feel better for the time, but they didn't cure anything. She was going about three times a week, and she said the doctor told her it was a nerve in her back, and that he didn't believe in psychiatry. She believed what he told her. I didn't.

I worried more about Peg than I did about Olin. I don't know why. Maybe it was because she was doing her best to keep steady and strong and just ride on through it. She kept a stiff upper lip for everybody else. She even told me that some friend of Don's told her that some friendly natives found the bodies, and that they wrapped them up in blankets and buried them in shallow graves. She said the natives had also said they had seen a tall captain who wasn't killed leave the plane. She said, "Maybe it wasn't a captain, maybe it was a lieutenant. Maybe it was Don." She may have even believed all of that. I don't know. I didn't tell her I didn't believe any of it was true.

GEORGE ERROL SMITH

Born: January 3, 1942
McCamey, Texas
Brother of Donald Clayton Smith

Gentle Genes

When I talked to all those people at Randolph, in San Antonio, I just asked them what the chances were that he would have survived the plane going down. They said none. They said, "Of course, we can't tell you this officially, but witnesses saw the big explosion, and they were carrying fuel." It was just a few days after we were notified he was missing that I called. How the hell I even found out who to call, I don't even remember. Five or six men were killed in the crash; there was a pilot, a copilot, a navigator, and two or three others. It was after the bodies were found that I first heard that story about some natives seeing a tall lieutenant walking around. The facts wouldn't have mattered to Mother. She would have jumped at anything.

She just lost interest in anything else. She made a big show of fishing, and I guess that was an escape. She'd never fished before Don was killed. It reached the point where you couldn't drag her away from the lake. She just lost interest in everything else, it seemed. Hell, in me, in Sue. Real interest. It wasn't anything overt, but her life became her grief, or her grief became her life. I wonder if it would have been the same if Don had been killed in a car wreck. God knows there were plenty of opportunities for that. I don't think in her *heart* she ever accepted his death, but I don't see how she could avoid knowing it, rationally. She just went into a steady decline until her own death. It was a hard time. Not for me, so much, because I left.

I was at Tech, in Lubbock, finishing my masters degree. We were notified definitely that he was dead in February, had the funeral down in San Antonio, and I finished school that summer. Then I went to Kingsville to start teaching. I moved around a lot, and I was never in McCamey for any long period of time after Don was killed. I made my visits faithfully, at Christmas, times like that, and I used to write, but I never did get along with Mama after Don died. There wasn't anything to get along with. It was a different kind of life altogether. I was never relaxed with her, because she didn't really, genuinely care how my life was going. Oh, she loved me and all of that, I'm not saying she didn't, but she didn't really have any interest in me, as she once had.

I used to be her pet, before that. If she had a favorite child in the family, it was me. I was Mama's pet before Don died, but I think I was more of a disappointment to her than any of her other children. I guess I just went in a different direction. I didn't choose a manly career, or something. She never could see me as a teacher. She said that lots of times. I don't know what she wanted me to do. Take over the shop or something, I guess, which would have been a disaster.

I went into the air force at one time. I was going the same route Don did. I went in in August of 1965, right before he was killed. I stayed in about thirty days. I had gone to graduate school for a year and taught for a year in high school in Andrews, then I went into the air force. I was going to be just like Don, a pilot and all that stuff. I hated it. Luckily my sinuses started acting up on me, and they told me I couldn't fly. If I couldn't get the career track I wanted, I could get out. So, I told them to stick it, and I took off. I never could get the fucking beds to make up right. I also didn't like those people telling me what to do, in the smallest detail. I never got along there, and I had a real schmuck for a roommate. I was more efficient than he was, and that wasn't real efficient, so we were always in trouble. I was really ready to get out, and I nearly never got out.

They were just leaving me in limbo, marching around the barracks, for about a month. I finally had the head of the English Department at Tech call the damn general at Lackland to get something done. I could just see myself roasting there forever, like being on a spit, turning slowly over the fire. I said, "Shit. What am I going to do?" I'd already called Tech and asked if I could get my assistantship back. They said, "Hell, yes," but time kept passing, and time kept passing, and I said, "Hell, it might be months before you get out of here." So I just called Tech and said,

"Will you call the general and tell him how *desperate* you are to get me out of here?" The head of the English Department did it. He's dead now, but he was really a nice guy. He called the general and told him he needed my ass out of there, and I was out the next day. That's exactly what I did. Two or three other guys like me who were also hanging around there managed to get out with me.

I don't know why the hell I went in in the first place. I don't know whether it was subconsciously a desire to do something more appropriate for myself, or whether I was just bored with what I had done so far and decided to give it a trial. It was a dumb thing to do, because it was almost forever. It was a five-year commitment to be a pilot. Hell, if I'd stayed in, we might have both been shot down over there. That'd been a hell of a thing, wouldn't it? I would have been over there right after him, sure as hell.

I was in McCamey when we first heard about Don's being missing. It was right at Christmastime, and I had been out, drinking beer with my Uncle Grover. When I drove back to the house, my mother met me at the door. She told me she had bad news. Everybody was there. I've hated Christmas ever since. Then Mother died at the exact same time of the year.

You know, from all the talk that went on at my house, they were over there in Vietnam, defending the shores of San Francisco, practically, which I never believed. I argued against that, even then. I argued with Don about it. He told me, "Goddamn, if I ever hear of you going to one of those damn demonstrations" —which I had already been in—"I'll kick your ass." I said, "What do you think we're over there fighting for, my right to do that, or what?" He didn't have an answer for that. But they believed in it. They believed it was a vital damned thing. I never did. I never did.

I had had the good fortune to have studied the French experience in Indochina. The professor had a good historical perspective on that part of the world. I was, of course, a mediocre student, but the domino theory never did work for me. All this domino theory is bullshit, and I never did believe that we ought to try to make every country in the world a democracy. It can't be done. I always thought the whole thing was an exercise in frustration. Hell, I never did think that war was worth a shit, but then, I never knew Don was in it. He never told us he went over there.

He'd already been over there several times, and we didn't even know about it. On TDY [temporary duty]. Hell, he was on the last day of a ten-day TDY when he got shot down. He was based on Okinawa. He and his crew volunteered to take some supplies over there so the people who had their families on Okinawa could be with their families on Christmas. They were on the last day of a ten-day TDY when they went down. He had been in and out of Vietnam for a long time. His Air Medal was for action months before he went to Okinawa the last time; it wasn't for the last time he was there, when he got killed. He didn't even have to be over there. He didn't have to be there when he got killed, but he couldn't stand to be around the house for too long. He was used to those ninety-day rotations. He could have kept on doing that. He had a choice, some kind of ninety-day rotation somewhere, I don't remember where, or Okinawa. A year in Okinawa. Which meant being back and forth to Vietnam. And he took Okinawa.

He was on the brink of divorce then, but he had two kids he adored. He told me about falling in love with some gal he met somewhere. I don't remember where. Anyway, he was all primed for a divorce, and he had the whole family in an uproar over it. Me and his wife and Mother, primarily. We took his wife home with us, and Don came to Lubbock while she was with us. I don't know. One minute he would be talking about divorce, and the next minute he would be talking about buying a house somewhere. He was very confused about it. I think he met the girl somewhere overseas. I think she was more of an escape than true love, because he was already unhappy at home. He was confused about all that.

Hell, he'd come home after a rotation, and after three days, he'd be itching to go again. I think that was why he took that year there, to get away, but with his rationale being that it'd be better for his career. I know also, knowing him as well as I did, that that shit excited him. He would dare the devil. Always had. That experience would appeal to him. I would have been scared shitless the whole time. He might have been, too, but it was the kind of terrifying thing he liked. So, as far as ever having the feeling of, "My God, what a life wasted," while I think it was, I don't think he would agree. I think he would have said, "Hell, I'm doing what I want to do, and it just happened."

The more I live, the more I think that our grip on this old life is so tenuous anyway, that if it's time to die, we're going to die, no matter where we are. Every time you drive down the highway, you put implicit faith in your fellow man. Ha. Most of them aren't even worthy of it. That was pretty much the attitude Daddy had, too, I think. Don would say, "Well, shit. Bury me where I fall. Just throw me in a hole and cover me up and go on back home and get back to business. Have a drink for me."

It hurt Daddy a lot. It really did. Don was Daddy's boy in a lot of ways, I think. Not that he didn't love and wasn't proud of me and Sue, but anyone is going to have favorite kids. It didn't mean that he loved us any less, it was just a sense of affinity, which I think Mother and I had for years. Of course, Sue grew up thinking Don and I were some sort of demigods. She's really come a long way by now, and I'm proud of her, but she really did labor under serious delusions about me and Don. Daddy and I have a sort of stoic attitude, especially about death, but it really did hurt Daddy a lot. Mother was such a problem, though, that you really had to put aside whatever you were feeling about Don for her, which wasn't easy. It would have been easy enough if it had *worked,* if by putting aside your own feelings or neglecting them, or whatever, it had had some effect on her. Then it would have been all right, I guess. But it didn't. Nothing made a dent on her, on what she was going through.

I had many really intense conflicts with Mother about that. I could tell that she was just letting it destroy her and our family relationships. I told her once. I said, "Hell, I'm still alive. Sue's still alive. We'd appreciate your being like you used to be." She didn't respond to that. She would just cry. And, of course, it wasn't long after that my first wife and I split, and I remarried. That didn't set well with her. The divorce didn't bother her. She just didn't want me to marry again that rapidly, or ever, maybe. I think she saw a chance to get me home, to what to her was my home, to come back to McCamey, at least temporarily. She said she wanted me to play the field. "Play the field," she said. I told her I didn't want to play the damn field. I'd played the field some when I was married. I didn't tell her that, but I had what I wanted. I wanted to marry Elizabeth. I just made up my own mind how I was going to live my own life, what I wanted to do. There was always a lack of understanding, a lack of acceptance, of Elizabeth. Mother never really treated her as a part of the family. I guess that sort of thing happens in the best of families. Things just get screwed up.

You know, Don's death just confirmed my original feelings about that war. We took two or three wrong steps, then it seemed like every step we took after that just got us deeper and deeper into it. It was just a colossal case of getting into a pile of shit and then falling down in it, instead of stepping out of it. I will never believe that Lyndon Johnson was an evil man, that he was dead set on ruining his own place in history, which was top-notch, except for Vietnam. I just think he listened to the wrong folks and had a wrong perception of what the role of the United States should be in world affairs. I still think we have the wrong perspective, and I don't think we learned a damn thing from Vietnam. We're at the point where we could get right into the same shit again now.

Politics. If we survive long enough, I think it will all balance out. I think we will stop fearing the communists, and the communists will stop fearing us. We have communists ninety miles off our coast, and they haven't come over to invade us. We had sixty thousand men die in Vietnam, which is all the way around the world, in order to save the shores of California. It was a crime. Maybe somehow we have to develop a gentle gene or something and pass it on to future generations.

ROVIE MAE GUNNELS

**Born: February 9, 1890
Monticello, Kentucky
Grandmother of Donald Clayton Smith**

Five Wars

Well, I remember five wars in my lifetime. The Spanish American, World War I, World War II, the Korean War, and the Vietnam War.

I remember that one evening my daddy came in and told us he was going to the Spanish-American War. I was only a little bitty girl, but I was so scared because my daddy was going. He had to tell me that he was just kidding; he didn't mean it at all. There wasn't a call for them to go then, I don't think. There wasn't a draft. That must have been around 1898. I was around eight years old, or something like that.

I've had relatives in four wars. I had a brother in World War I, and two sons, Jimmy and Clyde, in World War II. I had nephews in the Korean War, and Jimmy and Don were in the Vietnam War. It seemed to me that Vietnam was worse. Don was killed, and I thought it was worse. I don't know whether it was or not.

I think Peggy died because of her grief over Don. I think that is what brought it on. It was Christmastime. Christmas was always sad for her, and that's when she died. I don't like Christmas, either. If I am away from home, a tree doesn't bother me, but at home I won't ever put a tree up.

I don't think I would leave out any of life, but the worst things that have happened to me in life have been losing my children and my grandchildren.

LIAM J TERRY • RICHARD C TESSM
O McCORMICK + PETER M CLEAR
IAM M PRICE • JAMES L CRAIG Jr • J.
NOBLES • MICHAEL S BIXEL • CLAYTO
W HAAKENSON Jr • KEVEN Z GOOD
ORENCE • FRED OBERDING Jr + JAME
IBLISS • DENNIS W FINNEGAN • RICH
VARD • CHARLES A McSWINEY Jr • KE
A THOMAS • RONALD L VANLANDI
R WOOD • WILLIAM L MILLER III • STE
BROWN • JOHN L CARROLL + ROBER
MANKA + DONALD C BREUER • CH/
N W RYON • RONALD D STAFFORD
ARVEY + BOBBY M JONES • RICHARD
R TAYLOR + BILLIE JOE WILLIAMS • BIL

DENNIS WILLIAM FINNEGAN

Born: February 18, 1943
        Brooklyn, New York
Killed: October 31, 1972
        Approximately forty miles northwest of Saigon,
        Republic of South Vietnam

ERT E LILES Jr • GEORGE B LOCKHART
NALD D PERRY + ROLLIE K REAID •
ROTH + GERALD W ALLEY + THO

Patrick Finnegan in Vietnam

Dennis Finnegan in Vietnam

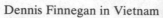

Mr. and Mrs. Finnegan and their youngest son John Finnegan pose with the two daughters of Dennis Finnegan *(photo by Peter Russo, Fort Hamilton Photo Facility)*.

MIRIAM IRENE FINNEGAN

Born: March 25, 1918
Brooklyn, New York
Mother of Dennis William Finnegan

PATRICK JOSEPH FINNEGAN

Born: November 23, 1947
Brooklyn, New York
Brother of Dennis William Finnegan

No Waves

MOTHER: He first went in July of 1966, and he went four times. He was wounded that first tour. He was wounded, but he didn't come home. He went to Okinawa to recuperate and then finished out his year there. When he completed that year, he took a month's leave to come home, then he went back for an extension of that tour. Because this first tour was extended, I think the army only considers he went to Vietnam on three tours, but to me he left four times. Four times he left and went to Vietnam. The last time he went, he was just a week short of completing the tour when he was killed.

When he was killed, he was in a helicopter. I never knew why he was in that helicopter. Running around in heliocopters was not a part of his duty. But he was en route either from Saigon back to his base or from the base to Saigon. He was preparing to leave Vietnam, and the helicopter was shot down. I had expected him at the door any minute, but he never came home. Before, he always came home ahead of when he was expected. Like, if he was going to be home in June, he would tell me that he wasn't coming home until July. That way, I wasn't waiting for him; he was always pulling in unexpectedly. Dennis had always come home like that, so this time I had his room all prepared, because he had been divorced, and he was coming home to my house. I had his room and bed ready for him. Then the army went to his ex-wife to notify her, because of their daughters, Denise and Diane. She called me, and then the army came to our house.

When he was in Vietnam, I was afraid he would be killed. The war was on television. We watched the six o'clock news and we watched the eleven o'clock news. We switched from station to station. We were down in Long Island at that time, and we had access to much more television than we do up here. He was out in the field with the 101st Airborne all the time except that last trip. On that last trip that he took, he said, "Don't worry. This is the safest tour I have had." I understood from him that he was not out in the field. He was in the headquarters. He was coordinating air strikes or something like that. So I did not worry myself that last trip, because I felt he was not out in the field in danger of ambush or whatever goes on, and he was shot down when he was supposed to come home in a few days. It was terrible. Terrible. One time, Dennis and Patrick were both over there at the same time. I had understood that they had a policy that two brothers were not supposed to be over there at the same time.

PATRICK: That wasn't exactly what the policy was. The policy was based on the Sullivan Law. That's where five Sullivan brothers went down on the same ship in World War II. The policy wasn't that they couldn't serve at the same time. The policy was that it was the responsibility of one or more brothers to make it known when one brother was already in a war zone. Then the one being sent would not have to go. If that one wanted to go, the option was still open to the other ones to come home.

MOTHER: Well, I don't even remember exactly now when you and Dennis were both over there, but once you were both over there at the same time.

PATRICK: That was from August to October of 1969. He got there sometime in August that time, and I got home the fourth of October, so we weren't both there all that long.

MOTHER: That's probably right, because Dennis came home from that tour in June of 1970. I knew they were both there. I knew Patrick was there, and I knew Dennis left to go there. I didn't know exactly how long they were both there. Patrick wasn't supposed to come until December, but he came home in October, so when he came home, I wasn't expecting him. We had a flag that the American Legion post gave to us. I think I still have it. These flags were very popular during World War II. There was a star on the flag for each member in the family who was in the armed services. There was one star on my flag, and I cut out another star. For a short time, I had two stars on this flag that I had hanging in the window. I think I took the second star off when Patrick came home.

PATRICK: Yeah, you did, but you could still see the outline where the second star had been.

MOTHER: I still have that. I came across that a little while ago. I don't know how I feel about all of this still. I don't know how to say how I feel. After a while, you get numb. I am still numb. I don't talk about the Vietnam War very much. I talk about Dennis, but not about the war, just childhood incidents. I don't talk about it much. I am not a very talkative person.

PATRICK: You say you don't have much to say, but you do. Yesterday you told me they got him killed for no good reason and the sons-of-bitches are now playing games in Central America. You told me that. That's a lot to say.

MOTHER: Yes, that is what I said. My youngest son is in the army reserves, so if anything happens, he's going to be tapped, and it is going to be Central America, I think. I don't think it will be in the Middle East. You see, there are not that many people to talk to, because there have not been that many affected by Vietnam. I never tried to talk to people about it. We lived in a suburban area in Long Island, you know, and the houses were far apart. I know that there were neighbors and people on our street who were not even aware that my boys were back and forth to Vietnam. When I learned that Dennis was dead, I was shocked. I was expecting him home. I didn't believe it. For at least six months, I had been watching TV, and they were saying all of it was winding down and that in early 1973 the POWs were coming home. I watched the television and the newspapers, and the war was coming to an end. And you always think there is a mistake. We did not view the body, and we thought, "Well, the army made a mistake." I don't know how long the war was on television. Sometimes I want to try to block things out.

PATRICK: Did you ever see Dennis in a bathing suit, or did you see him undressed after he was wounded?

MOTHER: Yes. His stomach looked like a tic-tac-toe game. With the way the scars were, he seemed to have two navels. It looked that way with the scars. He was very self-conscious of these scars and on the beach he would keep a T-shirt on him, over his upper body. He also had terrible trouble with the pain in his legs. He said, "I don't pray much. I guarantee you I won't be on my knees any more." He had trouble bending. I don't recall that his legs were that badly scarred. They weren't scarred, but you could see the shrapnel. He had pieces of shrapnel, and that is why he couldn't bend his knees and kneel. You could see the discoloration in his knees. You could see the metal under the skin, but I recall his stomach most of all. He tried to keep the scars covered up, of course, but you don't go jumping into a pool with a T-shirt on, so there were times when he had that shirt off and you could see the scars. I remember the scar on his wrist, too. He was shot there in some way that it also went into his stomach.

PATRICK: It went into his stomach and came out and took out a part of his hip bone. I remember him showing me all this up in the back bedroom. You know, the bedroom that we used to share?

MOTHER: Yes. He would show you more than he would show me.

PATRICK: He said that he saw the guy that shot him. He saw the Vietnamese that shot him.

MOTHER: He also said that he felt that they owed him one.

PATRICK: I think that was something that he felt he ought to say. I don't think he really felt that way. From the way he felt about those children, I don't think he really felt that way.

MOTHER: Oh, yes. He would ask me to send him things. He was interested in helping out with an orphanage. I don't know where it was, and I forget the name of the woman, but it was an American woman who ran this orphanage, and he helped out there quite a bit. Patrick has lot of pictures of Vietnamese children that he sent. I would send him pencils and books and things for the kids.

Within an hour after I got the phone call that he was dead, an army lieutenant came. I don't remember how many . . . maybe two, maybe three army people. I think one of our parish priests was there, but no one that I knew. I think that it is customary to pick up a clergyman to visit the home, but I don't really recall about this. There was a Lieutenant Kelly that I remember. I think he came with the first visitors. Then the army assigns an officer of the same rank to be with the family during the period of waiting for the body to come home and be buried. A captain stationed at Fort Hamilton came with Lieutenant Kelly, but Kelly did most of the work. The captain was a token gesture, just to have a man of similar rank. But Lieutenant Kelly was called a survival assistance officer, and he was really, really helpful. He was a lawyer by profession and he sat down with our lawyer, and they did everything that they could do. He was very good, and very kind and very helpful, a very nice young man. Our own lawyer, Bob Moinester, lost his son in Vietnam in 1968. He was a wonderful young man. The Moinesters were social friends of ours, too. Bob, Sr., had been a New York City fireman, like my Walter. Anyway, I haven't seen Lieutenant Kelly since that time. He was very kind and considerate. I don't remember that he had too much to do with the funeral arrangements. I think our local undertaker arranged all of that. He was very good, too.

PATRICK: I didn't go, but there was quite a funeral procession to Pinelawn.

MOTHER: Oh, traffic was stopped the whole length of Long Island from our house to Pinelawn. You have to be familiar with Long Island to understand this. There is a Sunrise Highway that runs from Brooklyn to Montauk Point. This is the main road that goes through all the towns that run out to Long Island, and traffic was stopped at every light. Each town met the funeral procession with their local police as we continued out.

PATRICK: Well, it's the Shore Parkway in Brooklyn, then it turns into Sunrise, and then further out it turns into Mountauk Highway, but basically it is the same road. I wasn't there that day, but just being in a national cemetery is a sobering thing. No matter how you look at the grave markers, they are all in a straight line. No matter what angle you look from, they all seem to be in a straight line. I never got around to going out there to visit Dennis's grave until 1975.

MOTHER: It is called the Long Island National Cemetery. That is the official name of it. We always referred to it as Pinelawn, but I understand that it is filled now and that they have opened up another one on Long Island. Dennis was the last casualty in Vietnam from Long Island. I didn't know that until last November when the Vietnam Memorial was dedicated. I didn't realize that. As a matter of fact, my cousin is buried just two rows away from Dennis. He died in early October of 1972, so the graves are filled as they need them. Two men dying just two or three weeks apart are buried very close together. Bill was very close to Dennis, and when we go to the cemetery, we take two bouquets, one for Dennis and one for Bill. He was a World War II veteran. He was about fifty-five when he died, but he was a World War II veteran.

PATRICK: Like I said, I didn't get out there until 1975, and there were a lot of people buried there that are Vietnam veterans, but they died in 1973, 1974, 1975. For what reasons, I don't know, but these are very young men.

MOTHER: My sister's husband is also buried in Long Island. He was a World War II veteran, also. He died about thirteen or fourteen years ago. He was in his fifties. He had cancer, come to think of it. And my cousin Bill died of cancer, also. That happens in that age group.

My husband died only two years ago. You know, I had also lost a child at twelve years of age. I was married for forty-four years, and that is a long time to have a life together. I guess I could crawl in a hole and pull the side over my head, and that is it.

PATRICK: You know, I never saw Dad cry except once, and it was right after Dennis got killed. That was when we were painting the bathroom. Dad came up, and he was just standing outside. He was even more quiet and secretive than my mother is. If he couldn't express his feelings in some sort of flippant way, it just wasn't coming out. On this day, he just stood there. He wanted to say something, and he didn't know what to say, and I didn't know what to say, because I had never seen him like that. We weren't a family that showed our emotions through physical contact. Our family was a testing ground for the world's greatest experts at sarcasm. You knew how much the other one cared for you and depended on you by how much they picked on you. That was the way it went. The touching and caring and telling each other that you cared just didn't happen. You had to learn how to read through the jokes to find out.

MOTHER: He and I didn't talk much, but we knew what one another was thinking. We'd often be riding in the car, and he would say something, and I would say, "I was just thinking about that." I knew him from the time I was fifteen. I was still a high school student. And then I grew up, and he was with me through losing two boys.

PATRICK: I don't think Dad ever recovered from Chippy's death.

MOTHER: No, but I would feel that we couldn't mourn too much for that child. He was physically handicapped and getting worse before our eyes. We had known for three years that we would not raise that child to be an adult. When he died, Patrick was less than three years old, and Dennis was only seven. I had these two young children to care for, so we couldn't mourn about

Chippy too much in front of them. At that time, the women still wore black mourning dresses. I didn't wear them around the house, but when I got dressed up to go to church, I would put my black mourning dress on. As I said, Patrick wasn't even three years old, and I wore the black dress to church for a couple of weeks. Then Patrick said, "Mommy, why do you wear that dress?" Well, I took the dress off, and I didn't wear it again. Like I said, I didn't mourn for this child, because I had young children to take care of. During those years, my mother and my mother-in-law and a neighbor had to mind my children while we took the boy to the hospital and the doctors. You couldn't mourn a child that you knew was going to be in a wheelchair within a few years. I just felt you have to resume a normal life as fast as you can.

PATRICK: You had his wake in the house. How could you go in the living room every day and not think of Chippy?

MOTHER: Well, we stayed in that house for a year afterward, and then we had to move. In 1950, when he died, funeral parlors were in existence, but they were not really as common as they are now. Now it is almost unheard of for a wake to be in the home, but at that time it was not. Then, again, he was a twelve-year-old child, and I just didn't want to leave him in a funeral parlor.

PATRICK: Also, having the wake in the house had to do with growing up in Irish enclaves in New York City. I mean, New York City is the melting pot. Well, maybe now it is the melting pot, but it wasn't then. It was, "Well, this is where the Micks live, and this is where the Italians are."

MOTHER: No. Our immediate neighborhood was not like that.

PATRICK: You mean there were a lot of Puerto Ricans and Chinese in Broad Channel?

MOTHER: Oh, no. That was Irish and German, but Ozone Park, where we lived when Chippy died, was more mixed. German, Irish, Italian. I don't recall any Polish. Probably German, Irish, and Italian for the most part. Maybe a Swede or two. I never lived in a pure Irish environment. I don't consider myself Irish. I am American.

PATRICK: And a good one.

MOTHER: Yes. I think so. I am glad to live in this country.

PATRICK: Those English ancestors came out of Liverpool.

MOTHER: Yes.

PATRICK: They were possibly living in the working-class Irish section of Liverpool.

MOTHER: That is possible. I can't trace my ancestry back too far. I am Irish and English, and I don't consider myself either one. I wasn't raised with Irish folk law. My mother's people were English, and she didn't have the Irish folk law to pass down, and besides, they are very superstitious. The Irish are outrageous with superstition. My mother didn't have too many, but my mother-in-law did. I was just astonished at the superstitions she pulled on me when I got married. I couldn't believe some of the things. For instance, with the first baby, I had him tucked on my lap, and I was cutting his fingernails. My mother-in-law came into the room, and she said, "What are you doing?" I said, "I am cutting the baby's fingernails. He is scratching himself, and he is scratching me." She said, "Don't ever do that." I said, "Why?" She said, "Well, it will make him a thief." I said, "Well, what am I supposed to do with his fingernails?" "You bite them off." "I don't bite my own fingernails. I am not going to bite the baby's." That is one of the superstitions. And don't ever put a hat on the table or open an umbrella in the house. That would bring very bad luck, and if a bird flew in the house, there was going to be a death in the house. Several times a bird got on our back porch and into the attic. We would get rid of it before my mother-in-law could see it, because she would have been terrified for the next six months, waiting to see who was going to die. Oh, they were outrageous.

But, with Chippy's death, we had three years of knowing it was coming. Our life was really tense in those years.

PATRICK: Chippy is the only member of the family that I have any memories of from Ozone Park. Chippy is the only one that I remember from that apartment. I don't remember you or Dad or Dennis or Grandpa or Nana. Chippy is the only one that I remember.

MOTHER: Well, the good old days are not necessarily really the good old days they are supposed to be. Life was hard then. With Dennis, I questioned that war right from the beginning. To my thinking, and I don't know how right I was, I just felt it was a civil war and we had no right to interfere in it. I couldn't see why America felt they had to side with one or the other of the factions in Vietnam. I could not understand why we were doing this. To me, it was almost the same as interfering in a family quarrel. In a neighbor's quarrel, who am I to pick sides? Dennis tried to change my mind, telling me we had to be in there to keep communism from taking over. I never quite swallowed it. In the beginning, he seemed to feel that we should be there. I don't know how he felt in the end. But we didn't argue about it.

PATRICK: Mom never argues.

MOTHER: I think I can discuss things without arguing. But he knew that I didn't agree with him. When he told me he was going back in 1971, I said to him, "Dennis, what are you trying to do? You have been there enough. Are you trying to be the last man jumping on the plane, leaving the country?" I couldn't see him going back again. Yet, I realized it was his job, and that he was doing it to get his ticket punched, more or less. West Pointers and OCS graduates don't get the same kind of consideration for promotions. And, in a way, I did feel since I had already lost one child, God wouldn't let it happen again. I had that feeling that it couldn't happen to me again. There again, so much piles up, and you feel like you're blowing your head off. I just all of a sudden said, "What am I doing to myself? What is going to happen is going to happen. Worrying can't change it."

PATRICK: Well, with Chippy you know there was nothing you could do. And there was nothing that you could do about Dennis. It was his choice to keep on going back.

MOTHER: Well, that is true, but it doesn't change how you feel. I guess I have to feel as though it was God's will. I still think almost everything that happens is God's will. I still go to church. I would not think about not going to church. To me, it is a habit, but I like it, too. And I pray. There's another habit I developed. From the first time Dennis went to Vietnam, I would do anything to avoid answering the telephone. My husband would get very annoyed with me. I would do anything up until the time he died not to answer the phone. It would ring, and he would say, "You're not going to answer that, are you?" Then he'd pick it up. Now I have to answer the phone.

My husband and I didn't talk much about Dennis's death. Patrick says that he broke down crying, but I didn't see that.

PATRICK: He wouldn't get to sobbing . . . well, more like his face quivering, and a few tears.

MOTHER: He probably thought, "Well, if one starts crying, the other starts crying," so you try not to cry. You try to keep busy and look for interests. At that time, we both started becoming interested in antiques. Even now, I wish there was a button I could push and say, "Well, I will shut off the worry tonight," but I am not made that way. I know I often go to bed and say, "I wish I could push that worry off." When you lose children, there is always something missing. At the holidays, especially, I miss the ones that aren't here. From the time of Dennis's death, the fun of Christmas was gone. After Chippy's death, I still had two young children I had to make Christmas for, but after Dennis's death there was no fun in Christmas. I just like to go to sleep Thanksgiving Day and wake up the third of January.

PATRICK: Well, you get a little joy out of it with Mikey now.

MOTHER: Oh, yes. There again, if you have children around, it makes a difference. Well, I think I can't lose any more sons, and that is why I worry. I can't worry about Patrick, because I don't know if he is getting home late, but my youngest son, John, lives with me. Believe me, if he is late coming home, I don't sleep.

I worry, but I have never had four sons alive at the same time. John was born five years after the oldest boy died, so I never had more than three at a time. Then the thought comes to your mind: "Gee, this could be the end of the family." Having had that many sons, you would think you were perpetuating the name indefinitely, but now all our hopes are pinned on Michael. But that's a silly thought. It's not a worry, but it is a thought that comes to mind.

PATRICK: What about those years when you had no idea where I was, when I was on the road?

MOTHER: That is one of the reasons I never wanted to answer the telephone. I didn't want to be the one to get any bad news about anybody.

PATRICK: During those years when you thought you would get bad news about me, what did you think it would be?

MOTHER: Probably that you were arrested. I have to say that. I would like to be able to live without a telephone, but I can't. When you were in Vietnam, I was afraid that you would be killed. If either of you were going to be killed, I would have thought it would have been you. I guess because of the differences in your personalities. I just thought you were a little more likely to dash into something, and that Dennis would be the one to hold back.

PATRICK: You obviously were not reading my letters from Vietnam.

MOTHER: No, that's not it. I mean, Patrick as a child was . . . when he was six years old, he got on a bulldozer and drove it. You know a kid that does things like that . . . you can never tell what they're going to do. At six years old, he started up a bulldozer and drove it I don't know how far. When he was running around the country, I didn't know where he was a lot of the time.

One thing I remember . . . and I think I will never forgive you for this . . . he called collect from Thailand. I thought you asked me to send you fifty dollars, but you said a hundred. And the phone call cost me sixty-five dollars. But he didn't call collect any more. That lady in California used to call. It was someone he met on the beach. . . .

PATRICK: In a bar.

MOTHER: Oh, I thought it was on the beach in California. Well, she obviously was quite enchanted with Patrick. She sounded like an older woman. I couldn't even tell you her name, but she called me several times to tell me how much she thought of Patrick. She was quite taken with him. She called me two or three times.

PATRICK: It was purcly platonic. It was just talking about the war and what a waste it was. I would get done picking avocados, and we would be at the bar. I didn't pick the avocados very much. I know it was my job, but I just mostly sat in a tree and read. The crops were going bad, and they brought a Mexican crew in. They went through that field in about a day and a half. Me and this other ex-grunt got hired to pick them, but we mostly just climbed up in the trees and read.

MOTHER: She talked for quite a while. I was a long time on the phone with her. I didn't mind those calls. I knew where you were at the time and that you were okay. I still worry about you some. I worry that you will make waves. I go along with a policy of making no waves, and I worry about you making waves and getting into trouble. I don't know what I think you would do. I didn't think that far ahead, and, to tell the truth, I guess I felt you joined the establishment when you opened a checking account. I thought, "Oh, good. He's coming around." That's the first step. I just like for everyone to go along and have things quiet and peaceful. I don't like to think about what could happen. I don't like to think too deeply on any subject.

PATRICK: Are you proud that Dennis was an officer? I know that I was.

MOTHER: Yes, because he was an officer so young. We went to his graduation. He was not quite twenty-one. I think that it was hard going to school after being out of high school for three years. He was a captain when he was twenty-three.

PATRICK: Then they dangled "major" in front of him all those years. He was promised a command school in Leavenworth. That's how they kept him in. That was the thing that kept him in. When he was going to get out, what they told him was: "Well, you know, you stay in and you are going to get 'major' pretty soon. We'll send you out to that command college in Leavenworth. That is one of the places to be punched up to the general ranks. Then we'll give you the duty station of your choice for three years."

What I was going to ask you about being proud of Dennis's being an officer has to do with the family. You didn't grow up filthy rich. My mom's dad was a New York City policeman, and there was always an income through the depression, when a lot of other people didn't have it. Dad grew up a little poorer. His mother had to go out and clean other people's houses, and Grandpa worked for the WPA. Things like that. Dennis was the first Finnegan to graduate from high school. And here he was, an officer. Not that it means that much now, but at that time, it was kind of breaking us out of a class. It moved us up a bit.

MOTHER: Well, we had a civil service background, and the military service is like that in that it is guaranteed as long as you keep your nose clean. You have a job. In the depression years, many people didn't have a job. Because of the civil service pay coming in, I never had to worry in my whole life. There wasn't any thought that either my father or my husband would lose their jobs, and that's a comfortable feeling. You know you are going to have food on the table and be able to pay the rent.

PATRICK JOSEPH FINNEGAN

Born: November 23, 1947
Brooklyn, New York
Brother of Dennis William Finnegan

Bitter Pills

I have a lot of bitterness. There's a lot of bitterness on my part toward the army. My brother was killed the thirty-first of October,

1972, and here is a letter from the Department of the Army, addressed to my brother, and dated May of 1973. This was seven months after he was killed. This arrived at my parents' address while his death was still a very open wound. This is what it says:

Dear Mr. Finnegan:
The attached award has been received for forwarding to you.
The Republic of Vietnam has made this award to you in
recognition of your service to their country while serving as a
member of the United States Army. The medal that
accompanies the award is not available for issue by the
Department of the Army. If you desire the medal, I suggest
you contact the dealer in military devices. Some of the dealers
advertise in the . . .

He had been dead for seven months. My parents got this letter about this medal, and they're telling him to go buy the medal if he wants it. That was pretty bad, but this other letter was even worse. It's the one that kind of sums up Vietnam for me. This one was received three months after he was killed. It says, "Captain Dennis W. Finnegan was promoted posthumously to the grade of Major, Army United States, as of 3 July 1969 . . . on the provision [that] additional pay is not involved." We received this three months after he was killed, and they had backdated his posthumous promotion to major to more than three years before he was killed.

I don't know why they did this, but I do have my own pet theory. Our chapter of Vietnam Veterans of America here in Albany looked over the list of people from New York State who were killed in action in Vietnam, and who were from our local area. I was in the army, and I noticed as I was going through the list that there were an awful lot of dead army corporals, which is strange. An army corporal is not even a rank any more. It is usually called "spec-4." It is very rare that they will use the rank of corporal any more, because there are some differences between a corporal and a spec-4. See, a corporal is an NCO, a non-commissioned officer. A spec-4 is an enlisted man. An NCO has more rights, and more power, than an enlisted man. They can have the same pay grade. A spec-4 has the same pay grade, but a corporal is an NCO.

When they categorize the people killed in action, they have dead enlisted men, dead NCOs, and dead senior NCOs. If some of the spec-4s were promoted to corporal posthumously, there would be fewer dead in the enlisted men category, and there would be more dead in the NCO category.

In my brother's case, the officers break down like this: company-grade officers through captain; field-grade officers such as major, lieutenant colonel, and colonel. And colonel is an iffy kind of thing. Usually you don't make colonel unless they think they are going to make you into a general. That is what usually happens, how it usually works. But a colonel is really a field-grade officer. Then there are general officers.

Now, my brother died as a captain. He was a company-grade officer. Then they made him a major after he died, and backdated the promotion. Now they have one more dead officer in the field-grade category, and one less dead officer in the company-grade category. Then they can sit around their base bars and say, "I don't know what people are complaining about. Look at all the dead NCOs we have." It looked to me, from what I saw, that about a third of the spec-4s in the army were turned into corporals. It looked to me as if a lot of people were promoted posthumously. Some PFCs were turned into corporals, too. PFC is called "E-3," and a corporal is "E-4," so that's only one actual rank. I know that a friend of mine, Dewey Ruis, was a Spec-4, and now he is a dead sergeant. He was a Spec-4 when he got killed, and now he is a sergeant. And Pypinowski, "Ski," we called him; they made him an E-4 from an E-3. I don't know that they are really that devious, but somehow this sort of thing seems to crop up a lot.

I was a finance clerk for a while when I was in the service, and if your promotion is backdated, then they owe you money at the higher grade from the date of the promotion, as it appears in its backdated version. In the letter making Dennis a major, they made it clear that retroactive pay was not involved. That's just the coldness they show. What they left unsaid is that additional pay is not involved because Captain—now Major—Finnegan is dead.

Dennis went into the service right out of high school, in September of 1960. He was seventeen at the time. He enlisted. He trained first as an engineer. He was a combat engineer. Then he was stationed down at Fort Bliss, and he met a girl, a sergeant major's daughter. They wanted to get married, and she kind of talked him into going to officers' training school. He qualified, and he went and graduated, and they got married right before he graduated. That was in Cedar Rapids, Iowa, in late 1963. He got his commission in January of 1964. He was just twenty years old at the time. After that, he went to jump school, and he was assigned to Fort Greeley. He and his wife split up while they were there, and he volunteered for Vietnam. When he came home on a thirty-day leave, he had the 101st Airborne patch on, and that really hooked me. I was eighteen, and he was twenty-three.

I had decided I would be a marine, and my life was planned. I was going to go into the marines, finish that, and come back and be a policeman, all in the good old Irish tradition, the New York City Irish tradition. That's just kinda what you did. My uncle had done it. It didn't work out exactly like that for me.

I really miss Dennis, now that my dad is dead. My dad died just a couple of years ago now, and I don't have Dennis around to talk to, either. We grew up in what would be seen as an unusual household by today's standards. It wasn't so unusual then, I guess. It was a three-generation house: our parents; Dad's parents; Nana's brother Charlie, who had a gimpy leg from World War I; and Dad's brother Jack. It was like a boarding house, a lot of adults, not that many kids. Three brothers. Then Dennis left when I was twelve and my younger brother was about five. There were three of us there for five years, that's all. We were always conscious of being Irish. Any time anyone asked you your name, you'd give them your full name, and then they'd say, "That's a good Irish name."

I grew up mostly on Long Island. Dennis grew up mostly in

New York City, in Queens, South Ozone Park. It was a family that started in Manhattan on my dad's side. Then my dad's father moved with his family to Brooklyn at some point. My grandmother's side of the family was already living in Brooklyn then, so my grandparents on my father's side met and married in Brooklyn. Then, in my dad's generation, they made it to Queens. By our time, they made it out to the island. Then they moved upstate. The first Finnegan over here was our great-grandfather. My son, Michael, is named after him. He was killed when he fell off a trolley car. We have a press clipping about it. He fell off a trolley car in New York City in 1904, and he bled to death. He was only around thirty years old. Dad was a New York City fireman, so he and my uncles kind of set the tradition I was planning to follow.

Anyway, I had been in the army for over two years when I got to Vietnam. They sent me there as a finance clerk, and then they made me an infantryman. Well, I did that for a while, then I developed a very large boil on one of my testicles. I had to go into the hospital. This guy, Doc Smiley, my medic then, has since deserted. That's a sad story. He deserted after he came back.

Doc pulled eleven months in the field, then his father died. His father was a World War II veteran, and he lived in the Bronx, the South Bronx, one of those bombed-out sections you hear about. Fox Street. By the time this happened, I was out of Vietnam. I picked Doc up at the airport and went to the funeral services. We went out to Pinelawn. That is where his dad is buried, at the national cemetery there. Anyway, Doc was the oldest of seven kids, and he asked for a compassionate reassignment to Fort Dix in New Jersey to be somewhat near his home. The army wouldn't give it to him. They sent him down to Fort Bragg, North Carolina. This was all going on between December of 1969 and January of 1970. I had left Vietnam in October of 1969. Sometime in May of 1970 I was walking around one of the lakes in Central Park with an old high school girl friend, and I saw Doc. I knew he wasn't supposed to be there. I said, "Hey, Doc, what are you doing here?" He said, "I quit."

Now, I had nothing against giving amnesty to those guys that went to Canada, but there were a lot of people like Doc that should have been given amnesty first. He pulled his time in the war, but he couldn't put up with the crap in the rear. I couldn't, either.

As I said, I had gone into the field in Vietnam, but I had picked up clerical skills during the two years I had spent in the army in the states. When I was clearing back into the brigade after getting out of the hospital, it just so happened that they needed someone to do morning reports at the brigade level for the battalion. I was a marketable commodity at that time. I was in. I had the ability to do morning reports, the top bureaucratic paper in the army. You keep the morning report day by day, and it's supposed to indicate where everyone is supposed to be and what they're doing. It's a pretty picky form to fill out. They don't allow any mistakes on it. Anyway, the guy they had doing it was leaving, so I fell into that.

By this time, I was twenty-one years old, and I had two years' experience controlling the army's paperwork, so I just did what I wanted to do. I made myself an E-3 and an E-4 in a matter of a month and a half. I just did it. I sent guys on leave and didn't enter it in the morning report. This would save them their actual leave time. I made people MIA, missing in action, as part of my job as a morning report clerk. This one guy was sick of the war. He walked off and sat down with a grenade. He blew himself up. There wasn't enough left of him to be identified, although people said they saw him go off and blow himself up. I made that man an MIA. I don't know how long he stayed in that category, but I feel sorry for those families, I really do. They don't know what happened in a lot of cases. They just live in limbo.

When I was doing the morning reports for two companies at brigade headquarters at An Khe, my battalion base camp was at LZ Uplift. It was only myself and two other guys from the battalion doing this job. One guy was an E-7. The other guy was Benny O'Donnell Taylor III, who had been with my brother in the 101st back in 1966–67. We had about two hours' work a day, nobody monitoring, nobody hassling us, and the rest of the day was our own. Then they changed brigade headquarters from An Khe to

Qui Khon, and our section moved back and worked out of Battalion S-1 at LZ Uplift. After a while, I couldn't put up with the bullshit that was going on, and I asked to go back to the field. That's when I went back to my old gun team, this time as an assistant gunner. Anyway . . .

When I was told my brother was killed, I was gone. I was in the wind. I was as close to being underground as I could get at the time. My parents got the word to me to call back to New York through a whole series of contacts. I called back, but I knew it was about my brother. This news came in 1972, the day after the election in 1972. I hadn't associated with anybody for years who didn't spit whenever Richard Nixon's name was mentioned, so his election was an awakening for me and a lesson in life. I was flabbergasted. Nixon had won by a landslide, and I couldn't understand how that could have happened. I figured it was rigged. I had just surrounded myself with myself and lost touch with the world.

After I got the message, I called home and talked to my mom. She said she had bad news, and I said, "Yeah, I know. Dennis is dead." They asked me how I knew that, and I said I didn't know how, I just knew it. So I came back to New York, which I really didn't want to do. I knew I would never get away from it again, and I really haven't.

Dennis was clearing country when he was killed. He was on his way home. That was supposed to be the end for him, his last tour. I believe that he was due back on the seventh of November; he was killed on October 31. The war would have ended for him then. He would have beaten it. But he didn't beat it.

Anyway, when I got back to New York, I went to the funeral parlor, because I wanted to see what they were burying as my brother. It was a closed casket, and the casket had a cover and an inner seal. I had opened the outer cover of the coffin and was starting to work on the inner seal when some government official came up. I don't know who he was. He wasn't wearing a uniform. He asked me what I was doing, and I told him: "The guy in the coffin, I'm his brother, and I want to see what you're burying. I want to see what's going into the ground as my brother." He said, "No. You can't do that." I didn't pay any attention to him. I hadn't paid any attention to anyone in the army long before I left the army, and I had learned to appreciate that if you just do what you want to do, there is a chance you will get away with it. I just went on working on the inner seal of the coffin. This guy then came up and began to physically restrain me from opening my brother's coffin. I didn't want to get into an out-and-out fight. That wasn't the place to do it. So I still don't know what they buried as my brother.

I went to the wake, and when they buried him, it was a big deal. They had motorcycle cops all over the place. It was a charade. I wanted no part of it, so I just hung around the house the day they buried him. I didn't go to the burial. I didn't go out to Pinelawn to see his grave until sometime in 1975. They told us he was dead, but not being able to see him, to see what was being buried, you know . . . from what I understand, we wouldn't have been able to recognize him, anyway. But, with a closed coffin, you want to look in it. There were a lot of closed coffins. You talk to guys who were in Graves Registration, and they sent back . . . you know, sometimes they didn't know what belonged to who. Even with all that, because I didn't see him, it wouldn't surprise me today if he walked in the door.

You work up all these fantasies. Here I was told he was dead, but I never saw him dead. I dream about him, and he got better in my dreams. He started off looking pretty shaky in my dreams, you know, burned and with half of his body kind of gone, but he's gotten better since the dreams started. When I dream of him now, he is just about how he should be. He was only twenty-nine when he was killed, but that was old for Vietnam. I was twenty-one when I was in Vietnam, and I was like an old man in my platoon. I was an old man.

As I said earlier, my original dream had been to go into the marines. I had wanted to be a paratrooper. I had gone to ask the marine recruiter if I could be a paratrooper. He said, "We don't promise you nothing but fifteen weeks of hell." He actually said that. Well, the army guys were just across the walkway, so I went over and asked him, and he said, "Sure. Sign right here." So I did, and I was gone a week later. Just the other day, I ran across the first letter I wrote home. It's dated August ninth. I went in on August first. Here's the letter:

> *Dear Mom and Dad:*
> *Hello. As you can guess, I need something. I am out of envelopes. Please send them special, stamped. I am signed up for airborne in Vietnam. Please tell me how Dennis is doing. I am praying he is okay. I am at the best training brigade there is in Fort Gordon. We got here yesterday. We had chicken today and it was delicious. The food in this company is great. We get about seven to seven-and-a-half hours sleep a night. It isn't half as bad as I thought it would be. I qualified for OCS. Please write Dennis and tell him my address. I can't write. I don't have any envelopes.*
>
> *They have me shining my shoes every day, and it is a funny feeling. Ma, keep an eye on Margie for me. I'll stop now. I have to practice push-ups. At AIT [Advanced Infantry Training], I'll do a thousand a day.*
>
> *Say hello to Nana, and tell her not to worry. I'll write to her as soon as I get the envelopes. Say hello to John. Here is the ten dollars I owe you and five dollars for stamped envelopes.*
> *Love, Pat*

I was really into envelopes. I was more athletic then than I am now. Dennis was always kind of klutzy, and I just knew he wasn't going to make it. I was going to take care of him. I knew he was a good guy, but he was klutzy. I was more coordinated, and I felt he needed me. He had told me that when I got to basic training, when they asked for a driver I should stick up my hand. So I did that. I became a driver for a basic training company and didn't have to do KP. I wound up driving for the battalion commander. I told him about my brother and that I was going to be an airborne infantry officer, so he liked me. He would request me, and I used to drive for him more than the normal rotation would have allowed.

After infantry OCS AIT, I went into a holding company, waiting for OCS orders. Waiting and waiting and waiting. In the meantime, Dennis had been wounded, and he was almost killed. I thought I couldn't wait. I had to get over there, so I dropped OCS, and got jump school back. I went to jump school, and I requested Vietnam. By that time, I was only in the army about six months. I requested Vietnam the day I signed up. I had requested it the day I got inducted. I requested it sometime in basic training. I requested it when I got into jump school. Vietnam and the 101st, that is what I wanted. They sent me to North Carolina, the 82nd, the pits-of-the-pits. I called home, and I was crying because they weren't sending me to the war. How ridiculous that seems now.

Anyway, I kicked around in North Carolina, and by the time they sent me, I couldn't have cared less if they sent me or not. Dennis finally got me over there. I was going to be in big trouble if I stayed around Fort Bragg much longer. This man, Major Rafferty, had served with my brother, and he was in charge of assignments in the Pentagon, of E-6 assignments and below. Through him and Dennis, I finally got my orders for Vietnam. In Vietnam, I ran into quite a few people that Dennis knew. He called West Pointers "ring knockers." Dennis always swore they sat around knocking their West Point rings against the tables. My general impression of them was that they were a bunch of fools. Whatever they were trained in, whatever books they had used to teach them, it had nothing to do with what was going on in Vietnam.

Anyway, I got out in October of 1969, and it seemed as if the war was never going to end. In fact, there were a lot of us for whom it didn't end in 1973. It didn't end until 1975, and, even then, it didn't end. Well, I am damned sure it didn't end for me in 1973.

In 1972, I was part of a San Francisco contingent of Vietnam Veterans Against the War [VVAW] that went to the Republican convention in Miami. I had been living and working on a farm outside of Fresno at that time. It was David Harris's farm, and it was through his peace movement connections that I got hooked up with VVAW. I certainly wasn't any great leader in VVAW. I never was that. I was just a body, just one more person who had to do it, had to be a part of voicing opposition to the war.

Anyway, back to Dennis. When he first went over in July of 1966, he wasn't there all that long before he was wounded. It was in September. They were moving down a trail, got ambushed, and he jumped off to the side. He landed on a stake and wound up losing some of his intestines. When they sewed him up after surgery, they discovered they had left a sponge or a clamp or something in him, and they had to open him up again to get that out. Trouble developed out of that. I don't know. It seems that his skin had lost some of its resiliency. The stitches tore out, and he had to be sewn back together again. They had clamps running all the way down the front of him. From that day on, for the next six years of his life, he looked as if they had performed an autopsy on him. He was split right down the front. The scars were awful.

He recuperated from that and made captain while he was recuperating. I believe they had him in a hospital in Japan at that time. He wasn't hospitalized in the States. He didn't come back to the states until the following July, when his first tour ended. I'm not really sure about all of these details now, but I think it was after that first hospital stay that he went back to Vietnam and was working in civic affairs with the Vietnamese. It was during that time that he had his helmet shot off his head. I still have the helmet. He got his second purple heart at that time. Then he extended on his first tour and was company commander for a while. He hadn't been back in Vietnam from the States for more than about a month when the company's perimeter was almost overrun. The Vietnamese were trying to overrun the company. He was wounded again. He got shot, and it reopened the old stomach wound. He saw the Vietnamese that shot him. The bullet came across his left wrist, took his watch off, then entered his stomach, traveled through his stomach, and finally took out a piece of his hip bone on his right side. It was about ten minutes after that that he caught the grenade and mortar shrapnel in the legs. This was all on his first tour and the extension of his first tour. He came back to the States after that.

When Dennis got back to the States, he was assigned to Fort Dix. He was the commander of a basic training company there. This was in 1968. He was on limited duty profile, still recovering from his wounds. That's when Dennis helped me get my orders for Vietnam. I typed up my own leave orders, took forty-five days, and went my merry way. Then I went to Vietnam. I'm not really sure, but I think I arrived there about the thirtieth or thirty-first of December 1968. Dennis was back in the States still. By the time I got to Vietnam, all my gung-ho had gone. I figured I would take a lot of pictures, get a good tan, and come back when I came back. In the meantime, Dennis had taken his separation physical, but he found out that on the outside there wasn't much opportunity for an ex-army officer who just had a high school education. He decided to stay in.

As it turned out, I was never really into war. I had opportunities to shoot people and could have shot them. I was a very good shot. I always made "expert." My father had started us in the basement with a twenty-two when we were about eight. I was good at it. I was a good shot, but I guess I never felt my life was threatened enough to warrant me shooting someone just because they were in a free-fire zone and fair game. The closest I came to shooting anyone I could see was an American, rather than a Vietnamese, and that was because of army foul-ups, them not telling me what was going on. But I still appreciated that there was a war going on.

I only carried from fourteen to twenty-one magazines when I was in Vietnam, but when I got there, there was this guy on the gun team, Benny Brandt from Alabama. Big black guy, real black, no white blood in Benny. He carried forty-four magazines. He carried anything and everything he could get his hands on. He was going home, and he was not running short of ammunition. He was on the gun team with me, and he had a big radio, and he would be marching . . . well, not marching, but walking in front of me, and he would have his radio on. He would have it tuned to the armed forces station. He had an ear plug in, and he would be listening to the radio and dancing through the jungle. He was fantastic. He would be walking a ridge line and doing this stuff. Then his brother got killed by a bolt of lightning in Alabama, and Benny went home. He went home after about eight months in Vietnam.

At one point, we had this brand-new lieutenant who was terrible. The army had also started an NCO academy at that point. I guess they were running out of NCOs or something. Anyway, we had this terrible lieutenant, and a lot of other new guys, including this sergeant who had graduated from this academy. He was terrible, too. Anyway, one night a bunch of us were sitting around playing cards. We did a lot of that. We would break out the cards and play a game called "spades." So we were sitting up doing that this one night, and we have this sergeant who doesn't know nothing. He knows nothing. Now I am not the greatest soldier in the world, or the greatest bush rat or boonie rat or whatever, but I know the basics. There was this thicket, an unbelievable thicket right next to us, and then there was a trail that came by there. I took this sergeant out and told him we needed to set up a claymore mine. I set up the claymore on the trail, wired the trip flare, and then came back in.

We smoked a lot of dope. Our platoon smoked a lot of dope. That is neither here nor there, that is just the reality of it. So, anyway, we were having our nighttime party, and all of a sudden this sergeant says that he hears noises through this thicket. I know there is nothing coming through that thicket. That thicket . . . I mean a person coming through that thicket was going to sound like an elephant charging through a wall of cornflakes. This sounds ridiculous, but this is really what happened. . . .

We were spread out in kind of a boomerang shape. Most of the others were at the other end of what would be one part of the boomerang, and we were partying our brains out at the other end of it. The guys at the other side were all new guys who didn't know anything. We weren't thinking about what they were doing. All of a sudden, one of them started firing and they all just opened up. I don't think anything had been going on. I didn't hear any incoming rounds or anything like that. Over there, they keep yelling they hear something, and I'm telling them no, that there can't be anything in there, if there were it would have to be louder. Then all of a sudden everybody takes off, and here I am, all by myself on the edge of this boomerang with the machine gun. I know there is nothing in there, but I'm starting to get nervous. I let it get the best of me. I started to fire the M-60, but it fired one round and jammed, so I picked up my 16. That was the first and only time that I fired on full automatic all the time I was in Vietnam. This other guy, Willie "Weed" Robinson, started dropping rounds in to where this noise was supposed to be coming from. Then things began calming down, and I went to try to find the sergeant and tell him that it's all right, that nothing's going on. I found the sergeant. He was just standing there, shaking himself to death. I tell the sergeant, "Okay, Sarge, it is alright. There is nothing going on," then I go to tell the lieutenant. I find the lieutenant, and he is also shaking himself to death. Now, these were the guys that were in charge of my life. I'll never forget it. The next day, we pulled out of there.

One morning they woke us up and told us there was a big battle. They had trapped an NVA platoon in a village. We had to get our stuff together in a rush and go off to this village. So we throw all this crap on our backs, and we head off. We had to go seven klicks. When we were about halfway there, they stopped us and told us to chow down. We did that and took off again. We crossed a road, and there was this village. The gunships are flying around and tearing it up, and there is a base camp not all that far away. It has guns, and it is not a fly-by-night base camp. It's a pretty good-sized base camp. There were about four rows of rice paddies you had to get through to get to the village. They put us on line and told us we were going to charge across those rice paddies. Now, there is no way that you charge across a rice paddy that is growing rice—a dry one, possibly, one that is not in use. But when they are filled with water and growing rice, you don't charge through a rice paddy, especially with seventy pounds on your back, you don't. You can barely walk through them, let alone charge through them.

So they told us to charge through this rice paddy, and we were all just standing there looking at each other. What are these guys, nuts? There wasn't even anything there. I decided they must have been making movies. That was the only thing that made sense to me. There wasn't anything in that village, no NVA. They brought us all this way to do battle with what they said was an NVA battalion or something, when they had a base camp of ARVNs less than a half-mile away from this village. And the base camp looked directly down on this village. If there was NVA there, why didn't they just blow it up? But no, they bring us all this way, stop us for ice cream on the way—the battalion sergeant major dropped in on a chopper and brought us ice cream for lunch —tell us to charge across these rice paddies that we can't charge across, to attack a big bunch of NVAs that aren't even there. They had to be making movies for somebody someplace. That was the only sensible thing I could think of. Maybe I shouldn't have even tried to find logic in it.

So I started thinking to myself—and a lot of other guys are thinking—if there is an NVA battalion there and we start across these rice paddies, all they will have to do is wait until we're in the middle of the second paddy and open up their gun teams. They'll take a shit load of us out. We went across, however. I don't remember going across those rice paddies. I guess we flew. I just remember being on one side of them and then going through the village.

There is this woman in the village, and she is pissed. She is just cursing us up and down, spitting on us as we go by. I still had a lot of crap in my head about the war at this time, but I remember thinking, "Why is she yelling at me? I don't want to be here, either, lady. I came over here to help you. Why the hell are you yelling at me?" A lot of things began to fall into place about that time. They fell more into place after I refused to go into the field. To be perfectly honest, most of the real reason I refused to go into the field was just total terror. The guys that were out there didn't know what they were doing for the most part, the guys that were the leaders. The sergeant and the platoon leader had less idea what they were doing than the dumbest private out there.

Anyway, because of too many things going on there that I didn't like, I refused to go back in the field. I was going to have to pull until the thirty-first of December, and the army wanted me to do it in the field. I wasn't going to go out in the field anymore, and I told them so. I said, "I don't care. I'm not going. Do whatever you want, but I am not going." I don't know why I didn't get court-martialed. I just don't know. Maybe it just wasn't worth it to them. They made me the battalion librarian.

Then I hear my brother is coming back again. He got into the country, and he got assigned. This was for his second full tour. He is assigned to the 101st again, and that's what he wanted. So I type up the paperwork for me to go home. He is in Vietnam, so I can go home. There was no reason for him to be there. I told him not to come over, and he came over anyway. I had no problems about going home. One of us should go home. He obviously didn't want to go home, or he wouldn't have come over to begin with, so I decided I was going home. I hand-carried my orders up to where my brother was at LZ Tomahawk. I borrowed a camera and went up to see my brother.

I got up there and my brother told me, "Hey, look, don't talk to these guys. They're activated National Guard, and they're really pissed. They don't want to be here." My brother knew the direction I was going in. He is still my brother. We were at opposite ends of the political spectrum, or quickly approaching opposite ends, but he was still my brother. One of the scars I have still is from him, you know, hitting me with a pillow and knocking me into a radiator. And he died with some of my scars on him. And he told me, "Don't talk to these guys." And those guys did not look happy.

We had pictures taken together, and he signed the papers, and I came back. I don't know why or how, but in trying to get the film out of the camera, I ruined the film, so I don't have the pictures. But I got back with my paperwork, so I can clear country now. I have to clear, and then they won't let me clear: "Ah, your hair is too long. Get your hair cut." So I get my hair cut. Then it's, "Your mustache comes down too far. Trim your mustache." So I cut the mustache. Then they started going on with more of this type of crap. At this time I had an M-79. I didn't have my M-16 any more. I started wising up. I started going around with my M-79 open, and a H.E. round in it, and I was showing it. That's all I had to do. They punked out. I got my papers signed.

I didn't really hear anything from Dennis. He came back in June of 1970 from his second tour. He wasn't wounded during that tour. In the meantime, I had come back and got hooked up with Vets for Peace. I got pretty dissatisfied with that and just became sort of a free-lance protester, I guess. Several of us started hanging around together, and we decided to go off to find "the revolution." We took this one girl with us. She didn't care much about "the revolution," but she said, "Oh, sure, I'll go," and she had a lot of money, so we took her with us. Then we picked up two other girls in Minneapolis. These girls were just out of high school, and they thought we were adventurers, so they came with us. Now there were six of us, all hairy freaks, packed in a Volvo with everything we own, traveling across the country and wondering why we were getting stopped every twenty miles.

I got deported from Canada. They said that I was a moral degenerate. We had gone in before from New York state. We didn't really get deported there. We just got thrown out. Then we tried to get back in again at Sweet Grass, Montana. I had been hearing all about Canada: "Oh, they are so great there." When we tried to get in again, the guy asked us if any of us were ever arrested. So I decided to see where those Canadians were at. I said, "Yes. I have been arrested." They took us down into this back room, and they typed up deportation papers. It said that I was a moral degenerate. We only got far enough into Canada to turn around and make a U-turn. Then when we got back to the American side, they pulled us over and made us get out of the car and they strip-searched every one of us. Then we wound up in Seattle.

I liked Seattle. I liked the feeling of Seattle at that time. That was in 1970. I didn't like very many cities, but Seattle just had a good feeling to it.

Now, looking back to those times, I remember that it seemed to me that the revolution was going to start any day: "The American public is just not going to put up with this lunacy any more, and tomorrow the revolution's going to start." I wrote my brother and told him that. While I really hoped it never came to that, if the revolution did start, I would be on one side, and Dennis was committed to the other side, and I was trying to talk him out of it. This was because I didn't want us to be fighting against each other. I knew I wasn't changing my mind, and I didn't want us to be fighting each other. I had all kinds of visions of the civil war in my head at that time, but I never found the revolution, so it didn't make any difference.

Then I came back to New York, and Dennis was back, also. We were sitting in the living room, and he was talking to my parents about the pacification program and how great it was going and this and that. I don't remember exactly what I said, but Dennis admitted it was not pacification, and it never was. It was relocation. We were blowing these people's villages up and destroying their capacity to produce food in their area, and then we were bringing them in and putting them behind fences with towers. You can call it "pacification" if you want to, but it was not. It was relocation and control. But it was his chosen job at the time, and he told me that, that it was the job he chose to do, for lack of non-military options.

We talked, and he said he wanted to kill some Vietnamese. I think it was just the macho part of him that felt that, or maybe because he had been shot at and shot up enough and had never seen one of them fall after he pulled the trigger. I don't think he really meant that, because it's not reflected in some of the things he did and the pictures he took. It was nothing but kids and countryside.

At that time I was living with this girl I had met in Minneapolis, and we decided to come back to New York. Then the bug hit us, and we headed out again. We were living in Las Cruces, New Mexico, in a seventeen-dollar-a-week motel. I didn't like Las Cruces. I didn't like the atmosphere, but I really liked that whole area geographically. There was a chain of motels there, and I got a part-time job scrubbing out the swimming pools and things like that, because I couldn't find any other work. Dennis cabled me fifty dollars to pay the rent. There was a telegraph strike at the time, and the money took a long time getting there, so we ended up living on the Rio Grande. It wasn't all that far away. It was just a little bit west. We wound up camping on the side of the Rio Grande, and I never paid Dennis back. I gave him back twenty-five dollars, but not the rest. Then he went back to Vietnam in November of 1971, and I never had the chance to pay him the other twenty-five. I didn't even know he was going back. At that time, we were living up in the mountains of northern California.

During the next year, I didn't know what Dennis was doing or where he was. I knew that he was back in Vietnam, but I didn't even think about it. I kind of just wrote him off. I was too hard-core. He was the enemy. He was my brother, but he was the enemy.

It was during that year that I got hooked up with the farm in Fresno, went to the convention with VVAW, and then went back to the farm. I still had no idea how Dennis was doing in Vietnam, but the winter started to come on the farm, and a farm can only support so many people through the winter. There were people who had been there longer than I had, so I left there. That time I ended up in Boulder. I got one job washing dishes in a place in Boulder and another job sweeping the floors in a defense plant. I thought, "I have big plans for this place." It was right around then that I was told that my brother was dead. My mom sent me the money for the ticket home.

His death really jammed up my head something terrible. I was just getting to know Dennis when he went into the service at seventeen. I was only twelve then, and up to that point all he had ever been to me and all I had ever been to him was a pain in the ass. I always wanted to crash his parties, and he didn't want his little brother hanging around, and it was a love-hate thing, and it still is. When I was in high school, I was proud to say, "My brother is an officer." I was proud to say that. It was a big thing then to be an officer in the army. You were *some*one.

Well, Dennis was killed, and I came back, and my parents couldn't deal with me at all. I had been living totally without social or cultural restraints for four years by then. All the stuff that you are "supposed" to do, I just stopped doing. In my own mind, I thought, "With all these other things that are going on in this world, I'm certainly not going to concern myself with social graces." I got a job working with an aluminum siding company and saved all my money. Nixon's inauguration came down, and I figured, "Well, there is no way the righteous people of America are going to let this man be inaugurated, and if it's going to happen in Washington, I'm going to be there." So I took all my savings, and I went to Washington. I came back, and I didn't have a penny. My parents couldn't understand any of that. They simply had no basis on which to understand any of that.

So I woke up one morning and my dad was telling me that I was going to a veterans' hospital. He said, "I called, and they have a place for you." This was down on Long Island. We were living in Lynbrook. My dad said, "You know you can't fit into society." Well, I don't actually remember what they said, but they let it be known to me that I needed psychiatric care quickly, and that my options at that point were to run out of the house like a madman with no money or to go along with this. So I went along with it. The Northport hospital got me. That was on January 28, 1973.

That was a hairy day. There were fantasies going on in my head based on my brother and not being allowed to see what was being buried, and I was also wanting to think that he was still alive. That was also the day that they started bringing the POWs home, so there were a lot of things running around in my brain. There was no one at Northport who could understand any of it. That was not a place where I wanted to spend my life, and, from what I could see around me, there were some guys spending their lives there. There was no real therapy, no treatment, no nothing. It was really like *One Flew Over the Cuckoo's Nest.* You learned pretty soon how to tongue the medication and spit it out at your first opportunity.

When I first got there, it took about three days of heavy medication because they were happy with me, since I was now acting like a chair, just like all the other guys. I kept telling them that I didn't need to be in there. I'd ask them, "What do you want to talk about? What do you want to discuss? What do I have to do to prove myself?" They gave me that Rorschach test, that ink blot stuff. He showed me something that looked like Madagascar, so I told him it looked like Madagascar. He kept harping on "a stitch in time": "What does a 'stitch in time' mean?" I said, "What is the relevance of that? If you can remember some nursery rhymes, you're okay?"

I don't know what it was, but they wouldn't let me out. I didn't want to be in the place, and they considered me a disruption, because I wanted to get out, and I was talking about the war. They would have these rap groups, and I would bring the conversation back to the war, and they kept harping that the war had nothing to do with it. They said that all of us people in the rap group had problems, and that from their perspective, the war had nothing to do with it. I don't know exactly what the framework is for being acceptable in society, but some of these guys had things going on in their heads that I'm sure would not be acceptable to society. But I wouldn't say that whatever was going on in their heads wasn't happening, either. Some of them were hearing voices and things like that. These were all young guys in the groups, and ex-infantrymen, and all from Vietnam.

There was no "post-traumatic stress disorder" at that time, though. That didn't become fashionable until years went by. I stayed there until sometime in late March. My parents would come and talk to the social worker, and it was as if I weren't even there. They would be sitting there talking to her, with me in the room, and I would have to look at myself in the mirror to make sure I was really there. They would be talking about me, you

know. My dad was the big one on that. My mom didn't know what
to think. After Dennis got killed, my mom just kind of zombied
out for a couple of years.

Anyway, I got out of there, and I got a job driving a cab. It
was a lot of hours and a lot of money, but no future. Then this
girl Sarah that I used to live with . . . she had become pregnant
while we were on the farm. It was kind of up in the air as to who
the father was. She kept telling me that it wasn't me, but it was
a full-term pregnancy, and, subtracting back, there was a good
chance that I was the father, so I bought a van and went to see
her. I went down to Tennessee. Then I came back to New York
again. Sarah had become a born-again Christian, and I was nowhere near that.

When I came back to New York that time, I started going
to school again. I had started going to school when I first got out
of the service, in January of 1970, and then Cambodia happened,
and school didn't seem all that important. It was a part-time job
for me, and income, with the GI Bill and everything. When I was
in Tennessee I went to school at a community college. What a
place that was. Nine dollars a credit, a GI Bill dream. So, when
I got back to New York, I started going again to Nassau Community College. I was doing good and making the Dean's List and
all of that, and, I don't know why, but the VA would decide I
wasn't going to school and cut off my checks. But I was going to
school, yet they kept hassling me. Then my parents moved upstate, and I moved into this roach apartment in Long Beach. They
kept cutting off my checks, and there was no work, and I started
selling off all my possessions. I really wanted to stay in school. I
was doing good . . . well, eventually, in late '76, I moved in with
my parents again, and then the VA sent me my checks. I couldn't
find any work up there, so I spent the money. Then the VA sent
me a letter saying they were going to cause grave hardship to my
life if I didn't return the money, if I didn't pay them back. I wrote
back to them and said, "I don't know what you think you've
already been doing to my life, but I have four dollars, and you are
welcome to it, but the rest you're going to have to wait for."

I went to school long enough up here to pay the VA back, but I never even finished two years. I still had about twenty-two months of entitlement left, but the ten-year limitation date has passed now, so I've lost that. I began taking civil service exams up here and got a job in 1977. I've been working there ever since. I started working in November of 1977, and the first year that I worked all year long, in 1978, I earned more money than I had earned from 1969 to 1977. I'm married now, and we have a son, Mikey, and the government has a better chance of water-skiing in the Sahara than they do of getting their hands on Mikey. Thanks, but no thanks. Our family doesn't need any more folded flags.

YOUNG · SCOTTY G AUSTIN · PAU
S · BRYAN J DE MELLO · MACK DEN
EGER · ROBERT W LABRECQUE · A
MILLER · JERRY D RICE · JAMES D S
· CORDIS R WHITE · RICHARD G
YER Jr · MONTY JAY EICHHORN · R
RD J HENRY · JOHN P LAMBOOY
J LYNN STENHOUSE Jr · THEODOR
LEY · WILLIAM C BIFFLE · ROBERT
ROBERT E LAVENDER · WALTER V L
WILFREDO B ANDRADA · CARL A
WEN · GREGORIO P CASTILLO · AL
V ELTING · JOE A FOSTER Jr · DAVI

STEPHEN JOHN CHANEY

Born: January 26, 1946
Marion, Ohio
Killed: September 23, 1969
Laos

AN A DIAZ-DOMENECH · JOHN M
X · STEPHEN J CHANEY · GALEN E

Stephen Chaney

The Chaney family
(left to right):
Frances, Stephen,
Kenneth, and Sheila Anne

FRANCES R. CHANEY

Born: December 20, 1921
Marion, Ohio
Mother of Stephen John Chaney

KENNETH D. CHANEY

Born: May 3, 1919
Radnor, Ohio
Father of Stephen John Chaney

So Proud

FATHER: Some of the fellows and I were talking about it, and, like I told them, we never let Steve die. We have pictures and other things around the house, and we have never put them away. We have always talked about him. What the heck. He was our kid, you know. What else can you do? We are not the kind of people to go into mourning and go around in black. In the first place, Steve wouldn't have wanted it. His friends still come in.

This one boy who was a friend of his . . . they went to school together, and they were more or less like brothers. His name is Tim, and it's just in the last year that it's gotten so he can talk about Steve. Before that, when I would talk to him and say anything about Steve, Tim would just kind of clam up, but he is just about getting through it now. Steve had a lot of close friends who come by, and we talk to them. He and I wore the same size clothes, except for shoes. He had big feet, size twelve. He had clothes, good clothes, sweaters, pants, and stuff like that, and I have worn them out. I still have some sweaters at home that are his, but I have people say, "How in the hell can you do that?" "Well," I say, "what do you want me to do with them, burn them?" I don't let it get to me, and neither does my wife.

MOTHER: It's not that we're hard, because we're not. We went through our mourning period for a long time, but, even at the funeral, we hoped we could make it easier on so many that were hurting so badly. There were a lot of people that were hurting very badly. All through the funeral I just prayed, "Don't let me break." I knew if I broke, Ken would, and I knew if he did, the whole church would go. We were trying to hold up so strongly for so many, not that we weren't hurting ourselves. We still hurt, and we're lonely. We'll always be lonely, but there is a difference between the grieving and the loneliness. We know what we missed. I mean things like . . . he talks about this Tim, and there are others. We see their families and their children, and we think or say, "Oh, what might have been." But I think God has a purpose, and, from the things we found out later, Stephen's mission was complete.

Stephen was killed in 1969. We found out exactly where he was killed in 1973, after all of the American men were back from Vietnam. The war wasn't over until 1975, but all of our men were pulled out of there in 1973. He was killed in Laos, and we could only guess where he was killed when it happened. When we were first told, an officer came to our house. They told us he was killed "deep in enemy territory." That was the phrase they used. They couldn't reveal any more, because we weren't supposed to have anybody in Laos. I have heard that some people have complaints about the way they were told, and about "the government did this, and the government did that," but, even not knowing where it happened, we can truthfully say that everyone was wonderful to us. Other than the fact of the big grief that we had lost our son, everyone, from the president on down, was wonderful to us. We received beautiful letters, and the officers that were assigned to handle the burial and keep us informed as to when he would arrive were very good. That is something, too. I could not use the word "body" for a long time. It was Steve coming home; it wasn't his body. But we were treated beautifully.

Steve was a Green Beret and a captain at the time he was killed. He was a lieutenant and had top-security clearance *before* he went to Vietnam, so we knew that he was working with something dangerous. Well, it was all dangerous. He went out, though, on long-range reconnaissance, seeking out the enemy. What their last mission was, we really don't know, but he was awarded the Silver Star for his action on that day.

FATHER: I think they said that there were ten others there besides him and a sergeant; all the others were Vietnamese. He had been out on a thirty-day mission in August. When he came back from that, he said he was going to be in for a while. Then, just about twelve days later, we got the letter saying that he was going to go back out. That was somewhere around maybe the tenth, or somewhere in that area. He was gone, then, sometime before the twenty-third.

While they were out on this patrol, they were going through the jungle, and they came to this river. On the other side of the river they discovered a bunch of Viet Cong. They were settled in over there, and Steve crawled up forward to the river to make a reconnaissance. Then he came back, and they radioed in for the gunships to come in. Well, the gunships came in, and the first rocket landed where it was supposed to in the Viet Cong area. The second rocket came in and went astray. It landed right in the middle of the patrol. They were all wounded, every one of them. Steve stayed with the radio and called in the medivac. He wanted his men evacuated before he would let them assist him, though he was close to death. He died before he reached rear medical facilities.

MOTHER: We discovered all these details in January or February of 1970, when we were called to Fort Hayes, which is in Columbus, Ohio. At that time he was awarded the Silver Star; the citation gives an account of why he was awarded the medal, so he was killed by friendly fire. But there was some beauty in the way that he did die. When they reached him, they could have taken him out first, but he said, "No. All my men go first." Then, when they got back to him, he succumbed to his wounds. We don't know whether it was right there, whether it was on the plane getting back to the base, or back at the base. We don't know.

Anyway, in 1973 we got this letter telling us he had been killed in Laos, and they gave a number where we could call or write. I immediately called Washington and told them we would just love to talk to someone who had been with him when he died. At that time we didn't know most of the people who were with him were Vietnamese. We felt sure that there were some other Americans with him, maybe several. We didn't know. Although Stephen said in one letter, "My work is cut out for me." He said, "I have a lot of respect for the Montagnards," but he also said, "I know my work is cut out for me." Anyway, Washington said, "Write a letter," which we did. We said we would like to know if there was someone we could get in touch with who was with Stephen in those last moments. They wrote back, and they gave us the name of a sergeant who was with him, but they said that due to the Privacy Act, they could not give us his address, but they would write to him and tell him that we wanted to get in touch with him. They did tell us that he had been hospitalized, I think for a long time, and then had a disability discharge, so he must have been badly wounded. We never heard a thing from him.

If we could just talk with this young man, it would help. If Stephen had been in a terrible automobile accident, we would have been at the hospital, no matter what, and we would have known all the details. I would have been able to hold him. I am sure by now this young man is in his late thirties. Maybe it is something that he can't handle. We don't know what he might be going through. But I told Ken just yesterday . . . we talked quite a bit again, as we do often, and when you are here and you see the memorial and all these wonderful young men . . . I said, "Ken, this time we should try to contact him again. We do have his name." They wouldn't give us anything else, just his name, and this man may have been so injured at that time that he wouldn't even be able to give us any details. I don't know. Still, somebody who came in and rescued them had to be there at that last moment. Someone knows what his last moments were like. Steve was the only one who died. Most of the others were Montagnards. It was only that sergeant and the people in the medivac chopper who would be able to tell us anything.

Just recently we discovered that there was a place in Laos called the Eagles Nest. We think Steve may have been based there. It was inside of Laos, and it was up on a mountain where nobody could get to it. It was evidently like a base camp, where they could take the men back and forth, into and out of Laos. We learned about this recently from talking to one of the veterans, and from doing some reading. When they told us in 1973 that he had been killed in Laos, they also told us that the reason they couldn't reveal the information before was that it was classified. I don't think many people knew there was a place called the Eagles Nest in Laos.

Truly, we have no complaints. We were treated so nicely. Every officer who came to our house or called us on the telephone kept us informed as well as they could. They said, "Anything you need, let us know," and, "We'll stay with you if you need us," but we had enough family there, and we felt that we were strong enough, that we could handle it. Even the captain who came and spent the day with us would have stayed through the whole thing, but Ken said, "No. You have family, and it's the weekend, so go on home." Since then I have been sorry we did that, because . . . this may sound strange, but Steve had a beautiful service, and there were so many beautiful things that happened . . . I wrote to him and told him, "I'm sorry we didn't have you stay." He was a Green Beret himself, and I think he would have been proud to have seen and heard the things that were said and done at the service.

FATHER: One of the ironic things that happened on the day that they came to tell us he had been killed was that I went to the door, and we had just finished lunch. It was around one o'clock in the afternoon. It was a rainy Saturday, and I went to the door.

Of course there is a curtain on the door, but I could see this officer standing outside the door, and immediately I knew what had happened. When I opened the door, this colonel was there, and I knew him and he knew me. He was a reserve colonel from Fort Hayes in Columbus, and we had come in contact with one another through the reserves. That was Colonel Cook. He came in, and it was really hard for him. All that man could do was look at the wall and tell us. He was shaking. When he got through telling us, we were all shaking together. He said that there would be somebody contacting us immediately, and they did call from Fort Hayes. We were told to contact an undertaker. Then this young lieutenant came up from Fort Hayes and sat with us that afternoon. He gave us all the details. "Do you want a military funeral?" "Absolutely." "Do you want a firing squad, taps, the whole thing?" "We want it all." Steve's body arrived in Marion on October 3, 1969. The burial detail came up from Fort Knox on Sunday night, and he was buried on Monday. They came and stayed in a hotel.

MOTHER: We were notified on the twenty-seventh, and it was not quite two weeks after his death when he came home. I had absolutely no complaints about the way the government treated us. Really, we don't think we were treated any differently than anyone else. Perhaps some people, in their anger over death, are just ready to lash out at anything. I don't know. I think that Ken and I accepted it the moment we heard it. I don't mean that we weren't grieving or that we weren't terribly shocked, but we thought, "This is it." That doesn't make it any easier, but I think that anybody who goes through that kind of terrible grief and loneliness and is bitter, too . . . I don't know how they stand it. To be bitter is an awful emotion. Even without death and war and people being killed in a war, there are people who are terribly bitter. Even if someone who has been ill for months dies, there can be this terrible bitterness and hatred. People just accept things very differently.

FATHER: Steve was very into playing football in high school. He graduated in 1964, and he had a four-year football scholarship at Notre Dame. He went there the first year and played freshman ball. At that time in the colleges the freshmen did not play varsity ball.

MOTHER: But that spring, Stephen, who was so mature, really, made this decision. He made it all on his own, really, that he was going to give up football. I was thoroughly frustrated. I said, "I thought you loved this game. How can you do it?" But he had come home, and evidently he had given it a lot of thought. We usually took him to the bus when he was going to school, but this time we drove him, because I just had to talk to somebody. I just couldn't accept this. I didn't know that he was sure about what he was doing. Ara Parsegian was the coach at that time. We didn't get to see him, because he was out, but we did talk to one of the assistant coaches. He was the coach who had scouted Stephen. We talked to him, and they were frustrated and really upset. He said, "Stephen came to us and said he was going to give up football. You know, some come in, even with a scholarship, and we know they just can't make it. We would have accepted that. If he had gotten a girl pregnant, we could have accepted that. Those things happen, or if he were failing in his studies. But it's none of those things with Stephen. We had high hopes for him. He was a good football player and a pretty good all-around athlete. We gave him twenty-four hours to change his mind. In twenty-four hours, he came back and said he hadn't changed his mind." I'll never forget this man's last words to us, he said, as we were going out the door, "I hope fifteen years from now he won't be sorry." Stephen didn't live that long.

Anyway, Ken and I felt that Steve had Vietnam on his mind all this time. He came home that summer. He worked a night job at Whirlpool and made enough money to pay for the first semester of his sophomore year at school. Well, that Christmas, just before he came home for Christmas, he had written a personal letter to his dad. I didn't see this letter, so Ken knew what his plans were, what he was going to do, but I didn't. So, Ken had gone to bed one night after Steve had come home for Christmas. I will never forget this. Steve and I were alone in the kitchen. He paced that kitchen, and he couldn't seem to get the right words out. He could usually talk beautifully. Then he went through all his reasons, all about the war, and that if he didn't learn anything else at Notre Dame, "I learned that what you believe in is what you have to do." Finally I decided I had to get him off the hook. I said, "Steve, you're leaving school, and you are going to enlist." He said, "Yes, Mom." I told him, "Steve, you make us so proud. You have made me proud many times, but I have never been prouder than I am at this moment." I still remember that, because Steve was really something to be proud of . . . you'd think I would quit this crying, it's been so long . . . like I said, there are times when we are pretty strong, but we are not all that strong, either. I guess we need tears. We really do. Anyway, foolishly, I also said, "Steve, won't you just wait until after your twentieth birthday," because that would be on January twenty-third.

I don't know why I did that to him. He waited. He just went to work in the local butcher shop, but he had already gone for his physical examination. High blood pressure runs in our family. I have been on medication for it for years, and at sixteen it cropped up with him. At that time, when you turned eighteen, if you were in school you had to go take your physical. His blood pressure had been up at that time. I don't know how they classified him, then, because he wouldn't talk about it. But now he had me praying about it, and I seriously meant it when I prayed that he would pass the blood-pressure test, and he did. Everything went great, and he called that night from Columbus. He was elated. He said, "Oh, Mom, I passed!" He said, "Mom, they asked me what I wanted to do during my tour of duty, and I said I wanted to go to Vietnam." I started to cry, and he said, "Mom, you knew." I said, "I know, Steve." Really, though, I had to shed a few tears.

Stephen was awarded the Bronze Star and other medals. He had several. After he was killed, there wasn't much that came home except this box. We opened it up, and I said, "This is like our gift." We got three photographs of him all the time he was in Vietnam. They were little snapshots. But we opened this box and . . . there were a few personal things, but there was also this green folder. I opened it up, and two eight-and-a-half-by-eleven pictures were in it. They were taken with this colonel who was investigated over there. Ken can explain more about that.

FATHER: Well, they had this guy who was a double agent. He was working for us and also working for the Viet Cong. Anyway, what happened is that they killed this double agent. Our people hunted him down and wasted him. All this stuff came out, like so many things do. It's one of those things where you know you do it, and it's okay, but if you get caught, that's something else. So the media got ahold of this and started a big investigation. The colonel who was there at the time was responsible for this man's death, but he went back to the States. Then this other colonel went over as a commander of the special forces. He was the one who took all the dirt and flak. It wasn't him. He had nothing to do with it. He wasn't even there when it happened, but he was there when the story broke, so he felt the flak. He retired right away.

MOTHER: He was made a scapegoat. They even had him in prison in Vietnam. I think for about five days.

FATHER: At the time they discovered all of this, he was the commanding officer. It's just another one of those dirty deals. Somebody wanted this man wasted, or he wouldn't have been killed. Probably they were right to do it, because he was working for us, and, by the same token, he was also working for the Viet Cong. They found out what he was doing, and when they found out, they killed him.

MOTHER: They probably had to do that. Well, anyway, this colonel was giving Steve an award in one picture. This was probably the Bronze Star. Then there was another eight-and-a-half-by-eleven that showed the colonel shaking hands with Stephen. It's just like I said, it was sort of a gift, because there were no big, big pictures of Stephen, ever, from Vietnam, and we never knew anything about his Bronze Star. He had never ever mentioned it. We didn't know about his medals.

FATHER: He got one of them when his camp came under fire and the little shed or whatever they kept their ammunition and stuff in took a direct hit. Steve and some more of them went into the building with everything exploding around them and hauled everything out. This is what he got one of the medals for.

MOTHER: But these things were never mentioned by him.

FATHER: Well, the thing of it was, he got his ear drum broken when the ammunition dump blew up. He knew that he was going to have to tell us about this, because once you get your ear drum broken, you are hard-of-hearing. So he told us that he had been clearing a road or something like that, and dynamite blew up, that he had been a little too close and it ripped his ear drum. Okay, we went along with it, but, actually, I got a copy of the commendation, and I found out where he was and what he was doing. I had doubted very much that it had happened while he was clearing a road. He got it at the ammunition dump, because you don't have to get too awfully close to something like that for that to happen. I still think that was where he got the torn ear drum. It was about the same time that he was given the award. The date was on the commendation, and everything was along about the same time that he wrote and told us about his ear.

MOTHER: He didn't want to worry us. We kept his letters, but he wouldn't write about anything like that. Like I said, he could really talk, but he wrote about funny things, like one time when they were under fire. He had gotten diarrhea very badly when he was a senior in high school. I don't think that he ever got over it. When he would become nervous, it would hit him again. In this one letter, he said, "You know me. Right in the middle of everything . . ." well, he put it pretty bluntly, but I will say "diarrhea," and he said, "I did everything right. I did everything that I was supposed to do. I land-crawled over to the latrine, and, all of a sudden, you guessed it, the latrine took a direct hit. I was so mad and disgusted I pulled down my pants, did what I had to do, and then I stood up and I walked back." Here we were, reading this, and we were petrified. Then we ended up just laughing. This was what he was wanting us to do.

Steve did two tours in Vietnam. He was on his second tour of duty when he was killed. He was there fourteen months the first time. He extended a little bit on his first tour.

FATHER: What it was, of course, was that when he first went to Vietnam, he went over as an infantry officer. He wasn't in Special Forces. He had volunteered, and he wanted to go to Vietnam, but the Special Forces weren't ready to send him over. He was training troops at Fort Bragg, so he went to Washington, to the Pentagon to some major that he got hold of up there. The major said, "Okay. We will send you to Vietnam, but you can't go through Special Forces. You have to go as a regular infantry officer." So when he went over at that time he went over in the American Division as a lieutenant. He went into long-range reconnaissance patrol. Anyhow, when his tour was about ended, he went to them and told them, "You can put me back in Special Forces. I'll volunteer for another tour." That is what they did. When he went back for his second tour, he was in Special Forces. He enlisted in 1966, and his first tour in Vietnam began in 1967. He was there from 1967 through 1969.

MOTHER: Yes. He came home for thirty days. After the first tour, he came home on his thirty-day leave. This was in January of 1969. He went back around the first of February in 1969, and he was killed in September of 1969. He really wanted to be in Vietnam. He really did. He felt he had to do it. These are the things we remember when we talk about it now. We talk about God's missions and all that. He loved football. He loved it. He even said, "Some day I am going to finish college, and I will play football again someday. I don't think that it will ever be with a scholarship, but I want to play again." But he gave up football. That was a tremendous sacrifice. Like I said, a little later we realized that Vietnam was on his mind all the time.

He worked very hard to get into Special Forces. Stephen had had knee surgery, and, of course, in Special Forces, you have to jump. His knee began locking on him again. In one letter he wrote home he said, "Mom and Dad, pray that I can jump. If I have to nail this knee together, I am going to jump." He wanted Special Forces, but he also wanted to be in Vietnam. That is why he felt so badly when Washington said he could go as an infantry officer at that time, and not as a Special Forces officer. He gave up Special

Forces then. That was another sacrifice, but he did get back into Special Forces.

You know, we have even had some people say to us, "Well, you knew what would happen when he went over there." But that's not true. You know what to expect, and you know there's a fifty-fifty chance he might be killed, but you don't think they are going to die. When they are so young, you don't think about death. They don't, either. Sure, he knew the dangers and the hazards, and we did, too, but they don't go over there to die.

Steve went over there feeling that it was his duty, that it was right, and that he had to be there. This one friend of Steve's, Tim, that we talked about earlier . . . Stephen had a military funeral, and military pallbearers, but there were about twenty honorary pallbearers. Some were his classmates, some teammates, and this friend Tim wrote a beautiful eulogy and read it. It was just beautiful. He said Stephen had said—and I know it's true, that he sat in our living room and said this—"I went over there the first time, and I was this gung-ho second lieutenant. I know now that it is a political war, but I have to go back, because of all these eighteen- and nineteen-year-old boys who are going over there. If I can save just one . . ." So I think by his second tour he felt that we shouldn't still be there. But he had also written home during that first tour of duty and said, "I am liable to get court-martialed, because I've been complaining that our hands are so tied."

FATHER: When you send men into enemy territory, territory that you know is full of enemies, and you don't allow them to load their weapons . . .

MOTHER: Now, he didn't tell us this, but these are things that we are hearing now. It was that you can go this far, and then you stop. You don't dare go any farther.

FATHER: That same sort of thing happened in Korea. That is why I say Korea was another little Vietnam. And there is another thing, MacArthur was a big general, and if Truman would have let him alone, he would have gone on into North Vietnam or Indochina, and we might not have had some of this.

MOTHER: You know, our daughter thinks she had a premonition. She felt like something was going to happen to Stephen. We were always concerned. And this is an honest thing. The Saturday morning that we got word . . . it was about one o'clock in the afternoon that an officer came . . . and I had had the strangest dream that night, just a real strange dream. The dream was in the first apartment that we lived in. It was an upstairs apartment, and the stairs were old. We lived in a few rooms up above the second floor, and we were living there from the time Stephen was born until he was about six months old. The thing about it was that Stephen was little when we were in this old apartment, and, in the dream, he was little, and there was a little alligator in the dream. Now, you know, what would a live alligator be doing in our apartment? Anyway, in the dream, Stephen was trying to get it, and he was going down the steps, and the steps were so dark. He was going down these stairs, and this alligator kept getting bigger and bigger and bigger. And another thing about it was that the alligator was blue. It was such a blue alligator. I don't know what it meant, but I dreamed that that night, and it stayed with me, and that morning I was going through old pictures of his, you know, after this dream. It is strange, and that dream will always be in my mind. He was a little child in the dream, and he got the alligator, but, as he went down the steps, it was like the weight of the world was on his shoulders, because this alligator was so huge as he went down the steps. That was it. And I don't know that that means anything. I don't know. But he was dead then. He had been dead for three or four days. When I had the dream. I will never forget that.

FATHER: Before he went on his first tour over there, he was in Panama for some training. He was supposed to jump off from there to Vietnam, but they had some kind of a mess-up there, so they sent them all home on a Thanksgiving leave, and then from that leave he went to Vietnam. Of course, a bunch of them were coming home from Panama on the plane, and I thought maybe they might have been half high or something, but they got this thing going, you know: "If you can't tap-dance, you are a queer." And they would all get up in the plane and start tap-dancing.

When he came home, he told us about it, and our daughter to this day swears up and down that once in a while she can hear him tap-dancing. She'll say, "The son-of-a-gun was tap-dancing again last night." And our granddaughter. Steve only saw her a few times, on his last thirty-day leave, but she swears that Steve talks to her. And she is not looney, either. Not by any means.

I was in Korea, and the big thing with the Vietnam vets that I can see is they were put down. They were the "woman killers," the "kid killers." They were the junkies and pot heads and whatever. All that kind of stuff. When they came back home, there was nothing for them. When I came back from Korea, we pulled into San Francisco, and at the pier there were bands playing. There were people there from the eastern part of the country meeting some of the boys that were getting off the boat. As we came off, the Red Cross ladies were standing out there with a cup of coffee in their hands, and a doughnut. When we went to Korea off Pier 96 in Seattle, the Red Cross ladies were standing there. They had a little booth set up out there with hot coffee and doughnuts. In World War II, it was the same way. You had parades when people came home, and you walked into a bar some place, and: "Yeah. Come on over and have a drink." It didn't happen to Vietnam vets.

MOTHER: You know, you have people say, "What a waste," out of sympathy, like about Stephen's death. Yet, I still don't feel to this day that "waste" is the right word. Sure, we would love to have him here, but he was doing exactly what he wanted to do, and he felt very strongly about that. He wouldn't have had it another way. It is going to be years before we really know about Vietnam, about just what it was all about. Maybe it was right that we went over there to try to help them, but the terrible thing is that our hands were tied. I think this is what Stephen was saying a few times, that the frustration as an officer was that their hands were tied, and he was only a lieutenant. The generals were apparently frustrated, too. I think that was what he was trying to say before he went over there for his second tour.

FATHER: You know, in Vietnam, they usually got the bodies

out of there within two or three days or so. What I am saying is that there were more that were killed in Vietnam that got out right away. They immediately brought them home. In other wars, they were buried in the cemetery some place over there, and you got the body home after the war was over with. If you wanted, they would bring it home then, but most of them came home right away from Vietnam. Well, there are probably some lost out there, like missing in the jungle, and maybe there wasn't anything left of them, because you do have several different things over there. In a jungle like that, it could eliminate a body practically overnight. You've got dampness and humidity, and all that kind of thing, plus the animals. Well, with Steve, they brought him home, and you couldn't see a mark on him.

MOTHER: We don't know where the wounds were, but they had to be in the lower extremities, because his face was beautiful. We could have really had an open casket. He was a little dark, but we did have a private showing for the family and some friends of his. There was no doubt that it was our Steve. He was in a dress uniform, and he had his white gloves on, and that was a blessing, because there are those who will always have doubts. We are lucky because we know it was him.

FATHER: And we know where he is. I can walk over about four blocks to the cemetery, and there is Steve. I can visit him any time that I want to.

MOTHER: And as far as acceptance of his death, that was always there. But you go through a lot of different cycles, I think, at times like that. You know, some people get mad at God and so forth, but it was probably a year or so later that I just all of a sudden . . . well, I have a lot of nieces and nephews, and I wouldn't have wanted it to be one of them. You know, if I could have said, "Bring Steve back, and take one of them," I never would have done it. I couldn't have. But, yet, I thought, "Here is our only son," and I was stopping by the cemetery one day, and I truly got mad at God. I was just really mad. I thought, "Our only son." Then we went to church. It was over a weekend, and we went to mass that Saturday night. I wouldn't go to commu-

nion, because I thought . . . well, thank God that real anger only
lasted twenty-four hours, because I don't think I could have lived
with myself. That is why I said that these people who have the
grief and the terrible bitterness, I don't know how they stand it.
And there were other times when I just thought, "Well, okay,
God. You didn't let us have him long enough, only twenty-three
years, but there has to be a reason that you wanted him back."

FATHER: One thing that has helped me is the fact that after
a while I was . . . well, I wasn't bitter, I have never been bitter
about it . . . but the thing was, I was grieving and feeling bad and
sorry for myself. I finally one day kind of caught myself up and
said, "Who the hell are you grieving for? Yeah, Steve is over there.
He is resting, and you don't have to worry about him. Hopefully,
he's in heaven." I don't think any kid who went over there to war
is going to any place other than heaven if he was killed over there,
because he has already had his hell on earth. But the thing of it
was, I thought, "You are not grieving for Steve. You're grieving
for yourself. You are feeling sorry for yourself." So I said, "Yeah.
Cut it out. If you have to do your crying, okay, but don't do it
trying to pass it off on him. It's your own self you're crying for."

Then this priest who was in World War II came over one
night. He dropped in on us. He would come every three months
or so. He is from a little parish down the Ohio River, about a
hundred and sixty miles from us, but he still comes back to Marion
to see different people. So we were sitting there talking one night,
and I was feeling kind of down. I asked him. I said, "Father, how
can Stephen be happy up there? If they know what is going on
down here, how can he be happy up there, looking down and
seeing all the grief and sorrow that we have?" "Well," he said,
"look at it this way. He knows God's plan, and you don't."

MOTHER: You could almost hear Steve say, "Yeah, Mom
and Dad. I know it is tough now, but wait till you get here." This
priest was able to say it, and I know it helped Ken. It didn't take
the loneliness away, but we have never forgotten that he knows
God's plan. To the priest, that was just so simple. It wasn't any-

thing complicated that Steve was fine and happy, and that he knows what it's all about, and that someday we will.

FATHER: But I thought, "Here is this young man, twenty-three years old, killed." I have thought that, and I'm sure a lot of other parents have thought the same thing. When he went into the army and I knew he was going to Vietnam, I used to pray, "Lord, don't take him. If you need somebody, take me. I am older. What the hell do I have to go on for? Don't take him, take me." But He wasn't ready for me yet, or whoever is going to take me, Him or the Devil! I don't know.

MOTHER: And the things that Steve truly loved and gave up to be in Vietnam. Then, when we found out the way that he did die, it is almost like God said, "Well done. Come up here." I was so proud of him.

And you know, when I found out that he probably knew that he was probably going to die, I was thankful, because I know that he had time to say that "Our Father," or whatever. He had enough sense about him to be on the phone calling the medivac, so I think he had that moment when he could say, "Dear God, have mercy on me and take me with you." I knew that Steve had that moment, and I felt so good about that. Yet I don't know how long he lived, lying there, but I know Steve, and I think that he would have wanted to die. I hope that there wasn't a lot of pain, but we know that he was coherent, and that he did have that last moment to communicate with God.

THOMAS MICHA

· MICHAEL L POGGI · C

· LAWRENCE D PERUSO · JULIUS

· ERIC V PULLIAM · RC

· BRUCE W SHAFFER · CHARLES

· CHARLES WALKER ·

· PAUL J BAKER · TERRY JOE BARN

· KENNETH J BREN

ROSS W COLLINS Jr · THOMAS L CO

· WILLIAM C GOULD Jr · G

· LARRY K HOC

· JAMES M McKINLEY · MARK

· ROBERT A MULHOL

CHARLES R PRCHAL · VICTOR H PR

PAUL JOSEPH BAKER

Born: August 23, 1948
       Troy, New York
Killed: March 29, 1969
       Quang Tri Province, Republic of South Vietnam

· RUSSELL L JOHNSON · CHA

· LAWSON D NELSON · DON

Paul Baker in Vietnam

The Baker family
(top row, left to right):
Linda, Bob, and Claire
(bottom row):
Mr. and Mrs. Baker

George Swiers

MARION R. BAKER

Born: June 3, 1917
        Troy, New York
Mother of Paul Joseph Baker

CLAIRE BAKER NETZ

Born: December 21, 1951
        Troy, New York
Sister of Paul Joseph Baker

GEORGE SWIERS

Born: June 25, 1948
        Chatham, New York
Friend of Paul Joseph Baker

Sharing Wars

MRS. BAKER: Paul was in the first semester of his second year at MIT when he quit school and came home. He said he thought he would enlist for Vietnam. We were not happy about it. My husband was alive then, and we both thought it would be better if he finished school first. That was in January of 1968. We tried for about a month to talk him into going back to school, but he had his mind made up that he wanted to do his time in the service. We tried to encourage him to get into the navy, but he said he would have no part of that, because he would be doing clerical work, and he didn't want to do that.

Paul was very idealistic. I can't say what his inner thoughts were, how he actually decided he had to enlist, but one thing he felt was that it was very unfair that all young men were not required to serve, that you could go to college, and stay there for many years, really, and not have to serve. He just decided he wanted to enlist, and we couldn't talk him out of it. He enlisted from Boston. Then he called home and told us what he'd done.

He was at MIT on a full-tuition scholarship. He had been valedictorian of his high school class. I don't think he was doing as well as he could have at MIT, because his heart wasn't in it. He could have done better. We all felt pretty badly when he left school. To begin with, I'm not sure we were wholeheartedly in back of that war effort. I still have very mixed feelings about that war, to the point where I don't think we should ever, ever fight a war that we don't go into to win. I think it was very unfair to all the young men over there that we didn't put our full effort behind them. We asked them to lay down their lives, and so many of them did, and I don't feel they were fully backed. I hope that will never happen again. I don't think we should let it. We should try hard not to.

My husband was extremely patriotic. He was in World War II, and he was patriotic to the point that no one could ever speak against his country or his flag. He was fairly horrified at some of the demonstrations during Vietnam, but he didn't really feel, "My country, right or wrong." Since he died, I found the original scribbling of a letter he was going to send to his congressman, asking him to do something about stopping what he called "the needless slaughter in Vietnam." He was in the air corps in World War II. He was in India and the Pacific Islands. But, of course, World War II was a different thing. My husband's two brothers were also in that war, one in the army and one in the navy. When the children were young, they saw all the pictures we had from World War II. I don't think Dad ever idealized his service in World War II, though. The stories from India were pretty horrible. I don't know how much he influenced Paul. The thing I think influenced Paul was the fact that he could stay out of the war if he wanted to, and so many young men couldn't. They were drafted. He was not drafted. He enlisted. He didn't have to go.

We didn't want Paul to go to Vietnam. To be perfectly honest, we didn't. If it had been a different situation, it would have been a different story. Vietnam was a war that wasn't a war. What bothers me most about the Vietnam War was that so many people sat in their living rooms and watched it on the news at night and said, "Isn't that terrible," then turned off the television and forgot it. It didn't affect them at all. Who did it affect? It affected us, those of us who had people involved. There were no sacrifices by the country at large. We weren't doing without things at home so that those boys would have them. Having been in the middle of World War II, I remember civilians doing without things. You did without. It didn't hurt you to do without, but, nevertheless, you did do without. Many times you ate your bread without butter, or you couldn't have things you liked, and nobody complained. Well, maybe some people did, but most didn't. In the Vietnam War, unless you knew someone personally, you could go on about your life and be totally unaffected, personally.

CLAIRE: In my own age group, I had many friends who didn't know even one person who was in Vietnam. I think in World War II you at least knew someone who was there. For Vietnam, there are an awful lot of people who didn't know anybody at all.

MRS. BAKER: I don't think it affected a great number of people. The only people I really think it affected were people who had husbands, sons, fathers, fighting. Or close friends.

GEORGE: There were 25.8 million males who came of age during that period who would have been considered draft eligible. There were nine million that wound up in the military. Only two and a half million went to Vietnam. Only one out of ten draft-eligible males during that time period wound up in Vietnam. Out of the two and a half million that wound up in Vietnam, there were only about five hundred thousand who did what Paul and I did, actually serve as infantrymen. The rest served as support for the combatants.

MRS. BAKER: And of the ones who went . . . I know you had your reserve officers and all that who went, but, on the whole, there was a group of young men who had to go whether they wanted to or not. They were just drafted. They didn't have the influence to stay out, and the others did.

GEORGE: One of the most horrible statistics you'll ever see about that war has to do with people of extreme influence. If you look at those individuals who served as United States congressmen or senators in the period known as the war years, to the best of my knowledge all of those people collectively had fifteen hundred sons and grandsons who would have been draft eligible. Out of the fifteen hundred, only twenty-seven went into the military. Out of that twenty-seven who actually went into the military, only three went to Vietnam. If the rest of the country had served in the same proportion as the sons of the country's leadership served, only about fifty thousand people would have ever gone to Vietnam, not the two and a half million that actually went. It's a real commentary on our leadership. It seems to me that one of the things leaders are supposed to do is not make demands on the citizenry they wouldn't make of themselves. Our leaders didn't do it that way. They protected their own. All things aside, I have always liked Lyndon Johnson. He had no sons to give, but he had two sons-in-law, and both of them went to Vietnam. Johnson could have kept them out.

MRS. BAKER: Another thing that has always bothered me is the question mark. We never really knew how Paul felt about the war. That's one of the voids in our life. He didn't come back to tell us how he felt after he got there, and I never heard him say how he felt about it before he left. The only thing I ever knew was that he didn't think it was fair that everybody wasn't put in the same category as far as being required to serve.

CLAIRE: In the letters he sent home, he never even really mentioned what they were actually doing. Another guy we knew used to send letters saying how awful things were, but I don't think Paul ever mentioned that.

MRS. BAKER: No. He never did. He wrote about more personal things, or funny things that happened. He never said how hard everything was. He never mentioned a name, which really was very difficult when he didn't come home, because we never knew anyone we could get in touch with who knew him personally. I always thought: "There he was over there. Did he ever have a friend? Did he have anybody he could talk to? Was there any continuity to the people he knew, or did they just come and go?" Then, when he was killed, I used to think: "There he was, way over there, all alone. Did anybody really care?" I mean, we got a letter, sure, but did that person really care? Was there anybody who really cared? We never knew that until George Swiers turned up.

GEORGE: I was probably as close to Paul as anyone. I actually knew him only a little over three months. I was his radio man, his grenadier. Paul was my squad leader, and that was your whole world in Vietnam. Your world is the people you're with. The most intimate breakdown in the infantry unit is the squad. We were Paul's family there, and I was the closest member of his family there, because I knew. I knew the names of Paul's brother and sisters, and I knew about his family. He knew about my family. That's what you did at night after you dug your hole and you sat in it. If you were a squad leader, you sat with your radio man, as I ultimately did when I became a squad leader. My radio man knew everything about me, and I knew everything about him, but you very seldom went beyond that to share a lot of things with other people. You never knew how long anyone was going to be there. You were always with strangers, people just passing in your life. Whoever was closest to you, you got very close to, but you didn't like to expand that circle too much. I think the fear of getting hurt had a lot to do with it.

I want to backtrack on something. Paul was valedictorian of his high school class, and he was in MIT for a year and a half, and he quit school. There's been a long-existing myth about the people who went to Vietnam. The myth developed that you only went to Vietnam if you were a dummy. I don't want to offend anyone, but I think I'm a part of the most educated generation this country ever had. You should talk to some of the kids going to high school now, and see how awful their whole educational process is. We were idealistic people. John Kennedy was our hero, and we picked up on his idealism. The kind of patriotism we had was not in relationship to a war that seemed as black and white then as it seems now. It's difficult now to look back on those years without saying: "I wonder. It was so clear. How could people actually have gone to Vietnam?" It wasn't that clear then.

People have the luxury of looking back now. The *Pentagon Papers* have been published. Watergate has happened, and people more generally recognize it's okay to challenge authority. There was no question in our minds, however, growing up during that period, that the decisions made by people in authority were made in our best interests. There was no question in our minds then about anyone lying to us, or anything like that. Consequently, a lot of individuals like Paul did quit school, and did believe, and did go to Vietnam. They got caught up in it that way. It's *because* of those years that many people have learned to question authority now.

Another thing. We were also the first real television generation. We had *The Sands of Iwo Jima* and *Guadalcanal Diary*. We had fathers who served in World War II. All of that became a part of our own history. In any case, that's a myth that I really wish somebody would put to bed sometime, that we went over there because we were dummies.

People who went over there and fought, people who were in combat in Vietnam, by and large were not wealthy people, though. Most of them were draftees, and most of the draftees were in the army. They weren't dumb. They weren't wealthy. They were drafted. The Marine Corps did very little drafting. I knew some draftees over there. If the Marine Corps did draft you, you wound up in the infantry. During my time in the marines, I ran into a lot of idealistic people. I consider myself an idealistic person.

MRS. BAKER: You have to be an idealist to enlist, I think. Not for an all-out war. I mean, if it's your country that's being attacked, certainly you would enlist, but for the type of war that

Vietnam was, you have to be an idealist to go out of your way to serve, I think. Certainly people who enlisted didn't do it just for fun. They felt it was something they wanted to do, that they were doing the right thing. Still, as to how Paul did feel about the war, that's one big question mark. I don't know. I had planned all those months to ask him how he felt about it after he came home. We never had that opportunity.

GEORGE: My own situation parallels Paul's just a little bit. I went out of my way to get there. I graduated from high school with a Regent's Scholarship, and I never even thought about college. Never. I enlisted in the Marine Corps. When I enlisted, in 1967, they gave me a duty station. My duty station was in Monterey, California, at the Defense Language Institute. In the Marine Corps, that is a most extremely rare duty station. They sent me there on a year-long program to study the Albanian language. I don't know why they did that. I took a language aptitude test when I went in, and I can still remember my drill instructor saying, "You've got class duty." They never send anyone in the Marine Corps to Monterey. It's an army school. I got out there, and I had my own room and my stereo. I was there for seven months.

I spent those seven months filling out administrative action forms for a change of duty, change of MOS [military occupational specialty]. They kept tearing up my administrative action forms. They said, "The Marine Corps has never had a graduate of this school. They *will* have one." I kept filling the forms out. Finally, I wrote a letter to the commandant of the Marine Corps. I said: "This is unbelievable. Here is someone who actually wants to go there. Give me a break. I've spent nineteen years of my life getting ready for my war, and you're doing this terrible thing to me." I sent the letter, and the commandant got it. He reviewed the whole thing, and they gave me my orders. Now I think they gave them to me as a punishment for writing to the commandant of the Marine Corps.

MRS. BAKER: George, were you disillusioned when you got to Vietnam and spent some time there?

GEORGE: Very quickly. Everyone I knew was disillusioned. It was not what they promised. In two ways it wasn't what they promised. First of all, there's this whole thing, again, about growing up in the television generation. Real war is not like television war. It's a lot to get used to when you're nineteen or twenty years old, seeing the kinds of things you see and feeling the kinds of things you feel. It sneaks up on you. We were idealistic people. We were not people of the world. A lot of us, especially those of us in the Marine Corps, enlisted. We came from relatively sheltered environments. We didn't expect to see what we saw. It crept up on you over a period of the first two or three months you were there. You just saw absurd things. It became very clear to you there was no reason for you to have to go through all of that.

I remember a talk Paul and I had one night. Neither of us believed that anybody in this country should have a draft facing them at all. There should be some kind of universal conscription, whether the country was at war or not. Assuming there was a war going on, there should be a unified country and the war should be shared. It should be shared. You shouldn't target a group of people to do the fighting.

I was amazed when I got to Vietnam. I landed in DaNang. It was at night, but the next morning, before they put us on a plane to take us north, I saw all these Vietnamese riding around on motor scooters. They obviously were my age or a little bit older, and I asked about them. It was explained to me that they had draft deferments. Vietnam was their country. It was supposed to be falling apart, and they were supposed to be needing our help desperately, and they had draft deferments. Obviously, the United States government knew this was going on. The same standards that were being applied here were being applied there. In other words, it was like saying, "Well, some people are really too good to have to go through war." That was something Paul and I were both adamantly opposed to, the idea of not sharing equitably the burden of war. The Vietnamese had the same standards we did. They had draft deferments. There was an upper crust that didn't have to go and do that sort of thing. They were going to run the government, instead, I guess.

MRS. BAKER: Well, do you think we should have been there at all?

GEORGE: No. Of course, I didn't know that then.

MRS. BAKER: I mean, in retrospect? I just mean in retrospect. Should we ever have been there?

GEORGE: No. I knew that was my feeling by the time I came back. Most of it was emotional, though, at that point. It wasn't really intellectual. The emotional part of me said, "Of course not. People shouldn't be going through that. That's crazy." I didn't develop the intellectual part of it until I got back and started reading a lot. In putting it all together that way, in a more academic sense, you can look at it and say, "There was no reason for that war to have happened. There was no reason for us ever to have been involved." I can see that very clearly now.

MRS. BAKER: Well, few people saw it at the time. That's why that gradual acceleration was allowed, really. I think we just kept getting in deeper and deeper. The best I can say is that it's a lesson. It's a tragic lesson, really.

GEORGE: And also the fact that, back then, there was no reason to think that leaders, elected leaders in a democracy, were going to lie to you, that they were going to make decisions that were going to be so apart from the American people, and not in their best interests. It was so contrary to the way I grew up, and the way that all of us grew up. You didn't think that was going to happen, and it did. It's so easy now for it to seem so black and white. That's why it's so important to remember it wasn't so black and white back then.

MRS. BAKER: Well, of course you believed in it. You thought it was right. If you went, you thought it was right, and you thought your leaders were leading you in the right direction. After a while, it became evident that it wasn't right. Then it was hard to extricate ourselves, really.

GEORGE: By the end of the whole thing, in late 1972, when

I was with Vietnam Veterans Against the War, we had a demonstration at the Republican Convention in Miami. The Nixon administration was saying that we were not really veterans, that they didn't know who we were, that we were a bunch of wackos. It was awful. The Nixon administration tried to find, somewhere at the convention, or somewhere in Miami, a "good Vietnam veteran" to bring in front of the cameras and microphones to say they supported Nixon. They couldn't find one. They couldn't find one anywhere. They certainly couldn't find one among us. I remember that it reached the point where, in one of the side speeches he made there, it was put in these terms: "Well, of course we have to finish the war, and we have to win it and do it right, because not to do so means that those who have already died have died in vain." They began putting it in those terms, and that was partly to hurt a lot of us who were members of Vietnam Veterans Against the War.

MRS. BAKER: I don't think any of them died in vain, because there's a lesson to be learned from it, so it isn't in vain. None of them died in vain. It shouldn't have been, but I don't think they died in vain if we've learned a valuable lesson from their deaths.

GEORGE: John Kerry, who is the lieutenant governor of Massachusetts now, was one of the leaders of Vietnam Veterans Against the War. He made a speech in front of Congress at one point. This was after the Nixon administration had started saying we were actors. Whenever we had a demonstration set up, they would start with: "They aren't Vietnam veterans. They're actors." It was about at that point that John Kerry made a very moving speech to Congress along the lines you're talking about. He said that no American who has died there, none of our friends, has died in vain, and just for the reason you're saying. He said something like, "This can be a turning point for America, where America begins to take a look at herself." Hopefully, this kind of thing will never happen again, if we do look at ourselves and if we catch it in time the next time.

MRS. BAKER: I think of the peace talks. Back then, and that would have been at the end of 1968 and the beginning of 1969, if you had someone in Vietnam then, you couldn't wait to get in front of the television at night to see how the peace talks were going. You were always thinking, "Oh, maybe it'll end, and he'll come home." Then you sat there, night after night. Nothing. Not even "night after night." It got to be "year after year."

I had a map of Vietnam. I sent away and got it somewhere. We used to take it out and try to figure out where Paul was, but the names were so alien to us, really. The names meant so little. DMZ. [Demilitarized zone.] I always remembered DMZ. But, in the meantime, you'd look at the television. Your life centered around the television at night, just to see where the fighting was. If it wasn't flashing on something where your husband, boy, or whoever you had there was at the time, you'd feel a little relieved for that night. For one night.

George, you said Paul was killed on the twenty-eighth of March. I always thought it was the twenty-ninth. Do you think that difference is because of the difference in time zones?

GEORGE: I don't know. I thought it was March 28, but we never really knew exactly what the day was over there. We knew when it was Sunday, because Sunday was the day we got the large orange malaria tablet. That was one aspect of what the life of the infantryman was like. There were always two wars. There was the war that the guys fought in the field, and there was the one they fought in Saigon and the rear-echelon areas, where they had air conditioning and television. The rest of us were in never-never-land most of the time. We had no idea what the exact date was.

MRS. BAKER: Did you always know where you were?

GEORGE: I had that advantage. A lot of people didn't have that advantage. I knew it because Paul was my squad leader, and . . . let me tell you how Paul picked me. I got there as one of a group of replacements for the company Paul was in. That first day, the lieutenant was going around with the squad leaders, and the lieutenant would ask each of the new people questions. I was the first person the lieutenant talked to. It was really just a show. The lieutenant wanted to show that he was one of the guys and a part of everything. Anyway, I was talking to the lieutenant, and he asked me where I was from. I said, "From Chatham, New York. Columbia County." I didn't even know Paul then, because it was my first day, but Paul said, "I'll take care of him." Just like that. Paul, of course, wanted to take me because I was from close by his home. He thought I could tell him what was going on in Troy. You always looked for someone from close to home, anything you could grab onto. You sent letters home, and got letters and clippings and other things they might send, but that's all you ever knew, really, about how things were back home. Finding someone from home you could actually grab and talk to for a few minutes was a special thing, a real person you could talk to.

Anyway, I became Paul's radio man. I shifted back and forth with another guy, so I was either the radio man or the grenadier, which are the two closest people to the squad leader. Paul would always have the maps. He would lay them out. He showed me how to use them to lay out a course. When I became a squad leader, I always had maps, also, so I always knew where I was and what was going on, but other people certainly didn't always have that kind of luxury. You didn't really care. We were just trying to survive and get home. That wasn't true of the enemy.

They would have phrases written on their shirts and on other personal effects. They were very patriotic phrases. They'd translate into things like, "For country," "For family," things like that. The main thing all of us had written on our combat jackets, on anything, would be a calendar. That said a lot. I mean, they had a sense of purpose to their war. They knew what they wanted. It became clear to us that our war was thirteen months, that's all it was going to be. That's when your tour was up, and that was your war. You beat the calendar, and you went home. All the idealism evaporated very quickly after arriving there.

MRS. BAKER: One reason I thought things were going very badly was because Paul went over as a private, and, the first thing you knew, he was a lance corporal. Then he wasn't a lance corporal very long when he became a corporal. We said, "They must be killing them all off for him to advance like that."

GEORGE: The 9th Marines, which Paul and I were in, I think

stands as having the highest casualty rate of any line unit in the war. One battalion of the 9th Marines became nicknamed "The Walking Dead." The 9th Marines had a huge turnover, but Paul's promotion to corporal was a meritorious promotion. I know that. It had nothing to do with losses. Paul was just an extraordinary soldier. He was able to separate how he felt about the war and what he had to do, specifically what he had to do in order to take care of his men. He felt very personally the responsibility he had. I don't think he liked it. I know I hated it as soon as I was burdened with leadership. Paul didn't like that part of it. He didn't like having to be a leader, but he was realistic enough to know that he was a very good soldier, and he separated it out. He would turn it on and off. That's a very rare talent, to be able to do that. I learned that from him.

At night, when we were out in the field on an operation, I would get out my pad, and I would write letters to my congressman, really walking a tightrope about getting in trouble, but I turned it on and off like that, also. I knew what I was doing during the day, and I knew what I felt I had to do at night. I thought about that a lot, about whether or not I should have just said, "That's it. I'm not going to do it anymore. I'll go to the brig." That would have been a very moral thing for me to do. I wasn't prepared to do that. Maybe that says something about me, but I wasn't willing to go to jail. I was biding my clock to get out of there.

MRS. BAKER: You know, actually, I think from the time Paul went to Vietnam to the day he died, every time I heard a car stop in front of the house, I went to the window thinking that was it, so the clock was running for me, too, but the day they did come, I wasn't there. I was teaching at the high school, so they got his father first, then came to the high school to get me. I don't know. When it happened, I think I was just numb. I didn't react at all. My husband didn't even have to tell me what had happened. They called me down to the guidance room and said, "There's someone who wants to see you." When I walked in and looked at his face, he didn't have to say anything. I knew. It's just something you're dreading happening all those months, and then it's happened, and you're numb. I was just numb about the whole thing.

Then there was a two-week wait from the time we got word to the time his body came back. During that time, I thought I had resigned myself to the fact. Then, when the marines called and said the coffin could be opened, that's when it hit me. I did not want it opened. As it turned out, we didn't have it opened. Paul's uncle went to the funeral home, and he said, "Time has elapsed. I think it's better you're just satisfied with a closed coffin." I definitely did not want the coffin opened.

CLAIRE: I wasn't home when we got word, either. I was away on a school trip. When I came home and got off the bus, that's when I was told that Paul was killed. Unlike Mom, I always thought Paul would come back. I don't think it even crossed my mind that he wouldn't come back, possibly because he had lived such a charmed life. He was valedictorian, and he was president of his class, and it just never hit me that he might not come back.

MRS. BAKER: I know his father always thought that he would come back. I think because he came back from World War II, he just felt Paul would come back, but, I don't know, maybe I thought my luck was running out. Paul's dad and I were married during World War II, and I stayed home and waited for my husband to come back, and he did. Then, when Paul went, it was just a blow to go through it again. I just remembered, during World War II, waiting every day for the mailman. In those days, we didn't watch the war on television. I just waited for the mailman to bring me a letter. With Paul, I didn't wait for a letter, because I didn't get that many letters, really. During Vietnam, you just sat in front of the television and thought, "Where are they fighting now?"

CLAIRE: I think the thing that I latched onto was that he might not be dead. When Uncle Bill went to identify Paul's body, I remember him saying that it didn't look like Paul, that he wasn't horribly disfigured, his face, anyway, but that it just didn't look like Paul. For a long time, I thought, "Well, it's just a mistake. It's just not Paul." I think accepting it is just a gradual process.

I don't know. He just never came home. I thought for a long time that it was a mistake. It was a long time. I would look for him, really. Then, every once in a while, you'd hear stories about somebody losing their dog tags or something like that, and they'd end up on another body. I felt that's what probably happened, that we had buried somebody else.

MRS. BAKER: You never told me that. Do you believe it now?

CLAIRE: Yes.

MRS. BAKER: I think the hardest thing was the two weeks wait between the time you heard and the time you went to the funeral. That was the end of it. Before that, you just fill in those two weeks. But the other thing about it, there were so few people you could talk to who went through a similar experience, because there were so few people you knew who were even in Vietnam, much less killed in Vietnam. The only people I ever talked to were the Tymesons. When Paul was killed, they came to our house and asked us if we had a cemetery plot, which we didn't. They said, "Well, would you like to have Paul buried with Ray?" It wasn't in our neighborhood, and it wasn't our cemetery, so we didn't, but they were the people we were closest to. I don't know anybody else personally who lost someone in Vietnam. I do know a couple of people who had friends there who came home, and there's another family in North Troy, the Guenettes. Peter Guenette received the Congressional Medal of Honor. He was killed, but I didn't know the Guenettes very well. Paul and Ray and Peter were the three from North Troy who were killed in Vietnam. There were other boys from Troy, but I didn't know their families. The only people I ever talked to were the Tymesons.

I remember a letter we got about that boy from Berlin who was missing for so many years. He was missing for years and years. His sister sent a letter saying how sorry she was that Paul had been killed. I didn't know her. None of us did. She said she thought it was better than their situation, if we could look at it that way, because they didn't know what had happened to their young man. But he did come home. He was a prisoner, and he was released years and years later. When she wrote the letter, I agreed with her. I could see her point. I would rather know what happened. I mean, the possibility of someone being missing and coming home was so remote that I could see her point in that. Another thing, too, I am just so thankful Paul was killed, and not spending the rest of his life in a veterans' hospital, or being badly injured, or maybe mentally incapacitated in some way. Death isn't the worse thing that can happen.

CLAIRE: If you're killed, you can only be killed once. You can be hurt so many more times. I'm a nurse. I'm a public-health nurse now, but when I was a student I did a rotation on the psych floor at the VA. They had quite a few Vietnam veterans there. They just seemed to wander around all day, and that was it. There were certainly no psychiatrists among us students, but a lot of the veterans' problems seemed to be connected somehow with guilt. They felt they were guilty because they were alive and their friends were dead.

I can remember one man, especially. I still remember him very vividly. I think he was a marine. He was with this group, and they were in a mine field. The jeep or truck or whatever they were in blew up, and he was the only one who survived. When he woke up, there was a group of Viet Cong going through the bodies of the other soldiers. He had to pretend he was dead for quite a long time. I forget how many minutes it was. When a group of Americans finally found him, he was tiptoeing through the mine field, so he wouldn't be blown to pieces. When I saw him at the VA, there was nothing physically wrong with him. He had been slightly injured, but he was long over that. He was still tiptoeing. He was tiptoeing down the hallway at the VA. He just couldn't get over the fact that everyone was dead except him. He apparently was the leader of this group, so he personally felt responsible for them. He couldn't understand why he was alive and the others were dead. He just wandered around the halls all day, walking on his toes. We were there the whole semester, and I never saw any real progress.

GEORGE: I think everyone who was there, who was in the infantry, carries a lot of guilt, a lot of survivor guilt. I've seen it for years and years. There are just all of these people you were with, and you're never going to be able, at any point, to pick up a phone and talk to any of them ever again. The only way, the only thing to do, I think, is to initiate. You have to finally bring yourself to make contact with the family, which took me a long time to do.

MRS. BAKER: The lack of knowing someone that Paul knew there was a real void. We thought it would help if we knew somebody, but we didn't. One night the phone did ring. It was a very poor connection. My husband answered it, and it was a young man. He said, "I was with your son in Vietnam," identified the company and all, and said, "I just want to tell you about him." My husband said, "Well, he was killed," and the young man started to cry and hung up. We never got his name. We never knew who it was, and we had no way of ever reaching him. Then you wrote and said, "Today is Paul's thirtieth birthday." I remember how the letter started. I still have it. I had copies made for each of the children, because they wanted it.

GEORGE: Part of me was afraid. It was horrible on my part, really, not to have contacted you sooner. I used to run rap groups for Vietnam vets, and I used to hit guys over the head with this very thing: "You better put all of this in perspective. You've got to do this and do that," and I knew what I had to do to put everything into perspective. I was ignoring it. My ignoring it for so long had to do with the fact that after I came back I was involved with Vietnam Veterans Against the War. I didn't know how that would affect the family. I was always afraid that maybe someone in Paul's family would see me on TV, and then, having made contact through seeing me there . . . I just didn't know. I had no way of knowing how the family felt about that and how they were going to feel about me. That was something I had to deal with. I finally wrote the letter and met you last Thanksgiving.

MRS. BAKER: Apparently we weren't the only ones who felt that lack of communication. I never thought about the world of people in the same situation, but we always thought if we only knew somebody it would help. A marine magazine came to us for about a year after Paul died, and we would always take that magazine and look through it to see if we could find that Fox Company and get a name from it that we could write to to find someone who knew him. Apparently other people have felt the same way. I cut an article out of the paper about a reporter who met a young man at the monument in Washington. He was tracing a name on the monument, and he said to this woman, not knowing she was a reporter, "This is my buddy." The reporter told the story in the paper. Now that family is trying to find that young man. They said if they could just talk to him that would kind of finalize things for them. Nothing ever brought the families together, I guess. Or the veterans.

GEORGE: Time is beginning to make people able to make more connections. It's happening more now, but the vets are the only ones who can do it. The families can't do it. There's something else that's a part of the problem. This may sound a little bit strange, but you very seldom knew people's entire names over there, even the people you were with. Maybe at some point some psychologist is going to do a whole thing on that, but everyone had a nickname they went by. It was almost like: "This isn't really me that's doing this. It don't mean nothing. It ain't real." That's how guys would talk. Back home was "the world," and you were going back to the world. Vietnam was the never-never-land you had in your backyard as a kid when you played cowboys and Indians. You didn't know people's entire names.

I figured out names so that my friend could bring back pictures of names to me from the monument in Washington. It took some work to do it. I knew Paul's whole name. I knew a kid named Charlie Martin's full name. The rest of them were mostly nicknames. Because I was a radio man, I carried initials for the brevity code, to use in calling on the radio that we needed a medivac helicopter for them. I knew their initials and the last three numbers of their serial numbers, and I had a date. I had to put it together like that from the list of names on the monument that's published in book form. There are just very few situations where a veteran is going to be able to initiate anything in the way of contact. The family, of course, can't. They don't know who to begin to look for.

MRS. BAKER: Probably your contact wasn't sustained over a period of time, either. Going back to my husband in the service, he was with his group for years. I knew many of the young men in his group, and the wives became friends. My husband is dead, and his close buddy is dead, but the other wife and I still correspond regularly and try to see each other once a year. They live in Vermont. It was over a period of years that he was with these men, maybe three or more years. It seems that in Vietnam it was that one-year tour of service, and that people were coming and going all that time, so you didn't become as closely knit as a group.

GEORGE: We depersonalized it. We just knew people by their nicknames. I think it was because of the war, not just because of the time element. I guess you could form your whole politics of the war based on the fact that they told you you were going home in thirteen months. That told you something. You were just going to put in your time, and nobody set any standards about how long it was going to take to win the war or what kind of effort was going to be put into it. Thirteen months, and you were going home. That's what they're telling you. They do that by setting a tour. Otherwise, you would want your most experienced soldiers doing the fighting. The first month you're there, you're useless, and the last month you're there, you're useless because all you're thinking about is going home. They have to maximize that time in between to make you an effective soldier. If they tell you up front when you're going to be leaving, that sends you a message: "Put in your time, and be real careful, and you're not winning this war."

I want to ask you something. This is something I've often thought about, but I never thought about it more often than when I saw your husband's obituary in the paper. I felt terrible about not having met him and spent some time with him. I didn't know. I had nothing to gauge what that would be like, how a family would feel about me. Because of the kinds of things I did after I came back, I didn't know whether he would have wanted to talk to me. Would it have been important to him? What would have happened if I had initiated some contact the first year after I got back?

MRS. BAKER: Probably just what has happened since. We would have been good friends. I can understand your point, but, as I told you before, don't blame yourself. You were the one who was in Vietnam. You experienced it, and we certainly don't blame you. I'm sure I don't. If my husband were here, he would never blame you for not getting in touch with us sooner.

GEORGE: Well, being active in Vietnam Veterans Against the War had a lot to do with my not wanting to get in touch with you, but I also didn't want to do it for other reasons. I worried about the kind of questions that would be asked. It was all very foolish, thinking back on it now. I wrote you at one point that you were the person he came into the world with, and I was the last person he was with when he left it. It's like there's a whole kind of cycle involved, and, of course, I should have been in touch with you. For Paul, if nothing else. But it was so difficult.

When I sent the first letter to you, it was probably the five hundredth one I'd started. I never got beyond just starting them. I looked up the phone number in the phone book, I don't know how many times. I knew the names of his brother and his sisters, and there was a time when I thought maybe that's the way I should initiate contact, through either Claire, Linda, or Bob. I would look their names up in the telephone directory, and I would just go back and forth on the thing. I finally felt I just had to do it, and you were very warm and very kind.

MRS. BAKER: Well, I certainly don't think you should blame yourself for not having done it sooner. As I said, Paul never wrote us about his feelings about any of it, and that's why I always thought when he came home, we'd all sit down and talk it all over. But I assumed he would be quite disillusioned. I guess we were all disillusioned about the war, really. There's another thing I could never really understand. When Paul was little, if we ever even saw an animal killed on the road, he'd cry, and I thought,

"How could someone that's so sensitive be over there with all that killing?" I thought that would be quite a problem.

GEORGE: He kept that sensitivity. He was a remarkably sensitive person. You could see that in the little world of the squad. He would mother everybody and yell at them, but then he would temper all of that very quickly. He also had a very sophisticated sense of humor. When we were going out on an operation, we really dreaded it. It was going to be two weeks or three weeks of a nightmare where you never knew what was going to happen, you would never sleep, and you were going to be miserable. You were going to go without this and that, and you were constantly worried about what was going to happen. Still, when it came time to go on the operation, we'd get on the landing zone and wait for the transport. Everybody was hating it, so Paul would line us up. He would introduce us like they do at a football game. He would say, "Starting as radio man from New York state . . ." and he would give my name. We'd have to go running out to the transport. It was just real crazy, but he would do that every time. He'd do it to be crazy and to pick everybody up. He was a guy who always carried two extra canteens, and if one of the guys ran out of water, he'd yell at him like crazy, then come back and give him a canteen when nobody was looking. That's the way he was.

I was the only one in my squad that wasn't either killed or wounded. In the entire platoon, there were eight of us that weren't seriously wounded or killed. Of the ones that were seriously wounded, I don't know how many ultimately died. There were eight from my platoon that walked out of there with the company. The company itself took a horrible beating. There was the lieutenant and his radio man, myself from my squad, one from another squad, and I think four from the third squad. That's all that was left of my platoon, all that walked out with the company.

It was a situation where we'd been chasing a North Vietnamese unit for about five days. We came to a tree line, and we did an envelopment, which is an infantry tactic where one platoon goes down and around, and the other two platoons stay up in front, and there were just many more of the enemy in the tree line than we thought. Once we enveloped them down one side of the hill, we realized they were also on the other side of the hill, and we were pinned down. We spent the night away from the rest of the unit. It was a reverse ambush, that's what it was.

We had chased them for four or five days, making contact the whole time. In the *Times Union,* there was a wire-service report of this. It was an important thing in my life, as it was in yours, and when I came home from Vietnam, I went to the Albany Public Library and got all the papers out. I wanted to know if it was there. It just seemed that it should be recorded somewhere, and it was. There was a wire-service report that talked about a running five-day gun battle between a marine unit and a North Vietnamese battalion. That's what it ended up being.

It happened around noon, on what I still think was the twenty-eighth of March. Paul was killed then. By early evening that part of it was over, the running battle, and we just brought the wounded back. Then we went down to our old ravine, and we just stayed there. It was a very long night. We had very little water, and almost no ammunition, and no radios. They were all shot out. Our people had every reason to think that we were all dead. I don't know why, but they didn't call in artillery on the tree line. They didn't call in gunships or anything. By not doing that, the company commander probably kept the rest of us alive, because we were just off the tree line the entire night. We lasted the night there. It was probably eight o'clock the next morning when another company came up and found us. By then we knew what had happened to the rest of the company on the other side of the tree line.

MRS. BAKER: George, how do you feel about all the Vietnamese that are coming into our country right now?

GEORGE: I resolved a lot of things about that in my own mind a long time ago. If they were the Vietnamese who were just caught up in the war all of a sudden, they were just victims, like so many other people. The Vietnamese who are coming into this country, however, are the people who lived in Saigon. They were part of a country that horribly brutalized its people for years and years. A lot of the Vietnamese who came into this country are here because they had a much better life when the Americans were there, and they're following that way of life. They want to keep it.

MRS. BAKER: The reason I asked is that I tutor for Literacy Volunteers of America, and we have requests from Vietnamese people who want tutoring. Perhaps I'm mistaken, but I feel that the ones who are here now are from the upper class who were able to leave.

GEORGE: I wouldn't want to say that's true in every case, but there was just no way to get out of Vietnam unless you had influence.

MRS. BAKER: Maybe I'm wrong in feeling that way.

CLAIRE: We have a lot of Vietnamese patients. I have a Vietnamese family I work with, and I was kind of disappointed in myself, because I thought it wouldn't bother me if I took care of the Vietnamese, like: "They're just other sick people," but I do have some ambivalent feelings toward them. Through an interpreter, I asked a little bit about their life in Vietnam. They were students. They lived in Saigon, and I'm sure they did very well.

GEORGE: Many of the upper-crust structure of Vietnamese society looked down on Americans. They were usually either French- or U.S.-educated. They were that part of Vietnamese society I talked about before, the ones who were happy to have Americans come and fight for them, because they had no intention of doing it for themselves. This was only a small percentage of the Vietnamese, but that's generally the percentage that got out. There was just no way lots of villagers in the countryside were going to get to Saigon for the evacuation. To get out of Vietnam during the evacuation, you had to live in Saigon, and if you lived in Saigon and were Vietnamese, that means you did well during the war.

I've talked with North Vietnamese people, people I was fighting against, not people from what was South Vietnam. I talked at the United Nations. I've met with the prime minister of

Vietnam. He was not a grunt during the war, but he was an important and influential military figure. I also talked with a former Viet Cong colonel who's stationed at the mission now. I had no feelings of animosity at all. I did at one time, but I've gone through that, and I think more people should. This may sound silly and trite, but in some sense I didn't take the war personally. I have thought, "My god, my counterparts from North Vietnam, they had so much more reason for doing what they were doing than I had for what I was doing." They believed in their cause.

Up north, where we fought the war, Paul and I, it was very conventional. We were fighting well-trained North Vietnamese troops, and they weren't going home in thirteen months, like we were. They were going to be there forever, or for however long it took. Some of them had already been there for years and years. Paul's counterpart and my counterpart up north were each probably someone much older than we were, and certainly more experienced.

MRS. BAKER: I've started feeling for those families. I mean, there are families over there who feel bad because their people were killed. I don't know if there's ever going to be some kind of stop to war, but there needs to be, on a very human level.

GEORGE: I remember talking to Paul about that when we . . . he used to like cocoa. He'd have cocoa, and he'd stockpile the stuff. He also liked this horrible stuff called "long ration," which is made on the gravy-train principle. It's this freeze-dried stuff, and you put hot water in it and mix it up. This was probably sometime around February at lunchtime. We had just come off an operation, and we were racked out, and I stole a whole case of these long rations. They wouldn't give them to the Marine Corps. I guess it wasn't horrible enough. But the army had them, and they were stockpiled. I stole a whole case of them, and I gave them to Paul. Oh, God, he was so happy, and it was this disgusting stuff. It really was. You carried them, though, because the alternative was the C-rations, and those cans were very heavy. With these freeze-dried things, you could carry an entire meal. They were just small little squares. Paul liked the chicken stew and the chili. It was disgusting.

MRS. BAKER: He was used to feeding the dog.

GEORGE: Well, it was disgusting. He would even mix them together sometimes. Anyway, he would have that and cocoa. I would have black coffee, and he would have his cocoa, and we would sit back and talk. Anyway, in February, when we had come off this operation, we were sitting and talking and drinking coffee and cocoa. We had killed some North Vietnamese, and we had their packs. We had to pull out whatever was in there and go through it for intelligence purposes. While Paul was going through some of the stuff this day, he found some letters. We would never open their letters. We couldn't read them, anyway, but it was a strange sort of brotherhood, I think: "I wouldn't want anybody to open my mail, so let's extend them that courtesy. We won't read their stuff." So, we didn't read their letters, or open them, but on this one particular day, this one guy's pack had letter after letter after letter in it, and they were all unopened. That shows you how much into the fighting those people were. He was probably just saving all the letters until he had time off to be reflective, then he'd sit down and read his mail. He never had the chance to do it.

I remember Paul sitting there, looking at all those letters, and we got to talking about what goes on at boot camp. They train young guys to go off and possibly kill people they don't know anything about. Time and time again you would see them inspiring the attitude, "Well, they have no regard for human life." I remember Paul sitting there and saying, "You know, for people who have no regard for human life, they're very real." They had the letters from home, and they had the pictures of their wives and their girl friends. That's the sort of thing that would come to you sometimes when you were over there.

MRS. BAKER: That's why war is so inhuman.

GEORGE: It's easy to depersonalize the other side.

MRS. BAKER: And they're basically in the same situation as you are. They're human, and they have their families and their feelings, and their government just decides that there's going to be a war.

CLAIRE: They've propagandized that on TV. They say,

"They don't mind that their sons or their brothers or whoever is killed. They don't feel the way we do." Then they show some poor women crying. If they don't care about them, then why are they crying? It's obviously not true.

GEORGE: Where we were, it was a very family-oriented culture. They bury their relatives in their backyards, so that they can be close to them. They're very real, and they're happy, and they're sad. They run the whole gamut of human emotions, and, of course, they love their kids. I think that Paul and I were fortunate in that neither one of us might have lasted very long in the south, in that grinding-down war with booby traps and such. I think probably he and I were both a little too trusting for our own good. We would have probably both been dead, but sooner. In the war in the south, there was also the pain of incidents like My Lai, where people just went over the edge—couldn't identify who the enemy was any longer. We had a lot of training that was basically racist in orientation, including the idea that "They don't care about human life," and it became easy to do that kind of thing— atrocities.

Where Paul and I were, it was just us and the North Vietnamese. It was very conventional. One on one. You very rarely saw civilians up there unless you went somewhere with a convoy on a special detail. You just did not see civilians. The rare times you did, the effect it had on you more often than not was to break your heart. It broke your heart to see families having to rummage through garbage pits and things like that. I can remember Paul and I sitting there and watching them one day. It was a degrading thing to just watch it. What it was like for them to have to do that, I don't know. But then, of course, the way we were treated, sometimes we would have to rummage to get what we wanted, also. If you were in the Marine Corps, you expected that.

MRS. BAKER: When you went to the movies and saw World War I movies, you saw the German soldiers and the American soldiers. There would often be some episode in a movie where one young man would be opposing another young man at close range, and neither wanted to kill the other. I don't think it's in the individual, really, to just want to kill that person over there just because he's on the other side, but you're a soldier, so you have to do it.

CLAIRE: The people who start wars don't fight them.

MRS. BAKER: We always decide: "We must be so careful never to let another war start." We haven't been able to do that through the centuries. No matter how terrible we think it is, we've never been able to stop it, but it's incumbent that we try to. Even with all of this, I don't think I'm bitter, really. Maybe if Paul had been drafted, I would have been. He did what he felt he wanted to do and should do, and I think it was up to us to respect his choice. We can't always control what happens to us, so he wasn't to live any longer. The years that he had were wonderful years, maybe not the one in Vietnam, but, while he had a short life, he achieved a lot. He certainly enjoyed himself. He enjoyed everything. He entered into everything with zest, so it was just his lot in life to die young, so I don't feel bitter. I could see where someone would be bitter if they felt their son didn't want to go and had to go.

GEORGE: And Paul really wanted to go to Vietnam so badly. It was very important to him that he go through that, so I guess you're right, if you put it in those terms. Obviously, the war didn't have to happen, but, God knows, Paul was the kind of person who could have ended up down in the South in the civil rights movement, and something could have happened down there. He had that kind of idealism. I know he hurt as much as anybody over there at times, both physically and emotionally, but I only saw him really in a depression one time. The whole time I knew him, I only saw him depressed once, and that was the day he died.

He knew he was going to die, and he knew he wasn't going to change that. I mean he actually knew something was going to happen. Just before it happened, just about ten or fifteen minutes before he died . . . we had done the envelopment, and we were down in this ravine. We sat there, and I had my canteen in my pocket. I looked over, and Paul was sitting there, and he was staring. I reached over and gave him the canteen. It was 120 degrees. It was awful. It was a furnace down there. I handed him my canteen, because I noticed he didn't have one. That was not like him. He was very practical. He knew exactly what we were going to be doing, and he knew what to take. He knew everything he was supposed to take with him, and what every one of his people were supposed to take, but this time he didn't have his canteen with him. As I reached over and handed him my canteen, he just looked at me, and he said, "No." Like that. I've always thought about that. He knew he didn't need the water, and he knew I was going to be there all night, also. You don't die of thirst in one night, obviously, but, from what I could see later, that was the only canteen we had that night. The corpsman borrowed that canteen I don't know how many times, to sponge off a guy's wound or something. That one canteen turned out to be very important. I just know Paul knew he didn't need the water, and I did. I think about that a lot . . . that he was that good a person and that good a friend.

ROBERT J. BAKER

Born: March 12, 1956
Troy, New York
Brother of Paul Joseph Baker

Younger Son

I was the youngest in the family. I was eight years younger than Paul. I was in seventh grade when he was killed. I remember that things happened very quickly. He enlisted in Boston and went to basic training and then was back for a couple of weeks around the

Fourth of July. Then he was off to San Diego, and from there over to Vietnam.

I remember getting letters from him all the time. He'd write a little section for each of us, or he'd take turns in who he was writing to, but he never really told anything that would make you worry or wonder. It was always joking with him, you know, evading the serious side of things, and trying to laugh around it, so I never really knew what was going on over there. But as soon as he went, it changed my whole outlook. I didn't know much about Vietnam, but I certainly became more interested in it. I do remember sitting around watching the news and trying to figure out where he was and where the heavy fighting was. We knew he was right by the demilitarized zone. Anytime they talked about DaNang and north, I knew that was kind of the area where he was, and I wondered every night what was going on. I became interested in body count, also. How many were being killed. How many Viet Cong or North Vietnamese Army were being killed and how many Americans.

None of my friends ever paid much attention to it. It wasn't something that was really affecting them. We were at a young age and still involved in all the playing and all the joking, and people were not really realizing anything else was happening. People weren't all that interested in Vietnam. I was in the seventh grade when he was in Vietnam. We studied some about current history and about Southeast Asia, and people became a little more aware. There was a girl in my class whose brother was also in Vietnam. In fact, he was killed, and he's a Congressional Medal of Honor winner. I haven't seen that girl since around the eighth grade. She didn't go to the same high school, so I don't know what happened to her. But I remember that Paul's going just made me more aware that something else was going on, and that a lot of other people weren't experiencing it. It was all in a type of little vacuum. You know, there's a war over there, and only certain people experienced it, and not too many people at home made much of it. Of course, that could be because where we lived was middle class, and there were fewer middle-class people involved in the war. We were experiencing something that other people around us weren't. I think that hit home even more when he was killed.

I remember the day they came to tell us he was killed. I was in school. I can remember that I was sitting in class, and I was by the door. I was in Catholic elementary school, and there were nuns and lay teachers, and I remember somebody coming to the door and knocking on the door and taking the nun out, and they were out standing by the door, and I saw them talking out there, and I just . . . I don't know why . . . I kind of knew at that point. I don't know why I knew, but I just kind of went numb, I guess. I don't really remember why I knew, but I just had this feeling that that was it. Then they came in, and they asked for me to go out in the hall. No one said anything to me. They just walked me down the hall. They never told me what was going on; I just kind of had this feeling. The school was connected to the convent by a walkway. We walked over there. I had never been there before. I walked into this parlor area, and my father was there. He just came up and hugged me, and told me that Paul had been killed. I've always kind of wondered how I just knew that was it. As soon as I heard them chattering out in the hallway, I think I knew. My mother had been teaching that day, and she said the same thing, that she had this same feeling.

I guess because I was so young, I had never really thought about him dying. I had never really thought he wasn't coming home. I had no feeling like that at all. I just assumed he was coming home. A lot of good things had happened to him. He was a good person, and I just assumed that in another year he would be home, and that it was nice that he got in the marines, because they station you near home for the last eight months or so, and he would be able to travel to see us. So it was a big shock. I remember the body wasn't going to come home for a while, a couple of weeks, and it was just around Eastertime. Maybe there was one day of school left before Easter, so I said that I was going to go to school the next day, and I think that my sister Claire went, too. We both went to school.

I remember people talking to me in school. That's where the

real awareness soaked in that they didn't know that much about what was going on. A lot of my friends were talking to me as if they hadn't even known my brother was there.

The waiting period was the worst period of all, I guess. I remember that I would get up every day, and I'd just leave the house. I'd go over in a field just a block or two away from my house. I'd go over and play basketball every morning, or do something just to get out of the house, just to be by myself. There were just all of these people milling around, all of these people you don't know hugging you, and you're just wondering: "Why don't you leave me alone? What are you running around hugging me for? I don't even know you." Things like that. I guess I just basically wanted to be alone most of the time. I'd just leave the house.

Finally the body came home, and we had the wake and everything. The body was accompanied by the marine honor guard, or whatever it was, the one person who's assigned. My sisters and I tried to get friendly with that guy, the guy in the dress uniform, asking him questions and things, but he really didn't want to talk about it. He would talk some. He was friendly, and he would chit-chat, but he wouldn't say anything about Vietnam at all. He was probably going through his own problems, having come home, and I'm sure that's not easy duty to serve, either, accompanying a body around. But I remember that I was looking up to this guy. I thought he was real important. And I remember during the whole time, waiting for the body to come home, setting up the wake, I don't think I had really cried, or, if I cried, I might have cried a little bit, but not really let out a good cry or anything. I guess I was just trying to be brave. I was the male who shouldn't be crying and all this stuff. During the wake—the wake just seemed forever—there were just so many people. Paul knew so many people, and my parents knew so many people. It just lasted forever and ever and ever. I remember standing there, and I wasn't crying, but it got longer and longer and longer, and I'd go over and I'd talk to the marine. I guess that around him I felt like I couldn't cry or something, but I remember him saying something to me like, "Why are you doing that?" I didn't even know what

I was doing, but I had almost twisted the button off my coat. I was doing it with my hands. That made me feel uncomfortable, and I just stopped. It was like I had to please him, like I had to impress this person, or just show that I was a man to this uniform, really, to this marine.

I was an altar boy when I was a kid and had served a lot of funerals, and I remember walking into the church this time. It was just packed. I'd never seen anything like it before. In any funeral I'd ever been at, there'd been family, and some others, you know, not very big, but this was just . . . the place was just packed. It was overwhelming. In fact, I think my whole class was there. But I remember going in, and all through the funeral, again, it just seemed long and long and long. Finally, when we were leaving the church and they played "God Bless America," or something like that, it really started. That's when I started getting really upset. I didn't cry too much, but I was really fighting back. Then I remember at the cemetery, at the gravesite, we were there. I don't know, really, who was behind me, but I remember that's when I started to cry. I remember someone behind me had their hand on my shoulder. I don't know who it was. I thought everybody in my family was next to me, but it may have been my sister. I still think it was kind of funny how my sisters and I just kind of looked up to this uniform. I guess maybe we looked at him as if he were Paul or something, and he had to be proud of us and all that stuff. I remember he would talk to us, and he was friendly, but I think it was my sister who asked him something about his experience, and then he went stone cold. That was it. He didn't talk about that at all. Then after a while he warmed up again for chit-chat.

I guess everyone handles things differently. I just wanted to be alone. My sister Claire was pretty much the same. I remember how upset my parents were. That was the most upset I ever saw my father. I guess I probably never saw him upset before. I was really young when his mother had died. I think he was probably upset then. I think I remember it some, but he was just really upset, and my mother was really upset, and they were both trying to be the strong parents. I remember some discussion about whether we could go see the body, and, while I didn't have any say in it, I certainly wouldn't have wanted to. I think that would have upset me even more. I think I would rather remember him as he had been, rather than to look at whatever had happened to him. Not that you would see it, but I don't think I would have gotten through that very well. My father was really adamant that he wanted to see his body, and they talked him out of it. I know that he didn't see it. My uncle did. My uncle said that it didn't even look like him. I remember my uncle said that, and I remember I always had the feeling that he wasn't dead. I know Claire felt that way, too. Even now I feel that sometimes. Now I feel guilty if I feel like that, because, God, if he is alive, or was alive, or was a prisoner for this long, then he'd be done for. I mean he'd be crazy, something worse. Back then, I guess I felt there was a chance, at least fifty-fifty, that he wasn't dead.

When the prisoners of war came home, I sat down and watched TV. I expected to see him walk off the plane. I looked at every list of names that they had, and I looked at every plane that came in, looking for that face, and I didn't see it. I guess all along I'd had that feeling, especially since my uncle had said that it didn't look like him. I guess if we had met George then, then we absolutely would have known, but I had that feeling that there was always a chance. Even now I feel it to some degree.

I've had a lot of nice things happen to me. Sometimes I think that when something nice is happening, maybe it's because of him, that he's around. If something positive happens to me, I'll think something like: "Gee, I wonder if that guy knew Paul?" I think like that sometimes, or that there's some presence influencing my life. He's definitely done that. He influenced my life while he was alive, and he influences it a lot now, too. I don't know whether I believe in spirits, but, even that aside, it's just the impact of knowing him that was influential.

Sometimes I don't understand my feelings about the war. When the protests were going on, or when I hear somebody talking very patriotically, I think: "What am I supposed to be doing?" I turned out after Paul was killed to be very much against the war, and I've had people say to me, later in life, "Oh, your brother was in the marines. He must have been really gung-ho." I hear that, and I think, "Well, gee, he wasn't at all, really. That doesn't explain him." But being in the marines has that reputation. I guess I have these feelings of "Am I supposed to be for or against?" It's not really that you're supposed to be either, I guess—it's just what everybody else is feeling.

Just last Friday night my mother showed me a copy of a letter George had from the national Vietnam veterans to the president of MIT. They're trying to set up a conference for 1984 to bring in a lot of people to talk about the war and issues associated with it, not really to come up with any answers, but just trying to get discussion going. I know they had something like that in San Diego a while ago. I think that's a good idea. I guess I don't know sometimes how I feel, because I try to be very loyal to my brother. He was certainly loyal to me. In fact, I don't even really know how to act around George in some ways. I am very much against the war, and at times I feel very strongly against any type of war and against any type of fighting, and then I say, "Well, gee, George was over there, and my brother was over there, and why were they there? Does that mean that I should support the fact that there was the war?" I guess the fact that Paul went there on his own accord, that he wasn't drafted, confuses my feelings toward the war.

I've only been around George a couple of times. My mother has had much more contact with him than I have. I really don't know how he feels about the war. I know he was involved very much in the antiwar movement when he came home, so I think I probably have a cursory understanding of how he feels, but I don't really know his reasons behind it, or what has shaped that besides his experiences there. In a sense, when you're not involved in it yourself, like many of the protesters, you have no ambivalence at all. It's just a concept, you know, war is a concept, and you're against it: "I'm protesting against war." But when there's been some involvement, there's ambivalence about it.

I know more about why my brother went now, but I don't

really understand. I can't really understand as much as he did. I've just found out through bits and pieces, and some of that's probably changed over the course of years. I was against the war, and then I would sit and think, "Well, Paul went. Why?" I wrestle with that all the time. I think I'll go back and forth thinking about it all my life. There's really some confusion there, not just about Vietnam, but about any war. I guess that's something that everybody that's been involved goes through. All the veterans have to answer the question, and it's harder for them, because they're the ones who went. You know: "Why did I go? Why didn't I go to Canada, if I had the chance? What type of feelings do I have now about it?" I guess these types of meetings sponsored by the Vietnam veterans are trying to help them with that. It's just wondering how you fit into the whole picture. That's something I've thought about for a long time.

As I got older, I kind of had an obsession to try to find out more about what Paul would have experienced. I wanted to find out as much as I could. I don't really feel that comfortable around veterans. I don't know that many, because they're mostly older. I had to register for the draft, and the people who were a year ahead of me in high school got numbers, but I didn't even get a number, because things were winding down by then. Although I don't know many veterans, I guess I would feel uncomfortable around them, because I don't know how they feel. I guess I feel very different from them. I mean, they experienced the war firsthand, and here's somebody whose brother was killed. That's very different, and I haven't really talked to too many about that. I haven't avoided it, but I haven't really had the opportunity. I guess it's just this overall feeling I have, that if I had the opportunity, I might not, because I wouldn't want to upset them any more than they had to be upset. But it's not knowing how they'd react to me, either, just because they could think I was approaching them as someone who's suffered because of war, but they did it firsthand. I'm not saying that's how they would react to me, but I guess that's in my mind: "They get first crack at having troubles, because they were there." It's like what I went through didn't count as much. I guess that's how I feel about it, that what a family went through, or what I went through, doesn't substitute for what they went through, because they did it firsthand.

I don't think the vets have received the recognition that's due them, and I guess in a way what I feel is that they're the first in line. They're the ones who were there. I mean, I think that I'm a different person because my brother was there and because he was killed, and obviously it's had a profound impact on my life, but I think it would have had more of an impact on my life if I had had to go through what he went through, if I had to be there actually myself, if I had to be in front-line involvement. I feel the veterans have experienced something much more powerful than I have, because they felt it firsthand.

In terms of George, George knew Paul for only so many months, but I think he considered him family. I think he lost a family member when Paul was killed, so not only did he lose a family member, but he had experienced all of this stuff firsthand. He had to see people die. I've never seen anybody die, and I've never seen anybody really damaged to any degree, either, in terms of an accident or anything like that. God. That must be just horrible. You can see some of that if you go to a VA hospital. VAs are eerie places, I think. My father was in the VA for a while when he was sick, and I got the creeps going there. I think one of the reasons people don't like going into the VA is that it shows them the impact of war. To me, any veteran who was over there lost friends who were as close to them as family, even though they knew them for only a short period of time. I just feel that must have a more profound impact on them than it does even on me. The fact that I lost a brother is very real, the fact that he's not here, but it's kind of abstract in that I don't know how it happened. I didn't see it happen. They had to kill people. To survive. They had their friends killed. It must have been an absolutely horrible, horrible thing to go through. I would be surprised if anybody could come out of that without really changing significantly. I feel that I should be more concerned about how they feel than they should be concerned about how I feel, because they've experienced so much.

I haven't had all that much opportunity to talk to George yet. When we first got the letter from him, the letter that began, "Paul would have been thirty today . . ." I wasn't living around here. I was in Virginia, but I got a copy of the letter. The letter really had a big impact on me, but most of what I thought about was: "That was ten years ago. God. What an impact it must have had on George, that ten years later is the first time he can really come to grips with it." Not maybe come to grips with it, but the first time he can really contact us. I do remember getting the cards, not signed, and flowers on the monument. All that stuff. I guess I wasn't all that curious, but George was doing it. George said that he would send a mass card or other cards, but that was the closest he would ever come. He didn't sign anything.

In the letter, it was obvious he knew lots about us. It was kind of eerie, in a sense. He had kept up-to-date about us, but we didn't even know who he was. It was kind of strange, in a way, but the impact it must have had on him was phenomenal. I haven't really had much opportunity to talk to him, but I was really tempted to try to see him sometime. I had the return address on the letter. I was going to not tell anybody else, but go try to find him one day. But I was in Virginia. We'd come up on vacation for about a week each year, and each year I thought I would do that, and each year I didn't do it. George wrote again a little while later, then a year later. The first time I met him was this past Thanksgiving. We had moved back up into this area by then. My mother had had some more contact with him, but she had never met him, either, until last Thanksgiving.

It's obviously had a big impact on him. Part of it is that what he wrote in the letter was very complimentary about my brother, and that's the way I had always seen him. In fact, I think that kind of feeds into the way I want to remember him, and the way I want other people to remember him. I was eight years younger, and he couldn't have been better to me, or nicer to me, and we were very close, even given that age difference. Everybody was very close in my family, but I think that some people think that, "Well, you were young, and you probably didn't know him all that well, and you weren't all that close," and that hurts, because I was. He was this perfect brother. He would bring me anywhere I wanted to go, and I knew all his friends, because I was kind of the tag-along brother that everybody else swats away, but he didn't. He wasn't like that. He brought me everywhere that he went. There'd be times that he'd say, "Okay, now you've got to go," because they were going to go off and do something, but I could basically tag along on anything I wanted to.

They'd be playing sports, you know, sixteen-to-eighteen-year-old kids, and then an eight-to-ten-year-old kid. I would get to play. They'd let me play. The difference in size and ability at that age was obviously great, but I never felt that I wasn't as good as they were, because he made me feel that way, so what George wrote about him makes me proud. It was kind of always the way I thought about him. Just the best brother anybody could have, the perfect brother. That's why, bottom line, my strongest feeling about the war is bitterness for having my brother taken away. I realize he made the decision to go, but nineteen-year-old boys should never be put in that position. I'm bitter because I no longer have him. I'm bitter because he won't be there to share in my life, because my wife won't know him, because my daughter will not have him to share in her life. He would have been the best brother-in-law and the best uncle in the world. I know, because he was the best brother.

I was still very young when I decided I was against the war. I couldn't travel or go to demonstrations, or anything like that, but in my own mind I was against the war. In my schoolwork, if I had to write essays, I would write on that topic a lot. This was in the eighth grade and all through high school. That very much influenced anything that I did, but I wasn't old enough that I was an activist or would actively protest anything. I just wasn't that age. After I'd graduated from college, a renewal of thinking about Vietnam started up, with some movies and some books coming out. I would see all of the movies on Vietnam, all of that. I guess to try to understand more about what people went through, especially Paul. That's part of communicating with the veterans or something, for me. Not really understanding, just saying in my own mind that it was horrible, but not really knowing all that much about just how horrible it was. The more I do look into it, the more I think as far as I am concerned it was just a terrible waste. It always has to happen to young people, too. It's all those people out there killing each other. They can experience feelings of humanity toward their enemy at times, even, but that just doesn't seem to filter to the higher levels, where the people are making the decisions.

I'm not saying there is never a situation that warrants the presence of our troops, but that the decision to commit young people to war must be made very carefully, and only for a very special reason. To subject young men to the carnage of war and their families and the country to the tragedy of war must be made for only the best reasons.

I think about El Salvador and places like that a lot now. I look at that and think: "God. How could we ever send a marine advisor there? How can we allow people to sit in their bunkers in Lebanon and get blasted all the time? Why is anybody there?" I think my first reaction is that nobody should be there, so let's just pull out. Then I realize that from some practical standpoints there are some political realities and that we need to help some people sometimes, but I just really feel terrible that there's anybody over there at all.

I feel worst for the families of those people who are killed. I wish that when Reagan called up one of those families, they'd just blast him, rather than saying, "Oh, my son died for my country." It's such a waste. They must feel worse than anybody else, because they're all alone. There's only a few over there, in Lebanon or in El Salvador. Obviously a lot of people made the comparison to Vietnam. I did, too, and it just seems that we'd better be very careful, or we're going to be escalating into another war.

It's the same type of war. It's a guerrilla war, but it's also a civil war. We may think we're going in there to help people, but it always seems like we're helping the wrong people. That's what got me with Vietnam, too. If a lot of Vietnamese didn't want us there, then why were we there? It's *their* place. It just seems like such a waste. If they're fighting us, then why are we there? We're supporting only a few people. Can't they fight their own war?

ROY JOHNSON · ROBERT W...
II · DAVID G LEDGERWOOD · JAY L LIEBER
L MASSA · JOHN T DUNLAP III · ANTHON
MAN · ARTHUR F McQUADE Jr · GEORGE
WILLARD A PERRY Jr · WALTER G POPE · JA
DAVID F STRICKLER · ALEXANDER TATE Jr
r · DAVID V WHINNERY · LUCKY G WHITE
TER F BARNES · CHARLES J BEHM Jr · JAMES
KNER · MICHEAL A BURNS · ERNEST BURTO
STINO Jr · LOREN K DAVEY · ROBERT J DIED
DAVID K FELLER · PHILIP G FRANKLIN · CH
ZA Jr · CARL R GIBSON · ROY LEE GIBSON
RIUS · LOUIS F GUILLERMIN · CECIL M HA
HOLAS L HOLLINGSWORTH · JOHN F HUT
ON · SEEBER J KELLY · DALE L KRUSE · LARR
USK · LARRY E LUTZ · GERALD A GRANSBU
ROGER D MILLS · MANUEL MOORE · RO

CHARLES JOEL BEHM, JR.

Born: July 16, 1948
Marion, Ohio
Killed: April 30, 1968
In a rice paddy area near the Saigon River, Republic of South Vietnam

AMS · ALFRED M WOLFE · JAMES R WORLE
TER · THOMAS E BONDERER · JAMES L BO
PARFITT · DONALD L CARNES · GARY S CO

Lois and Lee Krogman

LOIS PAULINE KROGMAN

Born: October 12, 1929
Marion, Ohio
Mother of Charles Joel Behm, Jr.

LEE WILLIAM KROGMAN

Born: July 28, 1924
St. Marys, Ohio
Stepfather of Charles Joel Behm, Jr.

Look at Me

MOTHER: When I married Lee, Joey was six. My other boy was about three-and-a-half. Joey's father paid no attention to him, not until his death. That was really bad news, filling a funeral hall with two different sets of people. I was like a zombie.

Well, anyway, he was engaged to a young girl, a girl he went to school with, Janice Giles. They were going to get married, and he knew he was going to be drafted. He had finished high school and was working for Brown Associates as an apprentice printer. There was a man at the printing company who was about three or four years Joey's senior. He said, "Well, Joey, you might as well enlist and go ahead and get it over with." He had an influence on Joe. What he said was probably all right. It was very logical, but I didn't want him to go. No. No mother wants her son to go.

He was a very adventurous boy, very outgoing. I never had to worry about Joey. He and another boy used to go to a place down at the railroad tracks called Hobo's Paradise. He was only about ten years old, and he always came back fine. Joey always took care of himself. I never worried about Joe. Then he enlisted in the army before being drafted, and he was bound and determined to marry this girl.

My son and I were very much alike. We clashed a lot. He was my firstborn, and I've always maintained that firstborn children are different. You grow and you learn with your firstborn. We didn't want him to get married. Dad even said to him, "Joey, what if you go over there and get killed, and you leave a child. You don't want to do that." I wish to God he had, now, because it would have been like having him here. I think we more or less said that to him at the time to threaten him, to scare him. We just thought it was the wrong time. Even though they were engaged, it seemed like a quick decision to make at the time. I never thought he would die. I really thought he was coming back. Anyway, he decided not to get married, and I've regretted that ever since then, very much.

When Joey died, we were living in an apartment above the monument shop. We have a monument shop. We sell monuments. The apartment was really high, and, on the day we found out he was dead, a car drove up. I looked out and saw this army man get out with Pastor Don Safford. I thought, "Oh, Joey got hurt, and he came to tell us." Lee knew better. You just get a telegram when they have to tell you they got hurt. When I saw them get out of the car, I never thought it meant that he was dead. It was a very peaceful day; spring was in the air. Spring is my most lovely time of year. I loved it, but, after that, I said I could never love it again. He was killed April 30, 1968, and time does some healing. I can like spring again now.

Joey was ambushed, shot down in a rice paddy. All but one of his patrol were killed. I had thought they were all killed, but Bill Snyder, who was there, told me one boy got away. Some things I will let Bill tell me, and some I won't. I do not want to see it, in my mind's eye. I can't deal with what he is telling me sometimes. He told me a little bit last night. Joey was in Charlie company, and his patrol came to a rice paddy. They knew there were Viet Cong in the paddy. They were told not to cross it. They were supposed to wait for another patrol to join them, then they were going to ambush the Viet Cong. Joey's commanding officer defied the order. He was the type, you know, who thought, "My group can do anything. This patrol can do anything." They went through there, and I guess the Viet Cong killed all but one of them.

Bill was in the same company as Joey, but in a different patrol. He said the one boy who got away called in our artillery fire on the Viet Cong. Bill said he tried all night to get in there and get Joey out, but he couldn't because of the heavy fire. Bill and Joey came from the same town. They didn't know each other, but they got acquainted after they were over there. I didn't know until last night that they just left him there in that rice paddy for twenty-four hours. The gun in his hand was all shattered to pieces. I know he probably laid there with blood coming out of his eyes, ears, and mouth, all over him. I don't want to know any more than that. Then we had problems getting his body back.

The sergeant that came with the minister to give us the information told us that because Joey was from divorced parents, he had to have the divorce papers. I said, "Oh, my God. I don't know where they are. I have them in a drawer somewhere, but . . ." I didn't know where they were right off the top of my head. Within three or four days after we were told he was dead, they wanted to see the divorce papers. I just wasn't thinking straight yet. They wanted the papers because his name was different. His name was Behm, and mine was Krogman. I had custody of him. He was nineteen, but, still, I had custody. I don't know how it got as screwed up as it did. We got a letter from Washington, D.C., saying that my son's body was going to his father, Mr. Behm, if we didn't get the right papers.

I had told the young man that if he would go up to the courthouse, he would find it right there. That would have been no trip for him, because our town is small. He said he would do it, but apparently he didn't. Well, my husband knows quite a few people in the Democratic party, and they helped us out a lot. A representative in our county got hold of a state representative. This was on a weekend and Gertrude Donahue was the biggest one we got to. She said, "There aren't too many people around Washington on a weekend, but I'll do my best." She called us back, and he was out on the next plane. It was eighteen days after he died that we got his body back.

We had all kinds of phone calls going back and forth to Washington that weekend, and we never got billed for one. We could never figure it out. We didn't call collect or anything, just picked up the phone and called. There were no 800 numbers or anything like that. I thought, "Boy, our phone bill is going to be terrific," but we never got bills for a thing. We never did find out what happened, but somebody must have paid for that. Somebody had to.

Now, I have nothing against fighting communism. Neither me or my husband do. Many people used to say, "He died in vain." No. He didn't. He did not. I believe in my country. It is a free country.

STEPFATHER: Well, the reason he didn't die in vain was because he believed . . .

MOTHER: He believed he was going over there for a purpose. He said, "Mother, something has got to be done. This aggression has got to be stopped, or there will be fighting in our own country." I do think he was right, but I just don't care for the way Washington handled it. I don't think they had their high-echelon people in the army trained well enough, like the captains and the people who were over there. Things seemed botched. Now, I don't mean everyone in the army is a nut, but it seems to me they ought to screen their people better, if they're going to be in command of things. I also think the war was often fought from the White House, and not as it should have been. Another thing I didn't like was what the media did.

They brought that war right into the living room. The blood, the violence. Sure, it's there. Lee went through World War II. He served in Europe under Patton. He saw it all. Some people might have liked this media coverage of Vietnam; I did not. I remember that all we got under Roosevelt, at that time, was "Movietone News" at the theater. We were shown some, sure, but not like that stuff in Vietnam. It goes on in every war. I am not condoning it, but that is *war*. They just showed too much, too much. Those Vietnamese, or Viet Cong—I don't want to specify a person or nationality—they had no reverence for life. Not when my son was taught, "Be careful of the children, the women, the old people. They will have them booby-trapped. Do not trust any of them." And they were booby-trapped. They used them.

I don't think some of the American people understand what these boys went through, the ones who went over and came back. It was a different type war than World War II. I'll admit that. It was a lot different. But, still, the American people did not uphold the Vietnam War. It was being poorly run, but, still, there were boys over there, giving their lives for the people in this country, and the people didn't give a damn. That is the way I feel about it. It was a politically run war, very much so. That stupid little place over there should be drowned in the ocean, and Joey felt he was going over there to serve his country. Of course, he was killed in 1968. I think a lot of them felt that way then. I don't know how he would have felt had he lived longer. He was only in Vietnam thirty days when he was killed. He had just left home. He'd been home on leave and had just left when these two people came up to our door and told us he was killed.

STEPFATHER: Before he left, I told him, "Joe, don't volunteer for anything. Don't even volunteer to go into the service. If they want you, they will come and get you." But, no. He had to volunteer. I told him before he left, "Don't volunteer for nothing. They will tell you what they want you to do. Protect yourself." The thing of it is, they had brainwashed him so bad. I spent three years in the army, and they never brainwashed me like that. He was gung-ho to go.

MOTHER: Bill told me he would say things like, "I have to make my family proud of me." That was Joe. It was like a challenge to him. That was Joey. According to Bill, his commander was that type, also. Joey happened to be in his command, so I imagine it would have happened sooner or later. Joey was like that. If you would ask for a volunteer, he would step up and say,

"I'll do it." Luck had always been with him. He could get out of anything, growing up. Maybe he thought his luck would hold on, I don't know. He did cry before he left. I didn't think that he would, but he did. He told Dad he was scared. I didn't realize he was that scared.

STEPFATHER: Funny thing. He picked out his own monument. He picked out his own monument before he left. He and I were down in the shop . . .

MOTHER: I called them for supper. I said, "You guys come on up here." The apartment above the monument shop is a flight-and-a-half up, and supper was going to burn. Finally, I went downstairs. There's a granite that's a green color. It's called "gorman green." It's a kind of army color, an olive green. Granite of this color is not too well liked. It has a little streak of black in it, just a little teeny bit. It's kind of blah. I went down there, and Joey was saying, "I like that monument right there. That one. That is the one I want right there." I said, "What!" He said, "I want that monument, all polished." It was gorman green. I just put dinner on the table. What could I do with all that?

STEPFATHER: It's three feet long, eight inches thick, and two feet tall. It was a complete block.

MOTHER: Joey said, "Mom, I don't like the shape of it. I want it shed-shaped." I said, "Forget about that." Well, that's the monument he got. I don't know, but he must have thought he was going to die, or he would have never done anything like that. When he came home from Fort Polk, in Louisiana, he said it was hell down there in that place. He hated that place. It was like a jungle down there. He got captured on maneuvers down there. They did everything to him. He said, "By gosh, Mom, that was terrible." He never broke and gave anything away, but he said it was awful. They had wire under his nose, and they put him in a barrel and pounded hell out of the barrel. That training was pretty rough. I suppose that the reason they did the training that way was if they actually had been caught, they would have been sadistically treated. Anyway, he was pretty upset when he left, I thought.

There was a big Tet siege going on over there when he left.

They had lost an awful lot of people. He was killed in April. He would have been twenty the sixteenth of July. We put the monument up by his birthday. I think I can really say, right after he died, when they told me he was killed, I felt about as complete and one-on-one with God as I ever had in my lifetime. Then I got mad at him, because I had prayed so much for him to bring my son home. Well, he brought him home. Then it got so I would word my prayers differently. If I wanted someone to come home, I would say, "Bring them home *to me,* not to you." I'm very careful about it now, about how I pray. I say exactly what I mean now.

I do feel good, knowing that Joey is in heaven. I really do, because he was a good church person. He took his religion very seriously. We had just built a new church in Marion when he died, St. Paul's. He was the first to be buried in it. It was sad, very, very sad.

One day, shortly after the funeral, I was patching jeans at the knees for my other boys. I was sitting at the sewing machine by myself, and it just came upon me: "Why me?" I sat there and pounded that machine. Damn, I was mad. I wasn't mad at my government for my boy going to war. I was mad at God for taking him, but that is one thing we have no control over. He takes who he wants, when he wants. That has been my biggest battle, Lois's will and God's will.

At the time of the funeral, I had no blood-pressure problem. I had always had a nerve problem. I had taken tranquilizers all my life, but I had no blood-pressure problem like I do now. The high blood pressure started with his death. After his death, my health didn't get too swift. I had a lot of heart palpitations. I almost had a nervous breakdown at one time in my life, after my first marriage. I've always been a high-strung person. When I married Lee, he was my rock. My rock hadn't been budged in some time, and Joey's death budged it. The doctor put me on some kind of medication, because he knew I had palpitations, and we didn't have a counseling service at that time. I was so uptight, I had back problems. It just seemed like it was one thing after another. Then I went to work, and that helped me for six years.

You know, everybody tells you, "You have three other children, pick up your life." That is a crock of shit. You have a piece of you that's gone, and it is just never filled again. That is so. I felt sorry for my other children. Oh, I didn't neglect them. I did mother-type things, but I wasn't thinking of them. No. It seemed that anyone getting ill really upset me after that. My mother got very ill. She had to have an operation. I saw her on life-support systems, and I just couldn't handle it. I just froze up again, started having palpitations real bad. The doctor couldn't get them stopped, and they took me to the counseling center. I was an outpatient for seven years. I became very obese. Then I found out that one of my adrenal glands had a tumor in it. I had an operation last year for that. I lost about fifty pounds. I have gout now, but I'm on only two very low doses of medicine a day now, and I take Valium if I need to. All of my diseases have been stress-related, emotional stress-related.

I still have fits of depression, and I fight them out myself. I just put one foot in front of the other, but I don't do anything too stressful. If I'm depressed, I don't do anything that day that is going to be too stressful to me, anything that I think I can't handle. If I don't want to go out of the house, I won't go out. If Lee asks me to go do something, I will do it. On days when I'm uneasy about going out, I will do it at less stressful times, like when the traffic is light, or avoid traffic, things like that.

It's been stressful* being here today. It's been hell being here today. Joey's died the third time. He died once when I was told. He died the second time when he came home. And he died again today. It's done, but it's not done inside me yet. I just keep pushing it back, that's all. I do shove it behind the door, but why should I live with it and torture myself? My son does come to mind a lot, still, at different times. It used to be a lot. I would feel his presence

---

*This interview took place in Arlington, Virginia, during a visit to the Vietnam Veterans' Memorial in Washington, D.C., sponsored by the Marion, Ohio, chapter of Vietnam Veterans of America.

a lot. But it's been fifteen years. I don't think of him as much as I used to.

We put up the memorial in Marion for Vietnam veterans. I always said I wanted to see the monument in Washington before I die. I wanted to come, but I didn't want to come. I wanted to see it, and I didn't. It brings so much hurt, and I am tired of being hurt. I like to stay away from stressful situations. I don't like being that uncomfortable, but I had to come here. I had to face it. I really wanted to see it. I wanted to see the monument, and I wanted to see that beautiful black granite. It is beautiful granite. It is solid black. It is imported. The United States does not have black granite. It is a misty color, because it has a little whiteness to it. It is good and hard. It is durable granite.

STEPFATHER: It has a hard polish on it, too. You see people putting their hands on it. They can do that for umpteen years, and it won't bother it a bit. The people can touch it. That monument will be there for years and years. It will endure. It won't change.

MOTHER: You know, I made the remark that I didn't think my son died in vain. But I was afraid of war. I am afraid of war. My son Gary missed it, but he wouldn't have been taken, anyway. If he takes his glasses off, he can't see. He is very, very nearsighted, and he would never pass the physical, but my other son, Bruce, would have. At the time he could have been taken, they weren't taking too many of the boys. But I said, "Hey, I don't want my son up there." It's not that I don't want to be patriotic. No. I just don't want to lose another one. I did not join this Gold Star Mothers' Club. I got hounded about that, but no. I paid my own personal debt with the death of my son. I didn't want to share anything with anybody.

After Joey died, seeing people on the freeway upset me. I would just be traveling on the highway, and I would see people, lots of people. I would want to say, "People, people, stop. My son is dead. Stop." That isn't right. It took me a long time to get over that. I wanted everything to stop, because my son was dead. Everything should stop. I was being very selfish, but this knowledge didn't come to me until after about ten years. You just sit there being very selfish and inconsiderate because your son died. I wouldn't want another son to go to war. I shouldn't be afraid another would die, but I don't want another taken from me.

Now, I'm not Catholic, I'm Lutheran. We do not have the reverence for Mary like the Catholics do, but today, before we walked down to the monument, we had to wait about fifteen minutes. We had to wait for one man to come. He was supposed to take our pictures. Oh, I hated that. But, as I stood there, I calmed down. Maybe the Valium was taking over. I didn't take it before we left, but on the bus, going over there. Then, as we were walking down to the monument, finally, my legs got a little bit jelly. I didn't like that. I didn't like anything. As we turned the corner to go on down to the monument, I said, "Holy Mother Mary, please help me." God. I had never prayed to Mary before, yet I turned to her. I unconsciously did. She was the mother of Christ, who suffered and died on the cross, and I prayed to the Holy Mother: "Help me at this time." I guess I am still mad at God.

There was so much rain today, so much wetness. People were taking sand and rubbing it over the monument, so they could make the names stand out. I thought, "Face powder will do," and I took out my compact. It's hard powder. I dipped in the powder puff and looked around, and put some on there. Someone took his handkerchief and wiped over it, and the name showed up. It was a little beige, but it was there. I knew it wasn't going to show up well enough for the picture, so I put some more on, and I thought, "Oh, God, they will get me for defacing the monument."

STEPFATHER: It won't hurt it. It will wash off. The rain itself will just wash it off. It won't hurt that granite.

MOTHER: There was only one time today I had a good feeling. There was a lady there, older than us, in her sixties or seventies. She was there with her husband. They were each standing on one side of a name. I guessed it was their son's. They were holding a white piece of paper under the name, lined up under it, to help make it stand out, trying to underline it. This woman walked away, and she had tears in her eyes. I said, "Did your son die?" She said, "Yes," and tears came down her cheek. She said, "Your son, also?" I said, "Yes. Do you have any face powder? If you put face powder on it, it will bring the name out." Then I just said, "Here." I got out my compact, and just dabbed it all over his name and then got a Kleenex and wiped it off. They were simply thrilled with it. They took their picture again, and I felt good about that. That was the best feeling I had today, because I helped her. It felt real good, helping that stranger.

There was this one boy from our group who cried a lot, a big, heavyset boy. He cried so hard. I hugged him, told him not to cry so. It was ironic. At that same time, these planes were going overhead, and I thought, "Is this what war sounds like?" I could visualize bombs coming from those planes. I thought, "My God. Is this what war sounds like?" They were so low, coming in. It was such a gray day, with so much fog, you couldn't see them. I thought, "This is what war sounds like. How could people stand it?" I saw some of the people walking, people walking up and down, and I had so many thoughts. Funny thoughts. I thought, "Old people, young people. How do they stand it in a war? Planes coming over and bombing. How do they live through it?"

After it was all over, and everything was said and done, and walking, going back to the bus, people were staring at me. My face was all wet, tears and everything. I thought, "Look at me. Just look at me."